THERE & BACK AGAIN TO SEE HOW FAR IT IS

*Sometimes it takes a whole tank full of fuel
before you can think straight.*

*Only a biker knows why a dog sticks his head
out of a car window.*

*Catching a wasp in your shirt at 70mph on a bike
can double your vocabulary.*

It didn't look that far on the map.

THERE & BACK AGAIN TO SEE HOW FAR IT IS

**Cultural observations of an Englishman aboard a
Harley-Davidson motorcycle around small-town America**

Tim Watson

Photographs by Anne Watson

Haynes Publishing

To: Faith & Hugo
For: Anne

Living the Dream – **Sean Riedl – RIP 22 February 2010**

Thank you to the Harley-Davidson Motorcycle Company for its support and help

First published in September 2011

A catalogue record for this book is available from the British Library

ISBN 978 1 84425 957 1

Library of Congress catalog card no 2011926162

Published by Haynes Publishing,
Sparkford, Yeovil, Somerset BA22 7JJ, UK
Tel: 01963 442030 Fax: 01963 440001
Int.tel: +44 1963 442030 Int.fax: +44 1963 440001
E-mail: sales@haynes.co.uk
Website: www.haynes.co.uk

Haynes North America Inc.,
861 Lawrence Drive, Newbury Park, California 91320, USA

Designed and typeset by Dominic Stickland

Printed and bound in the UK

Contents

PREFACE

For all my life motorcycles have fascinated me. I am absolutely no expert and I have a hard time telling all the different makes and models apart, or even keeping up with the latest new motorcycles. I am not even a professional amateur motorcyclist. I am, though, someone who could best be described as an ignorant enthusiast. I have a respect and genuine interest in motorcycles and also in the people who ride them far better than I will ever be able to. My own view on motorcycles is best described as a love–hate relationship. I love them and hate them in equal measure.

The downside of motorcycles is that they have the capacity to scare me absolutely rigid, so it is hard to explain to anyone who has never ridden one why I would want to do it. Perhaps it's some latent masochistic streak in my personality that I need to frighten myself as a reminder of my own mortality. Or maybe I am just plain stupid.

On the other hand, riding a bike on an empty winding road on a warm summer's day without another human being around is simply exhilarating. Riding a motorcycle and riding it well heightens my senses and somehow makes me feel more alive, allowing me to focus on just staying upright and staying safe and nothing else. There is no time to worry about money, friends, whose birthday I have forgotten, taxes or what needs to be done around the house. All the trivia and cares of modern life disappear as I struggle to maintain my balance and control 1,584cc of engine slung beneath a fuel tank on a two-wheeled missile that is guided by handlebars, has two brake levers and a throttle so sensitive that I can go from walking pace to 60mph in just a twist of the right wrist.

If I ride well there is an enormous sense of achievement. Everything just seems to click into place, from gear shifting to taking corners smoothly, and I feel I have become one with the machine. If I ride badly, which happens a lot, or ride at times when it's raining and cold and it seems every car or truck driver is out to kill me, I will always question why I am doing it. There have even been times when I would gladly have walked away and never got back on a motorcycle again. But there is always something that just keeps pulling me back.

This book is about how I took up motorcycling full time for six months to make a series of trips of some 8,000 miles around the US. For some this may seem like utter lunacy – the impractical dream of an idealist. I am a middle-aged man and was at a crossroads in my life. I stopped doing a corporate job I had been tied to for 28 years and left that life far behind me. I just couldn't do it any more. I felt there had to be more out there than just sitting behind a desk.

Based upon that decision I went straight out and bought myself a Harley-Davidson motorcycle and pointed it in an easterly direction. I couldn't go west as I live in California and that would have meant riding straight into the Pacific Ocean. However, I have always set out on my US travels with the sole intention of exploring the highways and byways and the small towns of America just to see what's out there.

The title of this book – *There & Back Again To See How Far It Is* – sums up what I wanted to achieve. There was no plan, no huge agenda of what I needed to do, no requirement to visit national monuments, no pressure to see all the famous US towns. What there was and still is, though, was a passion to get on my motorcycle to discover what lay around the next corner. As a child, whenever I asked my mother where we were going in the car – probably for the thousandth time – she always answered *'There and back again to see how far it is'*. That answer always satisfied me. It still satisfies me today and I felt it was a suitable title for this book about my rides around the US, as it defined best what I was hoping to achieve. I have always found that the actual experience of travelling is far, far better than reaching any destination.

So is this an *Easy Rider*-type story involving macho leather-clad motorcycle clubs and my daring exploits on two wheels? Categorically no.

But it is my story about what I found out there in America – its people, its culture and its astonishingly diverse landscapes. This country is so huge it continues to boggle my mind – 3.79 million square miles, 50 states and a nation of some 309 million people and growing.

When I first came up with the idea of writing the book many friends and other people who heard about it seemed genuinely excited. Granted it was always the men who seemed to have a wistful look in their eyes: they said it was something they would love to do but couldn't because of career and family responsibilities.

Aside from being an escapist's dream I also wanted to give the reader a perspective of what it's like to be an Englishman in the saddle of a Harley-Davidson motorcycle riding around the most powerful country on earth. A nation that calls itself the land of the free and yet is regarded by some as the Evil Empire, destroying smaller countries and cultures around the world. For some years now, in my opinion, America has given itself a bad press. Consequently the world has given America a bad press. It's a country that is often depicted by the international media as a symbol of all that is wrong with the western world, whose people are motivated only by greedy excess and who know next to nothing about anything outside their own country.

I wanted to see how much of that was true about the current US and how much was just prejudice, which is why I stayed away from the traditional areas like New York, Las Vegas, Chicago – all the big-name places. I wanted to see what America was really like, away from interstate freeways, in the empty deserts, high up in the mountains and in the immense wide-open places that few tourists ever really bother to go to.

While riding and then writing this book I learned a lot about myself, but I do promise this is not a deep and profound personal account of a journey where I am desperately trying to find myself by riding a large motorcycle. Quite simply, this is about riding a bike in the US and what I discovered out there.

I only recently learned that my late father, whom I never knew, loved riding motorcycles, so I guess it's in the blood. Let's ride.

CHAPTER ONE

UNEASY RIDER

*Snakes alive! – Escaping corporate life – Motorcycles and being a kid –
Learning to ride a motorcycle and failing – Italy and transsexuals –
Planning to ride around the US*

I'm certain the rattlesnake had already seen me before I saw it. It lay halfway across the road and had reared up in that classic strike pose, just like you see them do on TV nature programmes. Its head was pulled way back, and in the midday desert sunshine its malevolent little eyes sparkled like tiny shiny black beads.

I knew exactly what it was. I had done a little homework about being out here in the Mojave Desert, one of the wildest, least inhabited parts of the US. It was among the most beautiful areas that I was to ride through, and clearly had the capacity of also being one of the most dangerous. This was a Western Diamondback rattlesnake, described by the nature books as a 'watch and wait predator' that can strike at a distance equal to half its own length. Its tube-like fangs can inject venom into its victim, destroying body tissue and causing coagulopathy (or in layman's terms stopping your body's ability to clot blood), followed by neurotoxins that induce respiratory paralysis. This snake means business.

On average 1,000 people are bitten by rattlesnakes in North America every year, and of those some die unpleasant deaths. I like the US National Park's generalisation of around 1,000 victims per year – not precise, but sufficient to show that these snakes are dangerous – but odder still is an unverified statistic I found which claimed 72% of rattlesnake bite victims are apparently men. This may go to prove either that the male of the *homo sapiens* species is just plain unlucky, or somehow capable of provoking rattlesnake rage far better than the female. Or it may be a combination of both. Of course, it could also be an inherent stupidity gene that makes men ignore the warnings about potentially fatal bites from aggressive reptiles and then prompts them to annoy snakes enough to get them biting. Clearly men and snakes were never meant to get along.

Out in the Mojave Desert on my motorcycle I really had not been prepared for an encounter like this. The rattlesnake looking at me was obviously not in any mood for dancing. I could see its distinctive black and white ringed tail flicking and its diamond-shaped head darting backwards and forwards. The heat of the morning sun had given it a real energy boost and it seemed to be assessing me, considering what precisely I was going to do to it.

What the hell was I thinking of? I was miles from anywhere, strapped to an enormous Harley-Davidson motorcycle that scared the hell out of me every time I rode it, and now I was about to meet my scaly nemesis in the middle of the road. At that moment I was absolutely convinced I was about to feature in the US annual snakebite statistics. I was on a desolate road, surrounded by huge cacti and rocks, with a blazing desert sun overhead. I had not seen a car pass in 20 minutes and I had visions of a double whammy. Fatally bitten by a rattlesnake and falling off my motorcycle in the process, I would be lying by the side of the road and staring up at the enormous vultures that looked like giant hang-gliders wheeling overhead.

I had survived more than 1,500 miles of crazy roads and traffic; navigated myself past the chest-slapping backdraughts of 18-wheeler trucks; ridden nervously up mountain roads with sheer drops so high you couldn't see the valleys below; met all the elements – snow, rain, wind and heat – and tackled the challenges of riding a motorcycle through remote empty deserts. Now all this achievement was going to come tumbling down thanks to an angry two-foot reptile that just didn't want to share the road with me.

For some reason that is beyond me now, instead of swerving to avoid the rattlesnake I stuck out my left leg as a way of trying to fend it off. This, in hindsight, is really a bit like holding out your hand to catch a bullet being fired at you. My pathetic leg-shaking manoeuvre caught the snake off guard – it darted backwards a few inches and then slid across the road and behind the rear wheel of my motorcycle, but I knew that a bike's rear wheels have a propensity to flick out things that the rider has just ridden over. And travelling directly behind me was Anne, my American bride of four weeks.

Aside from being an excellent motorcycle rider, Anne had been commissioned to take the photographs for this book. As it turned out, she would also act as interpreter (many Americans don't understand my English accent and definitely not my humour), navigator and organiser, pointing me in the right direction across this great country of hers. Apart from having to put up with a lot of crap from me on a daily basis, Anne now had to contend with having an angry rattlesnake thrown at her. I had visions of the phone call to my in-laws, explaining how their daughter had met her end through the incompetence of her new husband and general all-round sissy.

A few seconds passed. I pushed the intercom button on my crash helmet to talk to Anne.

'I am so sorry. I didn't see it until the last minute and I didn't know what to do so I thought I would kick it. Are you OK?' I said.

I could hear my breathing coming fast and raspy through the headphones in my helmet. I also knew that rattlesnakes possess the ability to bite you even when they are dead. It's something to do with an inherent instinctive reflex they possess.

'Kick what, when, how?' replied Anne.

'The snake. Didn't you see that freaking great rattlesnake? It just scared the crap out of me. I have got to pull over and stop and have a break. That was just way too weird,' I said.

'No way. I was busy looking at the beautiful scenery. Darn it, I've always wanted to see a snake in the wild,' said Anne.

It was at moments like this that I wondered if this series of motorcycle road trips had ever really happened. Did I really start to imagine things while locked inside a crash helmet and heading towards a distant horizon? Was my mind playing tricks on me? In truth, the series of long journeys I made through the United States of

America often left me bewildered, astonished and, at times, frankly concerned that I was losing it.

Every day was an adventure, and just the process of 'saddling up' and starting the motorcycle early in the morning always made my heart beat a little bit faster. There was never a concrete plan; no clear map of where I was heading to next or what I was going to see.

* * * * * *

But how precisely does a middle-aged Englishman end up astride a Harley-Davidson in the middle of a US desert – and why, for goodness sake? As explained, I am no hard-core biker. Yet from my earliest days I have always had a fascination with motorcycles.

They have an ability to terrify me and elate me at the same time. I have no great escape stories to tell you about sliding down the road at improbable speeds that end in a mixture of gravel rash, broken bones, tangled motorcycle frames and the smell of leaking petroleum after yet another spectacular near-death accident. In truth I have enough trouble most days just concentrating on walking. Nor can I lay claim to being anywhere near the same level as film actor Ewan McGregor and his friend Charlie Boorman, who have achieved astonishing things on their motorcycles all round the globe during their great expeditions *The Long Way Round* and *The Long Way Down*.

After 28 years of corporate life, though, I can claim to have seen a lot of the world from some of the world's best hotels, or from the rear seat of a chauffeur-driven car taking me to yet another motor show or to the next Formula One Grand Prix race. I knew I'd led a charmed existence, having been lucky enough to work for some of the great automotive brands and witness some truly amazing things. But it was always a case of trying to stay ahead of the game, avoiding the accountants and hiding in the stationery cupboard when the mandatory head-count reduction seemed to come round with ever-increasing frequency. There are only so many budget and managerial processes that the human mind can deal with and I felt I couldn't carry on. There had to be more to life.

I was working as managing director for a luxury car-maker based in Rome, Italy, with an expense account and a commensurate salary, plus all the trappings you would expect. But it came at a heavy price, and my personal life was in tatters. Long, long hours – weeks of being away on product launches or at races or attending motor shows – meant that I was never home. I was drifting. I was miserable and at a complete loss as to what to do next. Most normal and responsible people would get a grip, make things work out, grin and bear it, and then shuffle off this mortal coil no doubt content that they had done the right thing by everyone except themselves.

My quick-fix solution to all my troubles was to go out and buy myself a big Harley-Davidson. I have no idea why I bought it, but I found myself consciously pretending that I wasn't having a mid-life crisis – indeed, that it was perfectly normal for a man of my age, experience and responsibilities to go and do just this. It was back to an old mantra that has dogged me all my life: *it seemed like a good idea at the time.*

There were a couple of other issues I had not quite thought through properly. For instance, I had not ridden a motorcycle since my teens; I had no motorcycle licence; and I knew I was the epitome of the middle-aged biker trying to recapture his lost youth. I was trying to make my mark in life, which to all intents and purposes might probably be a hideous bloody mess at the first road junction that I came to.

* * * * * *

I was born in Kent, traditionally known as 'the garden of England' because of its abundance of orchards and hop gardens, and from a very young age was hooked on motorcycles. It probably began on my 12th birthday when my parents presented me with a very old 125cc BSA Bantam bike. This was the start of a lifetime's obsession, and thanks to that BSA I learned more about falling off two wheels than actually how to ride them. The Bantam had served its time with what was then called the General Post Office or today's Royal Mail and had been used by postmen to deliver letters. It was simplicity itself and, despite a hard previous life, it was still in great condition. I loved it.

It always started first time. Painted khaki with creamy white inserts on the fuel tank, it had a rubber-ball horn mounted on the handlebars, a four-speed gearbox and the compression from the kick start was strong enough to break your leg and then scrape all the skin off your shins on the footpeg if you failed to start it right. I ran the BSA on petrol stolen from my stepfather's lawnmowers, and despite years of abuse from me it never missed a beat.

Our family house was surrounded by farmland and I rode for hours with my Jack Russell terrier balancing on the fuel tank. I loved that BSA, but there was another motorcycle that had already caught my young eye in the form of my stepfather's Triumph 750cc Tiger. It was definitely off limits to a teenage boy, but I seized my chance one weekend when my stepfather and mother went away leaving me in charge of the house, some fine classic cars and the motorcycle.

My stepfather rarely used the Triumph but I found it fascinating. It looked fast just standing still and was painted in metallic orange that sparkled seductively in the sunlight – a splendid combination of speed, amazing looks and danger. That weekend I decided I would try to ride it. No insurance, no licence and absolutely no on-road motorcycle skills: the perfect combination for an idiot teenager. And it was the start of that mantra – *it seemed like a good idea at the time*.

Unlike my old BSA the Triumph had an electric start, and turning the ignition key made the whole bike come to life in a shuddering raucous cacophony of noise. It sounded fantastic. I was not wearing a crash helmet and, for some reason best known to a 14-year-old boy, I was wearing my sister's purple *Alice in Wonderland* T-shirt with very short Speedo swimming trunks and tennis shoes. The T-shirt was so long it looked as if I had nothing on underneath. But I was oblivious to this as I sat on the Triumph, started it up and wobbled off down the driveway.

The Triumph was heavy and I could instantly feel that it was a lot more powerful than my old BSA. I told myself I would just ride to the end of the drive. Then I decided I would go to the end of the lane where we lived, but when I reached that point it struck me that this was just too big a bike for me to manhandle and turn around, so I kept on going. My hands had gone numb from the exertion of holding on, but this was unlike anything I had ever experienced before and was a heady mixture of sheer enjoyment and utter terror.

I came to the main road and a traffic stop. No choice now, I had to keep going, and I silently prayed I would find somewhere to turn this beast around. Cars and trucks were passing me really quickly and I caught glimpses of curious drivers' faces as I continued to roll along at a steady 30mph.

The bike seemed to want to go faster, but I was now experiencing the panic of being completely inexperienced on a big motorcycle in fast-moving traffic on the open road. It felt like I was travelling at 200mph, and although I wanted to stop I simply couldn't. I knew if I did there was a very good chance I would just fall over. So with tears welling up in my eyes I pushed on. Five miles became 10 miles and then 12, and I was way out of my depth. I was truly scared. Soon it was going to get dark and I didn't even know how to switch on the Triumph's lights.

It was then that I spotted a pub and a large empty car park. Perfect. I rolled in and began trying to work out how I could turn the bike around without dropping it. As I pulled in I saw the local policeman sitting there in his car, watching the evening traffic go by. Frantically pulling at the clutch, the brake and the accelerator I lurched and spluttered to a stop. Standing on tiptoes I could just about keep the Triumph upright. The police officer looked at me. I looked at him. With an expression of mild confusion he finally got out of his patrol car and sauntered across to me.

'Going somewhere special?' he asked.

'Just trying out the bike to see if I like it,' I said, trying to sound big and brave and as though it was perfectly normal for a young teenage boy to be out riding a big British motorcycle on a summer's evening.

'Not really dressed for motorcycling, are you?' he said, pursing his lips. 'Have you come far?'

'Um … not too far, but I'm going to turn around now and go home,' I said, trying to pull up the long T-shirt to show him that I was not nude from the waist down. This action clearly made him very uncomfortable.

'Do you live far away, as I think you *should* turn around and go home. Really, you should be wearing a crash helmet and riding gear and not those things,' he said.

All the time I was waiting for him to ask me my name and how old I was, and tell me to get off the bike and sit in the back of his police car so he could take my details. I was expecting him to charge me with a multitude of motoring offences ranging from being under age, no licence, no insurance and taking a motor vehicle without consent. But he said and did absolutely nothing more.

'Could you help me turn the bike around?' I asked politely. I had managed to ride up to the front wall of the pub and there was no way on earth I was going to be able to push the Triumph around. He took a long, hard look at me and sighed. Obviously the prospect of booking an adolescent boy trying to ride a big motorcycle was just going to involve too much paperwork. I stayed on the bike and he pushed me backwards. I can still remember him staring me straight in the eye and making puffing noises through his mouth as he rolled me backwards into the car park. He then turned around and walked back to his car.

My confidence grew on that return journey. I rode faster and at one point managed to get into fourth gear and up to a heady 45mph. I even overtook a slowing car that was turning right ahead of me. I had actually done it. I had ridden my first big motorcycle and it was fantastic. The feeling of elation didn't even diminish when I realised I couldn't lift the Triumph back on to its kickstand, so I left it leaning against the garage wall emitting that ticking noise that motorcycles make when they start to cool down.

* * * * * *

Growing up, I had many friends with motorcycles. Teenage boys and big motorcycles are a natural recipe for disaster. Too much testosterone and the illusion of immortality led to a series of spectacular accidents for many of them.

There were a couple of notable characters with stunning Japanese bikes who fanned my enthusiasm for motorcycles and riding fast. The most memorable was big fat Nobby. I have no idea why he was called that, but he preferred it to his real name of Sean. Even at the tender age of 18, Nobby had managed to cultivate an amazing beard that covered 90% of his face. All you saw were two large blue eyes and a nose. Occasionally there would be evidence of a mouth when he pushed vast quantities of food into a hole in his beard. He looked as if he was wearing a hairy mask.

Nobby had the biggest and most intimidating motorcycle I had ever seen – a black Suzuki GS1000 with a Yoshimura tuning kit. Back in the early 1980s this was considered to be a pretty special motorcycle. I was never entirely sure what the Yoshimura tuning kit was, but I would nod my head wisely whenever Nobby stopped eating to explain some intricate mechanical detail of the 'Yoshi kit', as he called it. According to him, it allowed him to reach Mach 1 speeds on the network of country roads around our village and nobody could keep up with him. Not even the police. I was deeply impressed.

Nobby was clearly in love with his Suzuki. Perhaps more than with his very pretty girlfriend Beverley, who managed to perch elegantly on the back of the Suzuki with her bum in the air while he drove them both up the road at what seemed like impossible speeds. I was more transfixed by the bike's sheer velocity and noise than Beverley's lovely backside.

There was also another friend called Jiff. I never knew his real name, but he used to ride very fast Yamaha sports bikes. He was even taller and bigger than Nobby and always dressed in black leather from head to foot, favouring the one-piece leather motorcycle suit that was very popular among the sports bike fraternity – and in all the time I knew him I never saw him take the suit off, even in the middle of summer. Maybe Jiff had no clothes other than those leathers...

Jiff's exploits on a motorcycle, and his accidents, were legendary. However, the big drawback was that he suffered from a very, very bad speech impediment which meant no matter how spectacular was his latest exploit, it took ten times longer for him to describe it. I gave up on Jiff's stories when he stumbled through a tale about slipping on a squashed hedgehog at 90mph and launching himself through the trees while his bike went off in another direction. I am sure it was a great story, but I could have gone out, bought another drink and read a newspaper, walked home and been back before he'd even got into first gear about this latest brush with death.

Jiff and Nobby did, however, leave me with a real respect for sports bike riders and what they were capable of doing on motorcycles. Sports bikes seemed to have a propensity for lifting the front wheel three feet off the ground under heavy acceleration, in particular up our village high street. It was only years later I discovered this was not compulsory. It was just something that Jiff and Nobby did to look cool and entertain us. They also helped make up my mind that I never wanted to ride a sports motorcycle. They are just too fast. I didn't want to ride one – and still don't – as they look technologically ferocious and appear to go around corners horizontally. But I do have a sneaking respect for their riders. They are definitely the fighter pilots of the road.

* * * * * *

Motorcycling and I parted company for the next two decades, although I still lusted after them and I still had an urge to go out and buy one. But it wasn't until I was sitting behind a corporate desk in California that I decided the time had come to go and do what I had always wanted to do. Part of the motivation was down to a group of bikers I met in a bar one scalding hot afternoon in the middle of the Arizona desert, just outside Phoenix.

There were perhaps twenty of them altogether – men and women – and they burst into a bar where I was enjoying a quiet drink in the shade of the back patio. I had heard their motorcycles miles away, long before they arrived, and the noise in the car park when they rolled in was like the start of a race. There was a lot of revving engines, shouting and definitely a lot of laughter.

To look at, this group appeared to be a sort of moving conga line of leather vests, leather trousers, shaven heads, enormous motorcycle boots and key chains, metal badges and embroidered eagle patches. There was lots of shouting and pushing and even more laughing. There also appeared to be a lot of fancy facial hair, some outstanding mosaics of tattoos and some very tight leather garments pulled over huge stomachs. And that was just the women…

They had all arrived in this explosion of exhaust sound, chrome and hot metal at the roadside bar and were stopping for a few drinks. This was not a motorcycle gang in the true sense of the word; they were a group of Harley-Davidson enthusiasts out for a mid-week ride. Many of them had adopted the motorcycle 'outlaw' image and the impression they gave was one of gentle menace. I slunk lower in the corner, hoping they wouldn't notice me in my red Mickey Mouse T-shirt, flip-flops and pastel coloured shorts. I have to admit, though, that I was fascinated by their look and the group dynamic. There was a road captain and a president and a whole hierarchy where everyone seemed to have a badge and know his or her place. They also appeared to be having a very good time.

One of them had produced a small video camera and amid the copious beer drinking there appeared to be a lot of filming going on of various members' body parts. This included recording what lay behind a pair of black tasselled leather chaps on a tall worried-looking man – and there was clearly something of interest and hilarity under one of the women's T-shirts. However, they really saved the best to last.

A very large man who was as wide as he was tall stepped into the middle of the group. He looked like he'd had his neck surgically removed and his enormous cannonball head had simply been stuck back on to his broad shoulders with glue and maybe duct tape. There was a bright green spider's web behind his left ear and his close-set eyes squinted in the bright sunlight as he stood beaming at his friends standing around him. An inflated stomach that looked as if it could hold gallons of beer peeked shyly from out of the front of his leather vest. With a flourish of his hands he turned his back to the camera, dropped his trousers and his underpants, and started to wiggle his behind for the camera in a suggestive way that I hoped only his wife had ever seen before, and never a former prison cellmate.

Amid roars of laughter, a lot of backslapping and shouting the group magically reassembled itself back into its leather conga line and started to file out of the bar. It was then that they spotted me.

'Oh man. We're sorry. We were just funning ourselves. Hope we ain't spoilt your drink,' said one of the men. The group started to form a semi-circle of quizzical leather-clad road warriors around me and, for a split second, I thought they were going to produce the video camera and ask me to repeat what Mr Cannonball Head had just done so well for them.

I explained I was not in the least offended, and in fact they had all made me laugh very hard.

'Well that's good, honey,' drawled one of the women. 'You make sure you have a good time too here in the US. Anyway, what's your accent? Are you Australian, or one of them South Africans?'

It was a question I was to be asked many times in the coming months, as I criss-crossed the United States. I find that some Americans are very curious about accents. Before she had time to tick off all the nations she could think of, I told her I was English.

'What, like the Queen of England, right?' she enquired.

'Well, sort of, we both come from the same country but she has a palace. And is our head of state. A bit like your President,' I explained.

'So you're not French, right?'

Things were starting to get a little hazy on the geography front. I confirmed to Mrs Leather T-shirt that no, I was not French, and assured her much to her satisfaction that I had no intention of ever becoming a Frenchman.

'Well, that's good, honey. Because they surrender a lot and caused us a lot of problems out there in Iraq.'

I wasn't quite following the logic here but didn't want to cause offence so I just nodded. By then they'd all got bored with the odd Englishman and trooped out, but just as I thought they had gone I heard a clattering of heavy motorcycle boots running back across the bar's wooden floor.

Mr Cannonball Head tore on to the patio, leaned into my face, looked me straight in the eye and said: 'Yer know … I do parties.' It was an interesting concept. And with that, he turned about and headed off again. A few seconds later they were gone in a swirling haze of dust, barking exhaust noise and glinting chrome. They looked fantastic and made me start to wonder how I could do what they were doing – without the video camera, of course.

This was the dilemma. I'm not brave enough to get a tattoo done, nor do I have any inclination to wear leather chaps, even in the bedroom. But was I committed enough to learn to ride a motorcycle again and then buy my own bike and travel the highways of the US? Maybe, I thought. Just maybe.

* * * * * *

'You want a what?' said an English colleague at work one day when I announced I was going to buy a motorcycle. 'Who the hell buys a Harley-Davidson apart from sad old men with very small willies? You do know they fall apart and bits come off them?' This last statement concerned me a bit. Did he mean that bits fell off Harley-Davidsons or sad old men saw their willies drop off? Either way there was apparently going to be a lot of loose parts rolling around.

Maybe I should have been considering purchasing a Triumph, or at the very least a Norton – after all, I am an Englishman. I did look at those fabulous bikes as well as a sensationally beautiful Ducati and a BMW. I felt the Ducati would make me push it inside my house where I would sit and admire it for the rest of my life and never ever ride it. Or if I did get on, it would be typically Italian and rev to 20,000rpm, launching me into hyperspace at 200mph before crumbling into a thousand pieces and leaving me standing in the middle of the road holding just a handlebar and some wires, while it went off in a huff to have an espresso coffee with its mother.

The BMW was a very sensible option. It was safe, fast and extremely tough, as actor Ewan McGregor had so ably demonstrated in his epic rides around the world on a BMW R1150 GS. Clearly this BMW had a proven track record mechanically, a long-distance touring bike taking whatever Africa, Asia and the North American continent could throw at it and never missing a beat, no matter how many times Ewan fell off.

Call me old-fashioned, but as a schoolboy I remember assembling Second World War BMW German army motorcycle model kits. Often they came complete with a sidecar and massive machine gun mounted on it. I must stress that today's BMW motorcycles are fine machines and bear no resemblance whatsoever to their WW2 counterparts defending what was then Nazi Germany. But part of me could not reconcile myself to the thought of spending the next 12 months on a motorcycle whose forebears had been designed to blow my grandfather off the face of the earth when he was fighting with the British army in North Africa and Italy.

The iconic Harley-Davidson seemed the only other option. This was an American motorcycle built in America for Americans to use on American roads. On most days in Southern California and often at weekends I had seen these fantastic-looking motorcycles being ridden around my neighbourhood. They had a retro look but managed to convey both excitement and intrigue at the same time and, for some reason best known to myself, I had set my heart definitely, 100%, on buying one.

But I had never even set foot inside a Harley-Davidson dealership. I had often passed one by, a little uncertain if I should go in. I thought if the staff inside weren't eating babies they would probably tattoo 'Anarchy' on my forehead and throw me out just for speaking with an English accent. I didn't even know which model was best for me or which type of motorcycle was going to be right for a long journey in the US. As it turned out, the first bike I bought was the wrong one, but at the time I was just excited to get back in the saddle.

After days of dithering, I eventually agreed to go along and look with my sister Pip, who was on holiday in California at the time, together with Anne, my wife. They both said I should at least talk to the sales staff and check out what Harley-Davidson motorcycles were all about. For some reason I had it in my mind that all of them would have huge ape-hanging handlebars, massive rear tyres, triple carburettors and no suspension. They would also be very loud and covered in chrome and skull motifs – like the ones I had seen in the roadside bar in Arizona – and they would be nothing like as good as a European motorcycle. How very naïve and wrong I was.

On that hot August afternoon when I wandered into my nearest dealership I broke every rule in the book because I decided to buy the first bike I saw. It was a 1200 Nightster finished in gleaming black paint, and was one of the new 'dark' range of stripped-out and de-chromed models that had just been launched. What I didn't realise, apart from it being one of the cheapest bikes at $10,000, was that as a Sportster it was considered by the aficionados to be the 'girl's bike' in the Harley-Davidson range.

I loved the look of the Nightster. It was low, with a solo saddle and a 'bobbed' rear mudguard, and it was reminiscent of the machines those outlaw bikers were building in the 1960s and 1970s. Powered by the latest version of Harley-Davidson's classic V-twin, air-cooled 1,200cc Evolution engine and weighing in at a chubby 562lb, it was clearly no lightweight sports bike.

Anthony, the Harley-Davidson salesman, was patient but not very forthcoming about the Nightster. He didn't offer me a test ride, but I never asked for one so only have myself to blame. After all, I was dressed in T-shirt and shorts and looked so unlike Anthony's regular customers that he probably thought I was just an English tourist wasting his time for a few hours. He did tell me this was the last black Nightster he was going to have that year and that they were very popular motorcycles. I should have done my homework better, but I believed him and lapped up the sales pitch.

I agreed to buy it, then lost count of the number of forms I had to fill in, but after several hours of self-doubt, where I kept questioning my sanity, Anthony handed me two sets of keys and the Nightster's manual. I was the owner – albeit a very incompetent owner – of a brand-new Harley-Davidson.

Now came the dilemma. I had not ridden a motorcycle in almost 20 years. The gear and brake selector were totally opposite to the British bikes I'd been used to. I had bought a cheap helmet from the dealership, one of those that are the bare minimum you can wear legally in California, and I looked like I was wearing a matt black eggcup on my head – and with my T-shirt and shorts I was totally inappropriately dressed for riding my 'girl's bike' home. Originally I had made a plan with a friend of mine, who had also come with us to buy the bike. As he was a far more experienced motorcyclist the deal was that, as soon as I had gone around the corner, I would stop and he would then ride my new bike the five miles to my house. Another one of those *it seemed like a good idea at the time* moments…

I started the Nightster and found first gear. Hey, this is easy, I thought, as I rode gingerly away from the dealership. Anthony had gone back inside immediately, clearly wanting to distance himself from any liability for selling a poorly trained circus monkey a new Harley-Davidson. First gear became second gear. Second gear became third – and then I realised I didn't know how to stop. I shot through the first intersection and turned left. I'd forgotten some fundamental motorcycle basics such as how to counter-steer and lean into corners. I was riding very badly and taking all the corners I came to sitting bolt upright.

Somehow I managed to navigate through the traffic lights and start the journey home that included a small part of the Ortega Highway, a notorious motorcycle ride. Ortega is famed not only for its fabulous corners and twisting road through the mountains but for regularly claiming motorcyclists' lives; nearly every weekend there is someone injured or killed on this 30-mile stretch of road.

I had other things on my mind. My inability to stop or ride properly meant that my friend, my sister and Anne, who were travelling behind me in a car, thought I was having the time of my life and getting back into the groove all over again.

'Because you didn't stop, as we all agreed, we thought you were enjoying riding your new bike too much,' said Anne afterwards. 'I told everyone in the car that there was no way you were going to stop. I knew you were going to have too much fun.' If too much fun involved sweating profusely and screaming obscenities for the entire 15-minute ride I had clearly stumbled across a new form of self-enjoyment. When I finally pulled into the driveway at home one thing was very clear. I needed to learn how to ride this motorcycle or I was going to be dead very quickly.

* * * * * *

I wasted no time in signing up for Harley-Davidson's new riders' course, which made perfect sense because it not only explained the Californian and US rules of the road but also dealt with completely incompetent beginners like myself. At the end I would walk away with a practical proficiency test under my belt and a chance that I might have extended my life a little longer.

The motorcycle and the US share a very dark secret. If the bike isn't trying to kill you by throwing you off at every corner and bump in the road, then the good car-driving citizens of America will give it their very best shot to help you along the way. Some will appear totally innocent, like the senior citizen behind the wheel of her massive Cadillac saloon. She will try to get you as she reverses straight out of her driveway and into oncoming traffic. It's not personal. She simply doesn't see you. And neither does the Mom doing the school run in her huge sports utility vehicle. She will have a good try at hitting you from behind as you stop at traffic lights for an intersection. She will also probably be drinking coffee from a cup the size of a flower vase while talking on her cell phone (even though this is now prohibited in the state of California) and doing her make-up in the rear-view mirror.

In 2008, the impressively named Department of Transportation National Highways Traffic Safety Administration (NHTSA) published its annual road accident statistics. Top of the list of the category that included cars and trucks were, of course, motorcycles. It was estimated that out of the seven million motorcycles on the roads of the US, 5,290 were involved in fatal accidents that year, with a further 96,000 motorcyclists injured. This was the highest level of deaths recorded since 1975 when NHTSA started monitoring motorcycle accidents.

To give you an idea of the scale of this problem, in 2008 car and truck passenger deaths in the US totalled 39,448 – meaning that motorcycle riders accounted for more than 11.5% of all traffic fatalities. Top places to die on a bike were California, Florida and Texas, and the NHTSA research went on to suggest that the most dangerous time to ride a motorcycle in the US was on a weekday between 3.00pm and 6.00pm or between 6.00pm and 9.00pm at the weekend. If this is starting to make your head spin, like it did mine, NHTSA concluded its research by stating that motorcyclists were 37 times more likely to die in a traffic accident than a car passenger and, furthermore, that while it fully supported helmet laws for all US states, helmets were only 37% effective in preventing fatal injuries in motorcycle riders. Out of the 50 states that make up the US, only 21 of them require you to wear a crash helmet when riding a bike.

I was simply astonished. That is a huge number of dead motorcyclists and I was further confused by the fact that the statistics are based upon figures of 'reported' deaths. Does that mean there are unreported deaths of motorcyclists in the US, people who are simply forgotten about and swept under the rug? Out of those 2008 fatalities, 27% indicated speeding as a factor, while 824.6 bikers were killed due to drinking alcohol and then going out and riding their motorcycles. Clearly, booze, bikes and no crash helmets at 4.30pm on a Wednesday afternoon are likely to kill you.

Tim Busche, President of the Motor Cycle Foundation, said in response to these figures that car drivers needed to look out for bikers and respect their rights in traffic and, more importantly, new riders needed to be properly trained. If I was ever going to make it across the US, and based upon my scarily crazy first ride home on a motorcycle, I was going to need some proper training.

* * * * * *

California probably conjures up glitzy images of swaying palm trees, endless sunshine, Hollywood stars, enormous cars, vast amounts of money and the endless pursuit of the American dream. A life of ease and fun, people with very blond hair, gleaming white smiles, endless golden beaches and surfboards.

At this moment, though, Southern California just felt very hot. Granted the sun was out and the sky was a perfect blue, but for some reason the Sunshine State also smelled very strongly of petrol and literally everything was upside down. I knew I wasn't dreaming, as I felt my stomach had been trodden on by something very hard and heavy, while somewhere near my head someone was riding a motorcycle very quickly.

As I started to focus a little more I discovered I was flat on my back on the scorching asphalt of a shopping mall car park with 600lb of extremely angry motorcycle lying directly on top of me. The noise near my head was because the engine was still running, while I had a vague sensation on my right side that the exhaust was either very hot or I had just wet myself. Maybe both. And there also appeared to be part of a handlebar inverted in another part of my anatomy. Something out of the ordinary had happened to me, but precisely what was not very clear at first.

I was certainly not feeling as chipper as I had two days previously when I'd signed up for the Harley-Davidson 'Riders' Edge Programme'. Indeed, I seemed to have reached the edge and gone straight over it. Anyway, for $350 Harley-Davidson offered a complete beginner's course spread across four days: two nights of intensive classroom training, where you learnt road rules and simple practical facts about how to ride a motorcycle, followed by two days in the saddle from sun-up until the sun went down. Or, in my case, when the sun goes up the motorcycle goes down and you fall over. The bike was definitely missing a few pieces and I was quite certain I was too.

On only my second day of practical motorcycle training, and in front of five bemused Californian fellow students, I'd obviously taken a slide – not a big power slide, like you see on *YouTube* or in the movies, but a very low-speed wobble, with the bike and me literally falling over in perfect synchrony into a crumpled heap of noisy revving engine and flailing limbs. There was also some muffled screaming as I choked on the cool neck bandanna which I had thought would make me look like a real biker.

My instructor, Mac, came running up, then slowed as he approached. He leant down to switch off the bike's ignition but said nothing. Evidently this was going to be awkward: I had broken one of his motorcycles and disobeyed some very clear orders.

'You got that real wrong, brother. What happened?' he asked, looking down at me with a frown.

'I don't know. I just sort of fell off.' I knew it wasn't the answer he wanted, but it was the truth. After eight hours in the saddle I was exhausted and simply couldn't turn the handlebars. When the bike started to slide in a curve on the specially marked-out course I'd had no option but to let it fall.

'Just sort of fell off?' He tried to mimic my English accent and, like all Americans when they do this, he sounded exactly like Dick Van Dyke, who'd displayed the worst-ever cockney accent as the chimney sweep in the film *Mary Poppins*. Mac was a tall guy of indeterminate age with icy blue eyes, and he looked every inch the ex-marine, ex-gunfighter and government agent I assumed he was. I had always made it my mission in life to avoid men like this. This time, though, there was no escape.

For the past two days Mac had walked, stood and run around the motorcycle training ground, often in 90°F heat. He always arrived first in the morning, from some tiny Californian town miles away close to the US–Mexican border, and he was always the last to go home at night when classes finished. He'd demonstrated how to ride a motorcycle and how not to ride. He had shown us emergency stops and done some memorable riding tricks to show what could be accomplished at speed. He knew his stuff, was clearly very fit and could ride superbly.

Now he edged a little closer to me, then stooped low so I could get the full benefit of what he was about to reveal to me as he rolled up his left trouser leg.

'You don't want to be doing that or you'll end up with one of these,' Mac said, pointing at something. This man was not only a government official and a paid killer, he was also half man and half machine. Glinting in the late afternoon sunshine was what I thought at first was a robot leg, all brass studs, polished aluminium struts and what seemed to be counterlevers and springs. It was a prosthetic lower leg, ankle and foot.

'Hit a dog at 55mph in the dark and went down. I think I killed the dog and I lost my leg below the knee. So pay attention. Always look up and watch where you're going. On a motorcycle everyone and everything is out to get you. Now get up and we'll check the damage on the bike.'

At the end of the four-day marathon, Mac took each of the six students aside individually to tell them if they had passed or not. After the damage I'd done to his bike I was not too sure that I'd be leaving with a pass, let alone his blessing.

'You've still got a lot to learn,' said Mac, his blue eyes staring directly into mine. 'However, you have got your own bike. But you need to practise, practise, practise or you'll never make it. I am going to pass you, but let me tell you, you only just scraped through.'

I solemnly shook Mac's hand, trying hard not to punch the sky or run around whooping like a teenage girl. The hard bit had actually been done. Now it was just a trip to the Department of Motor Vehicles to complete the mandatory written test and I would be the proud possessor of a full Californian motorcycle licence.

* * * * * *

There is an old saying that 'when men plan, God laughs'. Clearly the joke was very much on me because, just as I had jumped through all the legal hoops to become a qualified US motorcycle rider, the car company I was working for decided it was time for me to move again – from California back to Europe and then straight to Italy. There was no way I was going to leave my newly acquired Harley-Davidson in California. The thought of being parted from it after all I had been through in the US – buying it, learning to ride it and then being very scared of it – meant I felt I had no option but to take it with me. So, after conquering a mountain of paperwork and customs forms, I had the bike shipped to Rome.

I began to regret my decision almost immediately. A new Italian work colleague took me to one side and confided: 'Your motorcycle will get stolen. There are some bad people in Rome. They will come to your house and take it or they will steal it while you're out riding it on the road.' He seemed to think my Harley-Davidson was going to be taken from me within minutes of being unloaded from the boat by what he described as 'bad men and gypsies'. Quite who these thieves were and precisely why they had collectively been waiting specifically for my bike's arrival in Rome was never made clear to me.

Italy. Oh Italy. It's a country I have loved for many years. I had lived there before, for five years, in the magical northern area of Reggio Emilia when I was working for a very famous Italian sports car company. Now I was back as an employee of a British car company and delighted to find that very little had changed. I was optimistic that I would find time and places to ride my Harley-Davidson and evade the thieves.

I adore the Italian people, their friendliness, openness and their startling generosity. Then there is the beautiful language, the Italian way of life and the sheer utter craziness that you can only really experience from living there on a full-time basis. A holiday in Italy just gives the tourist a glimpse of what opportunities are waiting to be discovered in what I consider to be one of the world's most magnificent and most insane countries.

From the moment I landed at Rome's Leonardo da Vinci airport at Fiumicino, everything fell back into place. I smiled perhaps a trifle too smugly at the countless bewildered American tourists trooping off their planes straight from the US and wanting to visit Tuscany, Pisa, Florence, the Vatican and Venice all in one day. They always appeared to be very confused and lost and were often not aware they were going to spend the first half of their holiday traipsing around the airport in small groups looking for their Italian holiday rep, whose answer to every one of their questions always seemed to be 'go and have a coffee at the airport bar and we will tell you later'.

This was the very same tactic used by the Italian shipping company when I asked when my motorcycle would arrive: 'Have a coffee and we'll tell you later.' I knew it had left the US, but the Italian end of the operation could only say that it was possibly somewhere in the Naples area. Maybe it would arrive tomorrow, maybe next week or even next month. They were always a little unsure.

My bad grasp of the Italian language did not help matters. The conversation with the shippers seemed to involve what I loosely translated later to myself as a problem with angry seagulls, Italian dockworkers not working any day of the week after Tuesday and something about Italian customs wanting to inspect my motorcycle for the enormous stash of drugs and guns I had hidden on it. So I resigned myself to sitting and waiting to see what would happen. This, as I should have known by then, was the best and often the easiest rule to live by in Italy.

However, perhaps I should have spent the time establishing how foolhardy I had been even to consider riding a motorcycle in Italy.

Nothing had prepared me for the Roman way of driving or the experience of riding a motorcycle in the city or on the roads of southern Italy. Romans have absolutely no concept of how to merge at an intersection: the general idea is that everyone goes for the same gap in the traffic all at the same time. You do not yield. You do not stop for one second as someone else, or maybe even two or three other road users, will try and squeeze in. It's automotive madness.

At best the roads in Rome are smooth and unpredictable with adverse cambers that abruptly end in a mass of gravel or potholes going into a sharp right-hand corner. The heavy traffic, stifling summer heat, with wet winters and occasional frost, mean that Rome's roads are generally appalling. They constantly need maintaining and there is often not the right paperwork/money/manpower or inclination to get the problems sorted out. Southern Italy was not, as I had hoped, going to be the best place to ride a motorcycle.

However, despite the incessant obstacles and crazy traffic, riding my Harley-Davidson was something of a merciful release, because it offered me the freedom of the road without the hassle of trying to get a car through Rome's narrow streets. It did, however, require a huge amount of concentration. I was used to planning and looking ahead when riding a bike in the US, but nothing had prepared me for Italy's unwritten traffic rules. Basically you need the skills of a military helicopter pilot and the ability to register everything that's going on around you every split second. At any given moment there could be a loose dog just wandering around at a junction or an old man who has stepped out of the local coffee bar to enjoy a cigarette in the middle of the road while watching the traffic go by. Or a whole series of scooters might appear from nowhere and weave in and out of other vehicles, sometimes even resorting to a quick trip along the sidewalk before rejoining the main road again. Rome's traffic was and is nuts.

One Sunday afternoon in mid-August I had a memorable ride which left an indelible impression on me and confirmed that strangeness often encountered while on a bike rather than being behind the wheel of a car. I had so far successfully eluded the thieves and decided that it was a perfect day to go on a motorcycle ride.

It was stiflingly hot and, although this was the height of Rome's tourist season, there was very little traffic. Most of the Italians were away at nearby beaches or had gone off to the mountains to escape the oppressive summer heat, while all the tourists were probably still having a coffee and waiting at Rome airport. It was only expats like myself who found they had Rome entirely to themselves, so it seemed a perfect time to get on the bike and ride. I had worked out a couple of carefully planned routes that led me out of Rome in a sweeping loop, up into some hills and around a magnificent lake that boasted the Pope's summer holiday house on its shores. Aside from the dubious road quality I thought it looked like a great ride of about 100 or so miles. There would be some stunning scenery and, as it was a Sunday morning, it would be almost traffic free.

On my way to see if I could sneak a look at the Pope sunbathing I took a side road which led out into some farmland and past expensive villas where Rome's glitterati, VIPs and politicians lived. The road was lined on both sides with tall pine trees and it was bumpy as hell. Coming around a sharp left-hand corner the Nightster bucked and reared as I hit a big bump at about 50mph. I had slowed a little beforehand as I had seen the obstacle ahead, and had braced myself for it by standing up on the footpegs with my backside hovering over the saddle. Instead of protecting my nether regions, as I had hoped, the rebounding rear suspension sent the bike's saddle straight up and hard into my groin. It was just like someone had punched me in the nuts.

When you're travelling at 50mph on a motorcycle and have just been whacked in the testicles I discovered that things tend to happen very quickly – but in a blurry sort of fashion. I let out a large groan, shouted some choice Anglo-Saxon expletives and pulled hard on the front brake, which in turn caused the bike to start diving while the rear wheel began to slide. I came to an untidy halt at the side of the road. There were tears streaming down my cheeks. I was in excruciating pain, bent double over the petrol tank, and I was shouting very loudly above the bike's exhaust note: 'Fuck. Fuck. Fuck.'

It was at this point I saw him – or her. Dressed in long white shiny PVC boots, a G-string and a tasselled bra, the apparition was standing by the road a few feet ahead of me. He was a good six feet tall, a black African transsexual, and judging by the size of the white lace gloves he was wearing he had very large hands – and also a pair of enormous boobs. He was standing looking at me with a mixture of surprise and bemusement. Clearly regular customers did not usually arrive kerbside announcing their intentions, but the F-word needs no translation in any language and here was a potential client arriving on a motorcycle and shouting his head off about what he clearly wanted.

A little way off to the side was another hulking great black lady-man dressed in black leather and sitting at what looked like a tiny card table complete with a red and white checked tablecloth. Maybe this was the more expensive high-level version of what these people had to offer – perhaps a little roadside dining at the card table before we got down to the serious business?

I had stalled the bike, having let the clutch out abruptly in my pain and surprise at meeting these new roadside friends. I fumbled around for a while, trying to find the right gear, still suffering and with my eyes watering, but I managed to start the bike up and ride off. As I passed them the PVC-booted one looked at me with eyes that were as round as saucers. The make-up looked like it had been applied with a paintbrush and the wig was not set quite square on his head. Evidently both of us were equally surprised at the encounter. I nodded a greeting and quickly disappeared around the next corner, breathing a sigh of relief.

* * * * * *

I never made it to the Pope's summer house, but I did get as far as the farmland on the outskirts of Rome. It was here, with little traffic and winding country roads, that I rediscovered all over again what it was I liked about riding a motorcycle. Italy taught me many things about riding: to be ever observant; to expect the unexpected at any given moment; to pay attention to traffic behind; and always to read the road. I felt, after my Italian experiences, that I could ride anywhere, handle any traffic conditions and cope with any road surfaces. How little did I know…

I spent several weeks mulling a plan over in my mind. I talked with Anne – my soon to be wife – about how I really wanted to return to the US, sell my Harley-Davidson Nightster and buy an even bigger motorcycle – and then head out into the great unknown. I had absolutely no idea where I was going to go or what I was going to see, but I was determined that I was going to spend several months on the road, exploring the backwaters of the United States of America.

I was happy to try and do this all alone, but Anne could sense imminent problems for me in her country. She too had a passion for motorcycles, she rode them far better than I did and she was also pretty handy with a camera, which was how I pitched the idea to her that she should come along with me and take the photographs for this book. I don't think she ever doubted that I would try to live my dream of a motorcycle road trip around the US, but she had the previous experience and foresight to know what might happen to an oblivious Englishman who had trouble getting his trousers on in the morning and regularly experienced difficulty remembering which street he lived on.

I also have to give Anne credit for not saying anything when I told her that maybe we could get as far as the state of Ar-Kansas. I sort of knew I might just be in over my head with this project when I saw a slightly quizzical look in her eye.

'I think you might mean Arkansas,' explained Anne. 'Sounds like a great idea. I have always wanted to see the US away from the beaten track. Many people, including Americans, just have no idea what's out there.'

Some of my American friends had told me that I could expect to find groups of marauding neo-fascist militia, randomly shooting people and waiting to overthrow the government, while stretches of remote desert were home to ostracised paedophiles and murderers. They said that in some small towns people wouldn't understand my English accent and would think I was from another planet. I'd also run into outlaw motorcycle clubs and generally end up being mutilated, killed and then probably eaten. And all this could happen to me in a country that is considered by some to be the greatest country on earth. As one of my American friends put it: 'There's a whole heap of nothing out there until you get to the east coast. Why on earth would you want to go there?'

Precisely. *It seemed like a good idea at the time.*

CHAPTER TWO

CALIFORNIA SCREAMING

Buying a new motorcycle – Getting on the road in the US – Freeway hell –
Entering Julian – California deserts – Trousers off in public – Dates

The United States of America never ceases to amaze me. I am
constantly astounded by the sheer enormity of this country, the
widely differing states and peoples, the astonishingly diverse
topography of the mountains, deserts and open spaces – and how
simple day-to-day living can be if you have money and how hard it is
if you don't. America touches every other country and every living
soul in the world. For some people it's a nation to be reviled. For
others it really is the land of the free and a place where dreams come
true if you are prepared to work hard for them – that's why so many
people want to go there to live.

The USA's 50 states are loosely knitted together to form the most
powerful nation on the planet, but each state has its own history,
laws, food and, believe it or not, even its own culture. It's a truly
fascinating place, and I really wanted to try and get under its skin, to
discover more about it from the saddle of a motorcycle, and also to
look at it from my perspective as an Englishman.

I'd spent many years coming to the US on business and had worked
there for five years before returning to Europe. I'd been to New York,
Los Angeles, San Francisco, Miami and a host of other big cities but I
had never experienced what I considered to be the real US – small town
America. I looked at maps showing oddly named towns in the middle
of deserts or up in the Rocky Mountains. What did people do out there
in what seemed to be the middle of absolutely nowhere? Some people
told me there was nothing to see if I did set foot out there and I would
be foolish even to attempt it. I remained unconvinced.

With Barack Obama installed as the 44th President of the United

States in 2009 I sensed a real shift and change in the country. There was a feeling of optimism, despite the sudden economic downturn. Some were likening Obama's election to the momentous occasion when John F. Kennedy arrived in the White House in 1961. I wanted to see if this wave of new-found optimism had reached the smaller, quieter corners of America. Was Obama liked or hated? Did people even care they had a new president?

America holds many contradictions and myths, but I was often surprised to find, while travelling around on my bike, that some of my preconceived ideas about the country as a whole were true. Hollywood may often lie, but occasionally its films actually reflect a partial reality. By this I mean I found that small town America really does exist. There *are* long empty roads through the desert, massive wide-open empty spaces, ubiquitous diners staffed by aggressive waitresses and interesting motels that look like they have come straight from the movies. But as I was to discover, all these things and many more besides are far, far better in real life than anything Hollywood has ever presented to us on the silver screen. And they look even better from the seat of a motorcycle.

* * * * * *

Ever since I was a young teenager I'd always wanted to make a series of motorcycle trips across the US, no doubt partly inspired by the *Easy Rider* poster I had on my bedroom wall. As an adult I'd seen a lot of both west and east coasts from a car seat, and had driven along some fantastic roads and seen some truly interesting sights. But I had never experienced that massive expanse of land, the 'middle bit' of the US as some people referred to it, the states with such enigmatic names – Nevada, Utah, Arizona and Wyoming.

There was no way, though, that I was going to head out into the unknown on my Harley-Davidson Nightster. It was a great short-distance motorcycle, but there was nowhere to store or carry anything, and I could hardly ride the thousands of miles I envisaged we'd travel while standing upright on the footpegs because the rear suspension was so hard. It had to go – and anyway another bike from Harley-Davidson had caught my eye: the Street Bob.

Launched in 2006, the Street Bob had already attracted a loyal following of Harley-Davidson enthusiasts. It had a bigger engine than the Nightster, it was a better ride and overall it was a larger motorcycle. At its launch the Street Bob had received good reviews from the motorcycle media, and while it was not a full-on Harley-Davidson touring bike it had the same 96 cubic inch engine (1,584cc). It was a retro-looking, stripped-out model in the Dyna range and seemed to offer everything I would want or need for long motorcycle journeys.

The main problem was that its luggage-carrying capacity was going to be a challenge, as there was very little space to put anything on it, and there turned out to be other issues with the Street Bob, as I later found out on the road in the US, but I had made up my mind. This was the motorcycle for me. It was offered in a very limited range of colours but my eye was caught by the black denim – a type of matt black paint on the tank and mudguards that was supposed to age with time, like a pair of your favourite jeans, according to the Harley-Davidson marketing blurb. It looked, as my American friends would say, absolutely killer.

* * * * * *

'Spider, where the hell is my motorcycle?' I bawled down the telephone. I was in no mood for polite conversation.

I come from a generation of Englishmen who were brought up to apologise for everything, whether it was their fault or not. If someone accidentally stands on an English person's toes on a crowded train they are compelled to say sorry, even though it's their foot that has just been crushed, and more often than not they preface any question to a stranger with 'I'm sorry … I'm lost/do you know where the bank is/my monkey is on fire'. You get the picture.

So I found myself increasingly uncomfortable about having to confront the Harley-Davidson staff about why my new motorcycle had failed to arrive when they said it would. I took the plunge and made the phone call to Spider, and found the only way of communicating that I was unhappy was to stop being so *very* English and apologising for bothering them. They had taken the money for my new bike and I simply needed to be 'American' and demand to know when they were going to deliver it.

My previous bike, the Nightster, had made it safely all the way back from Italy, arriving in the US with just a few marks on its paintwork where it had been tied down with rope by the Italian shipping company for its long sea voyage back to California. I was genuinely sad to see it go. It had prompted me to get back in the saddle and it had been undemanding and fun to ride. But the fact that it really wasn't cut out for long trips across America meant I had no option but to wave it goodbye.

After several hours of negotiating and arguing at the local Harley-Davidson dealership, where the original price of my new motorcycle seemed constantly to rise once taxes, more taxes and compulsory Californian exhaust emission charges were applied, I signed on the dotted line and traded in the Nightster for a 2010 Dyna Street Bob. As always, I had fallen for the patter and listened with my mouth open as Jeff, the salesman, extolled the virtues of the Street Bob as a long-distance cruiser or just great for riding around town. I also accepted his spiel without question when he told me that the Street Bob was a very hard model to find and the black denim colour scheme I was asking for almost impossible to obtain.

However, Jeff knew a Harley-Davidson dealership in northern California that might, just might, have the bike I wanted. It was going to take some serious negotiations, with Jeff insinuating he would have to sell some of his family members and personal possessions to help me get hold of this very rare motorcycle. I duly signed all the purchase forms, handed over the last of my money and sat back and waited the seven days Jeff promised me it would take for the Street Bob to arrive. I had done it again – bought a bike I'd never ridden and believed the salesman's talk and promises. Jeff was a genuinely good guy and tried his best for me, but in his eagerness to get me what I wanted and a sale for himself he had not really worked out the timing of the bike's arrival very accurately.

One week turned into two weeks, and then three, and I was getting very frustrated which is why I ended up on the phone asking Jeff's boss, the curiously named Spider, where my bike was. Jeff had been avoiding my angry calls, knowing he could give me no definitive answer, so Spider had stepped in to placate the irate Englishman.

'What can we do to make things better for you?' asked Spider.

'Well, for a start you can tell me when my motorcycle will arrive and then deliver it to my house,' I said. I was feeling a bit stupid really. I was making a big deal out of the bike not arriving on the agreed date and hearing myself complain on the phone made me sound like a petulant spoiled child.

'OK, this is what will happen,' said an unruffled Spider. 'Your bike should be with us by the end of the week. We will check it over and then get it delivered to your front door on Saturday morning. We don't normally do this for customers, but as a goodwill gesture we'll pay the cost of delivering it directly to you. Does that work?'

Saturday morning would be perfect, I said. But Saturday morning would also be the time in my town of Santa Ana, in California, when all the neighbours would be around for the twice-yearly garage sale. Essentially, everyone puts all the mysterious kitchen appliances and odd bits of furniture they have collected over the years up for sale on their driveway or front lawn. The neighbours come by to haggle and you dispose of decades of rubbish, all for the grand sum of about $12.50. It's similar to an English car-boot sale.

During a heated debate with a Mexican woman about the price of the fluorescent pot plants that had always induced serious dizzy spells and nausea, my 2010 Street Bob arrived on the back of a trailer. Amid the broken garden furniture, boisterous children and arguing bargain-hunting housewives, the motorcycle delivery man quietly unloaded my bike, gave me the keys and drove off quickly. It was finally here, sitting by the kerbside looking magnificent. The motorcycle I had wanted, the bike I was going to spend the next 12 months of my life on as I roamed the back roads and small towns of America. The motorcycle I had never even ridden.

Eventually I managed to spend the best part of two months getting acquainted with my new bike. The Street Bob weighed in at 667lb and was more than 100lb heavier than my old Nightster. There was a six-speed gearbox, rather than the Nightster's five gears, which would be better for cruising the long empty highways I envisioned I'd be riding. I kept the Street Bob's standard exhaust because it was a lot quieter than many of the modified motorcycles I'd seen around California, but it still sounded like a Harley-Davidson with that evocative 'potato, potato' engine note.

I contemplated changing my bike's handlebars for high-rise 'ape-hanger'-style bars that rise straight up for 16 inches, but I had read that in some US states motorcycle riders are forbidden from having their hands higher than their shoulders, so I kept the Street Bob's 10-inch mini-ape handlebars which turn back towards the rider. Unfortunately they always made my wrists ache when I rode, but I wanted to keep the Street Bob as standard as possible – the way Harley-Davidson had designed it. Admittedly, every Harley-Davidson is a blank canvas for the owner to modify and personalise to their own taste, but for me the Street Bob needed little modification, particularly as I did not relish wrestling with any after-market modifications by the side of the highway in an empty desert in the middle of nowhere. It remained exactly as it had left the Harley-Davidson factory in Kansas City, Missouri. Standard.

The first time I swung a leg over my new bike I knew I had made the right decision. It felt as agile as the Sportster, but the instant difference was a much smoother rear suspension, better and more positive brakes, and an easier clutch. This machine was actually comfortable and more than capable of doing long trips. I also liked its lower centre of gravity compared to the Nightster, which had always felt top heavy, as if it would topple over if I didn't pay enough attention when I came to a halt. Did I know what I was looking at with the

Street Bob? Not really. It appeared to be faster and just as nimble as my Sportster, and it looked great and went really well. What more could I ask for?

Lack of luggage space on a motorcycle is always an issue, but with a stripped-out Dyna like the Street Bob, which is basically a motorcycle with a big V-twin air-cooled engine, solo seat and handlebars and very little else, it was going to be a real problem. I had worked out I needed saddlebags, definitely a windscreen, and some engine-guards. Mounted on the front of the bike's frame the guards stuck out about 12 inches each side, just ahead of my legs, and I was reluctant to have them fitted as they looked awful and spoilt the lines of the motorcycle. But if I ever dropped the bike they would protect the fuel tank, which would be expensive to repair, and maybe stop me damaging the handlebars as well.

* * * * * *

One of the reasons I had returned to the US was to get married to my long-suffering fiancée, Anne, who'd accepted an offer of marriage from an idiot who'd proposed to her by offering an engagement ring in a bowl of olives. I'd thought *it was a good idea at the time*, but I realise now she could easily have unwittingly swallowed the ring; I'd felt it was an interesting and different approach…

Anne had travelled the world extensively. She had her own Harley-Davidson and could out-ride me any day of the week. She had also seen most of the US on car road trips as a youngster. When I suggested that, instead of a honeymoon, we should hit the road on motorcycles Anne put on a brave face and said that would be fantastic. She genuinely made it seem like it was something she had always wanted to do, but there were a couple of conditions if she was going to come on this trip. For a start, there was apparently a major language barrier to be crossed and Anne would help me steer clear of some of the pitfalls that she knew I would create all by myself.

'There are going to be towns out there in the back of beyond where people simply won't understand a thing you say because of your English accent,' explained Anne. 'Actually, come to think of it, there are times when I don't understand what you're saying. And while your English humour seems very funny to you, I guarantee that people will not get it. That could lead to all sorts of problems.'

I had to concede Anne's first point. There had been a lengthy discussion a while ago in a Chicago restaurant, when I had asked the waiter for a glass of water.

'Er... I am not sure we sell that here,' said the waiter eventually, looking furtively across the restaurant for some kind of back-up from his colleagues.

'WATER,' I said yet again, slowly, spelling out the word, and trying hard not to sound exasperated that the simple task of ordering a glass of colourless liquid at an American restaurant could be so complicated.

'Oh wadder,' he said. 'Why didn't you say so? I'm sorry, I didn't understand your accent. Are you from Australia?'

So Anne had a point on the language front. She also had a point about my dry sense of humour. 'You may think you're being funny, but many Americans get very confused by you and think you are just being plain rude,' she tactfully explained.

I immediately agreed that out on the road I would not speak to anyone unless I was spoken to, would not ask for water, and absolutely on no account would I make a joke about anything or anyone. I would leave all the talking to Anne and merely hang around in the background, observing and trying to look enigmatic and interesting to anyone who happened to be passing. I failed on all counts, as it transpired. Fortunately Anne and I are still married but at times, out on the road, I am sure it was a close-run thing for her.

Another of Anne's requests before we left our house and rode out of California was for her to be allowed to give me a hand working out a route of where precisely we were going to go. But this was *my* project. I knew where I wanted to go and how we were going to get there, but I am also a man and therefore in charge of directions – and like many men I will not stop and ask anyone, even when I have been lost for hours and have passed my destination several times without realising it.

'Look, I think I've got this covered,' I said to Anne one evening, after I'd spent several hours studying huge piles of maps and reference books. 'We need to head due west out of California for a couple of hundred miles and we should be in Arizona by the evening.'

'If we take the route you're suggesting and head due west we will end up in the Pacific Ocean,' said Anne.

So I conceded that while I would like to continue to plan the route, I would always confer with her beforehand and let her know precisely which ocean we would be riding into each day.

* * * * * *

How on earth do you plan for a motorcycle road trip across the United States? I had studied maps and read a whole series of travel books, but there was no easy guide on how to do this. My list of questions seemed endless. What should I take with me? Where would I find the best weather? Where were the good riding roads? America is simply huge. It looked like a vast undiscovered space and it seemed to grow bigger every time I looked at it. There seemed to be new states I'd not spotted before and they all looked empty of human habitation and simply enormous.

I had read that the US had a land area of approximately 1.9 billion acres, including Alaska, although this huge state was one step too far as it involved going through another entire continent-sized country called Canada. And if the number of acres in the US sent my head reeling then the actual landmass, which equated to 3,794,101 miles, made my brain implode. If I planned to cover all those miles I could well be in the saddle of my Harley-Davidson (based on a good 200 miles of riding a day) for close to 51 years!

To give an idea of the distances, what I thought would be a straightforward first day's ride to get out of the state of California was actually a journey of 450 miles. For a European that was like riding from London to Frankfurt in Germany, and on that ride you'd pass through four countries – not just a single state. No matter how I looked at the map there was no easy way out of California, for the route east looked long and tortuous and involved a lot of freeway riding. How on earth were we going to be able to do this?

* * * * * *

The man in the bookshop eyed me suspiciously. In one hand I was clutching a large road map of New Mexico that had caught my attention, and in the other I was juggling my crash helmet, riding goggles and gloves. I was hot and flustered and my leather riding jacket wasn't best suited for book shopping.

'A tourist, eh?' he said, noticing my accent. 'New Mexico is a really big place. It's got some cool places to see, though. Are you going there for a vacation?'

'Not really. I'm planning on riding there,' I replied, trying my best to sound like the seasoned motorcycle traveller of my dreams.

He stared at me intently. 'Wow, man! You're riding a horse to New Mexico. Man, that's a really long journey for you and your pony to take. Hey, Maud,' he said, turning to a little old lady standing near him at the cash register. 'This guy's riding a horse to New Mexico!'

Maud looked at me curiously.

'Really? Are you sure you want to do that, honey? It's a long way, but my gosh that sounds fun. Like a real adventure. What sort of horse you got? My sister breeds horses. She may be able to give you some advice,' she said.

This was all getting out of hand. I was standing in front of them dressed in motorcycle gear. Didn't that give them a little clue about my mode of transport? Or did they think I was just a very cautious car driver who liked to wear a crash helmet for his own protection?

'I don't actually have a horse,' I said. 'I'm planning on riding my motorcycle there and back and need this map to work out a good route.'

They both looked at me as if I was totally mad. Clearly their initial idea about me riding a horse to New Mexico was a much better and far more likely option. Who would be stupid enough to ride a motorcycle all the way to New Mexico from California?

* * * * * *

I had done my homework about what I should take along on the trip, though. There are some excellent Harley-Davidson and other US motorcycle websites that give a wealth of information. Based upon their suggestions I needed to include a full tool kit, flashlights, CB radio, hot weather gear, cold weather gear, wet weather gear, spare boots, spare helmet, tent, blanket, motorcycle spares, welding kit and maybe an air compressor. Plus some people were suggesting it would be a good idea to have satellite navigation, a radio, maps, books, a large library of travel guides and a small monkey. Well, not the small monkey or the welding kit, but that gives an idea of the scale of the problem I was facing. What could I afford to ditch and what could I not do without?

Did I need all the assorted items of weatherproof clothing I'd amassed? My motorcycle boots, jeans, T-shirt and leather jacket would just have to suffice.

I really liked the idea of a handlebar-mounted satellite navigation system, but that involved me working out how to rewire the Street Bob and I know the limitations of my electrical capabilities. I'd probably cause the bike to start every time I pressed the horn, smoke would come out of the battery and the wheels would then fall off. So good old-fashioned maps would have to be sufficient, plus a couple of route guides.

For communication I'd rely on my cell phone, although I knew full well that coverage was going to be patchy at best up some of the mountains and out in the deserts I was planning on riding through. One wise purchase I did make was a helmet-to-helmet communication system for Anne and myself. It had a range of half a mile and allowed Anne to give me sensible instructions and directions while I shouted and swore at people and things that scared the wits out of me.

I also took along an impressive set of tools that for some reason included a wood chisel, part of a glue gun, a box of small nails and a pack of plastic ties. None of these would be any use on the bolts or screws of my motorcycle, but at least it was reassuring to know that if I broke down I could build a kitchen table at the roadside.

The other real problem I faced was that my saddlebags measured just 20 inches x 13 inches x 7 inches each, so with my woodworking tools and a change of clothing there was little room for anything else. I managed to squeeze in a small FM/AM radio in case I wanted to listen to music. Unfortunately it took to switching itself on at random moments, tuning into Spanish-speaking stations and making it sound like I had a very small Mariachi band concealed in my saddlebag. Then there were maps, more maps and guidebooks, which took up the rest of the very limited space. And then, just to be safe, some more maps.

* * * * * *

Next I had to decide exactly where I was going to ride to and how long it was going to take. It was late spring. Would I be back before Christmas? I felt my first stab at a US motorcycle road trip should take a minimum of 14 days, maybe three weeks, maybe even longer, depending on what I found out there and where the road took me. I estimated that around 250 miles a day would allow me to stop and see things as well as cover a reasonable distance on each leg of the journey. I was to find out, almost immediately, that a minimum of 300 miles a day was barely sufficient to get from one town to another, through the wide-open spaces between them, just to find a bed for the night.

In truth, I had thought I would camp my way around the US with nothing more than a blanket, sleeping bag and a tent, sleeping out in the wild with just a huge desert sky overhead. But much as a tent sounded an interesting proposal for overnight accommodation, Anne persuaded me that we really should consider stopping at the cheap motels that we would undoubtedly find along the way. She'd also mentioned serial killers and coyotes, so I reluctantly conceded.

There was one thing about which I was absolutely adamant, however. I wanted to do as little interstate freeway riding as possible. For a start, I wanted to see the US away from these massive highways, to take my time to look at what was really out there and understand what I was looking at, but my second reason was completely and totally irrational.

For the best part of 25 years I'd driven all over the world, taken four-wheel-drive vehicles into South American jungles and on unpaved roads across the Andes in Chile, and also raced cars around some of Europe's most demanding motor sport circuits at spectacularly slow speeds. I'd tested cars around the globe, driving long, mind-numbing and exhausting routes, and remained unfazed by some of the world's worst traffic-blighted and crazy cities such as Athens and Bangkok. Heck, I'd even survived riding in Rome's chaotic traffic. But despite all that motoring experience, the thought of riding a large motorcycle on a Californian freeway scared the hell out of me. It had nothing to do with speed, as most US freeways are restricted to a 65–70mph limit, depending on which state you are in – plus these limits are strictly enforced by the highway patrol, as I'd found to my cost on several occasions while driving a car in both California and Arizona – but a lot to do with the fact that sometimes there was very little room for error.

On Californian freeways there is something called the HOV lane (High Occupancy Vehicle), where vehicles with more than one passenger – and motorcycles – are allowed to travel to avoid experiencing the ubiquitous stop-start traffic jams. It sounds like a great idea, but the trouble is riding a motorcycle in the HOV lane often means you have some vehicle 10 feet off your back wheel, and at 65mph that's decidedly unpleasant. One mistake in braking and the car driver could catapult you and your bike straight into the other packed lanes of traffic – and there are sometimes as many as six of them all moving in the same direction.

Then there's the mixture of road surfaces that run from occasionally smooth tarmac to what is euphemistically called 'the slab', i.e. concrete that is laid in sections and makes up 90% of California's freeway surfaces. It's grooved to allow rainwater to drain off and the sections mean there's constantly a horizontal ridge to ride over where the two slabs meet, making bike handling very tricky. And don't even mention the 18-wheeler trucks and the backdraughts they create ... riding a bike on these roads is a hugely unpleasant and miserable experience, constantly exhausting, always scary and occasionally very dangerous. However, I had no choice if I wanted to get out of California quickly. I needed to take Interstate 5, the San Diego freeway, south before I could strike out for the states that lay to the east, and I also had to brave the strong breezes as I rode parallel with the Pacific Ocean.

In early May I finally decided it was time to go. The saddlebags were packed, though I still had no precise route in mind. I was planning on heading south, travelling into the mountains and high deserts of Arizona, and then taking in New Mexico. On the maps it looked simple – nothing to worry about, a straightforward run – but I soon discovered that maps don't always tell the whole truth; or maybe I'm just not very good at reading them.

Anne was following me on her bike as we turned left out of our street in Santa Ana. Within the space of just five minutes I was facing my worst nightmare, because we rode straight into a massive traffic jam on the San Diego freeway.

* * * * * *

We needed to travel some 40 miles towards San Diego on Interstate 5 before we could turn off and head east, inland towards the Cleveland National Forest, and over what looked on my map like some small mountains. The route would then take us straight into the Anza-Borrego Desert.

It was a truly beautiful warm Southern Californian day as we left, with bright blue skies overhead. Despite avoiding the rush hour the traffic on the freeway was nose-to-tail, with cars and trucks as far as I could see, but before I even had time to gather my thoughts the enormous cavalcade started moving in unison, quickly getting up to 65mph, and I had no option but to get going and hang on for dear life. With a strong breeze coming in off the Pacific Ocean making my bike handle oddly I found myself constantly fighting to correct which way I was travelling, and my hands were numb from the combination of gripping the handlebars too tightly and the engine vibration you'd expect from a Harley-Davidson that has a rubber-mounted V-twin which makes the whole bike shake.

Overhead circled two massive US transport helicopters, dropping supplies to troops training at Camp Pendleton, the major west coast base serving as the prime amphibious training centre for the US Marine Corps. Established in 1942 and 82 miles south of Los Angeles, this enormous military facility, home to the fearsome 1st Marine Expeditionary Force, takes in more than 125,000 acres of Southern California terrain and is strictly off limits to civilians. It was also the stumbling block that had forced me to take the freeway in the first place.

I felt vulnerable and remote. I was wearing a full-face helmet for the first time, to allow two-way communication between Anne and myself using the short-wave radio system we'd bought, but the trouble was I couldn't use it. I was too scared to take my hands off the handlebars in order to press the radio intercom button, so our freeway ride was restricted to my grunting in terror while Anne talked to me. I began to have serious doubts about whether I was going to be able to make the series of trips of several thousand miles we'd planned for the months ahead.

Then I heard some words, loud and clear in my helmet headphones, that took me completely by surprise: 'Jesus loves you and is waiting for you in heaven. Repent your sins now, brothers and sisters. Are you ready to show your love for Jesus Christ?'

I thought I'd taken leave of my senses. Had I terrified myself so much that I was now hearing demented voices in my head, or had I already died and was now on my way to the eternal life? Or perhaps Anne, who was behind me, had suddenly found Jesus while riding her motorcycle? The biblical messages kept getting louder before I realised that my helmet communication system was picking up a local Christian radio station that seemed intent on saving my soul. Great. Now I not only had to contend with the rigours of a 40-mile freeway ride through crazy traffic, I also had no option but to listen to some evangelical preacher on a radio station that I couldn't switch off because I didn't want to take my left hand off the handlebars. This was getting insane – and it was only the very first hour of the first day.

Suddenly the turn-off for the town of Oceanside appeared. I counted down the miles and, with a mixture of unbelievable relief and gratitude for my good fortune, shot off Interstate 5, away from the racing traffic and on to a much smaller and quieter two-lane highway. I had made it! This was more like it. Fewer cars and people, roads I knew I could handle – I could actually do this. Heck, I even started talking to my Christian preacher, who was still chatting away inside my crash helmet.

Highway 76 had looked an interesting road from the map I'd studied at home. It wound up into the Cleveland National Forest and on towards the remote deserts of Southern California. I knew that within a few miles we would start to climb up into the mountains to a town called Julian where we could stop and plan the next section of the day's riding. I'd also chosen this route because I really wanted to be able to tell Anne over our intercom system: 'OK. We're now entering Julian.' It just sort of appealed to my stupid sense of humour, the one that could get me into so much trouble here in the US.

* * * * * *

The Cleveland National Forest is an area of outstanding natural beauty and on a motorcycle in early summer it really was the only way to experience the landscape at its best. There was very little traffic and the summer flowers were just coming out. It was a naturalist's dream, set in 424,000 acres, with Highway 76 winding right through the middle of it. Yet this sea of tranquillity had not always been so.

In 1582 Juan Rodriguez Cabrillo arrived from Spain and claimed

San Diego and California for himself and his country, from that day forward and forever more. But life has a hilarious way of altering ambitious men's plans. In Cabrillo's time the lands within the Cleveland Forest were known only to the desert and coastal Indian tribes who used to traverse them, moving with the seasons looking for food and shelter. The Kumeyaay, Luiseños, Cahuilla and Cupeño nations found a good living in the forest and were largely left alone by the Europeans for the next couple of hundred years.

Then, in 1769, the European settlers started to take an interest in the peninsular mountain range that runs through the Cleveland Forest and its coastal plain. Spain was concerned that England and Russia were about to seize the lands and appointed Junípero Serra to establish the first of his 21 California missions in what is now downtown San Diego. (The remainder of his missions were scattered up the California coast as far as San Francisco.)

Prior to this the human impact on the land that makes up today's Cleveland Forest had been insignificant. The Spanish explorer Vizcaíno and Cabrillo himself had reported that the native Indians did considerable burning of the brushlands along the coast and in the mountains, but that overall there was very little human influence. However, with the arrival of a ranching culture in the nineteenth century, the landscape underwent some dramatic changes. At first it was subtle, as European- and Asian-introduced plants slowly replaced the native grassland. Some botanists still argue that this invasion of the settlers' plants had more effect on the region than any other single factor. Widespread overgrazing throughout the area, brush and trees cut for fence posts, and fires being set to clear the place for forage increased the impact on the land well beyond that of the Indians in previous centuries. Then, in 1869, gold was discovered near Julian, attracting hordes of miners from around the world and swelling the town's population to greater than that of nearby San Diego. The influx of miners left its mark on the land. Trees were cut for mine timbers, heat and cooking fuel. And great expanses of brush were burned so miners could penetrate new areas to search for minerals.

As the mines petered out, so did many of the early ranches, which had been overgrazed and had lost their chief labour force as the Indian population died off, in part due to the hardship of having immigrant masters but also because they succumbed to European diseases. This in turn led to a series of problems with managing the water sources found in the Cleveland Forest, which were now of critical importance to the growing Southern California communities. Reports in the late 1800s refer to fires that burned out of control for weeks at a time. Lack of protection from fire was causing serious damage to irrigation works, the water supplies of rural areas, the small metropolitan area of San Diego, and other coastal towns. In 1891 the Forest Reserve Act was passed, primarily to protect the water sources in the area but also to prevent illegal timber cutting. Cleveland National Forest became one of the first protected areas in the US.

In 1907 President Theodore Roosevelt made extensive land additions to the forest and a year later it had grown to an immense 1,904,826 acres. But it wasn't to last for long. With an ever-increasing population in Southern California, more than 60%, or 749,730 acres of natural wilderness, was returned to the public for houses and roads. The remainder was protected and became the Cleveland National Forest of today.

Despite man's interventions, the forest is still a place of outstanding natural beauty. I am always astonished how quickly you can leave the hustle and bustle of Orange County, Southern California, and be in small town America, travelling across wide-open spaces where nothing appears to have changed for decades. It had taken us less than two hours to get there. Admittedly, we still had to cross a huge section of California, but I felt I was thousands of miles away from home.

After the rigours of the San Diego freeway I needed to stop and catch my breath, so I pulled up in a car park immediately opposite Lake Henshaw at the base of the Palomar Mountains. This lake is a large, shallow reservoir originally constructed to support agriculture and fed by the San Luis Rey River. Over the years it had suffered poor management, long periods of drought and a host of planning arguments. It is also a major fishing attraction for anglers from San

Diego and despite not being very deep has apparently claimed a number of fishermen's lives over the years, due to the strong winds that blow across the water's surface. Quite how you drown from wind is still a mystery to me, but a number of the Lake Henshaw fishing websites I looked at constantly reminded anglers to be on their guard for wind.

Surrounded by one of the most extensive grasslands in Southern California, the lake is edged by the remnants of ancient woodland, including apparently the largest expanse of Engelmann oak trees in the world. There is little public access in the area, apart from the lake itself, as most of the land around the water consists of private ranches and the La Jolla Indian Reservation. That would explain the deathly hush. There was not a sound in the car park apart from my motorcycle's hot exhaust pipe ticking away as it cooled down. There was absolutely nobody about. Just two cars passed by in the 15 minutes I was there.

I was feeling more comfortable on the bike now. My arms still ached, but I had regained some feeling in my hands and my thumbs were no longer numb from the exertion of holding on to the handlebars too tightly. I'd also worked out the communications system with Anne and was able to raise my level of conversation from scared grunts to actual coherent sentences.

The deafening silence at the lake's edge was abruptly broken, however, by the sound of an angry-sounding bushwhacker being fired up as a friendly-looking man started attacking lakeside vegetation with a vengeance. It was a curious sight as all I could see were his head above the edge of the road and clouds of blue exhaust smoke. He nodded and smiled and continued thrashing the weed cutter around, then several minutes later he switched it off.

'I guess I'm kind of lucky today,' shouted the head at me from several feet below where I was standing as I looked out over the lake. He didn't wait for me to ask why. 'Some days I hit a couple of rattlesnakes with this thing. Not a nice experience.'

I nodded in agreement and realised then that my life was a whole lot better than his. Hard manual work every day with the additional element of a potential rattlesnake bite thrown in for good measure must be tough.

It was time to saddle up and drive the 15 miles or so to the former mining town of Julian. Finally I could announce to Anne that we were entering Julian. It was a great motorcycle ride into this town, with hairpin bends that climbed fast and smoothly to some 4,220 feet above sea level before we hit its outskirts. I think there may be a joke in there too somewhere...

For me the term 'town' evokes images of a place with a big market square, a town hall and sizeable buildings, and streets of houses with maybe a few factories thrown in. As I was so often to find, the term 'town' in America is often used for what I would recognise as a big village in England. A town in the US seems to refer to a place that perhaps has just a main street (usually called Main Street) with a scattering of houses off to one side, a church, and maybe a grocery store and a gas station.

Julian is just such a place. It was founded just after the US Civil War when displaced Confederate veterans from Georgia headed west to seek their fortunes in the new and mostly unsettled lands of Southern California. Among this group were two cousins, Drue Bailey and Mike Julian, who found a lush meadow between Volcan Mountain and the Cuyamaca Mountains. The cousins were there in 1869 when cattleman Fred Coleman found the first flecks of gold in a creek ridge nearby. It was the George Washington mine near Julian that struck the first gold seam but it wasn't very big, and San Diego County's first and only gold rush was over in a matter of ten years, with very little gold actually being found in any of the mines. But the mining community remained and grew into a town named Julian, in honour of Mike, who was later elected San Diego County Assessor.

The settlers and some of the gold prospectors who stayed began farming the rich agricultural land around the town. While many varieties of crops were planted and farm animals reared, Julian proved a particularly good place to grow apples. Even today apple trees continue to be grown all around. This would explain the enormous signs announcing 'Try our Apple Pie' posted everywhere by the Julian Pie Company, purveyors of a product they proudly labelled as 'American as Apple Pie'.

Today, Julian seemed a nice place to visit but very much a tourist stop and a resting place for travellers. There were a few bars and a lot of visitor shops selling the usual trinkets that you never knew you wanted or needed. But there was still the feel of an old town and some of the nineteenth-century buildings remained, although they had clearly seen better days.

There was one enormous wooden building on a side street that looked in keeping with the mining town's façade and yet it was only a few years old. Called 'The Birdwatcher', it was literally crammed to the rafters with what the owners described as 'everything for people who love wild birds'. I had never seen so many feeders and different food types for specific bird species under one roof. Who drives all the way out here to buy this stuff, I thought? Clearly a lot of people did as the shop was busy, with bags and bags of peanuts and the unusually named 'tit fat' being bought.

The climb into the mountains had brought relief from the freeway traffic but a change in the weather, because grey clouds had started to form, promising rain. The temperature had dropped too, from a heady 75°F to a cool 62°. And it was definitely time for lunch. As this first journey unfolded I was to learn two important lessons when riding a motorcycle across the US. The first was to stop regularly for food, as you develop a ravenous appetite when riding. I assume this is because you are in the fresh air and using a lot of upper body strength to keep a heavy motorcycle pointing in the right direction. Missing any meal out on the road made me get tired very quickly; I would become light headed and that ruined my concentration. The second lesson was always, always, always to refuel, no matter how much petrol you might think you had in your bike's tank. I was to find out later that running a motorcycle in 90°F heat in the desert with next to no petrol in the tank causes severe anxiety, and it was certainly one of the stupider things I did on my road trip.

Lunch was a huge hamburger the size of a small dinner plate, with chips, at the quaintly named Miners' Diner on Julian's Main Street. The diner laid claim to having an original old-fashioned soda fountain and apparently opened for business in 1928. Judging by its décor not much had been done to it since then. Perhaps the only changes were the addition of a TV in the corner that was being studiously watched by an elderly woman chewing solemnly on a sandwich, or the massive carved bear that had been placed in the diner's window and reared menacingly on its hind legs for no other reason than that it could.

I would have liked to linger longer in Julian but we needed to press on and find somewhere to stay for the night. As I refuelled my bike the skies above looked ominously grey. We needed to escape that rain and get down the other side of the mountain to the Anza-Borrego Desert that lay some 30 miles to the west.

* * * * * *

Nothing had prepared me for traversing the deserts of the US on a bike. I had been through some of them in a car many times, but you miss out on the entire experience when you sit cocooned in the air-conditioned environment of a modern motor vehicle. A motorcycle, though, gives you a taste of the desert's raw edge. The heat, the smells and the wildlife all converged as I found myself bombarded by swarms of furry beetles that bounced off the bike's windscreen and fuel tank and then hit me in the legs like small hairy tennis balls.

For years I had dreamed of the day when I would be sitting on a motorcycle, looking at a ramrod-straight two-lane road with yellow marking lines down the centre, disappearing like a tarmac ribbon towards an infinite horizon. It was everything I had hoped for and much more besides.

And the silence … it sounds an odd thing to say, but I had never heard such silence before. There was not a single sound – no traffic, no people, no dogs barking, no car alarms, no music – just an occasional warm breeze and a complete absence of noise. In the space of 20 miles we had gone from the lush pastures and farmland around Julian to a barren landscape of yellow-brown rock formations and weird desert plants. If it were not for the road I could have sworn I was the first person ever to have set foot in this sensational but eerily empty natural wilderness.

The 600,000 acres of the Anza-Borrego Desert State Park make it the largest state park in California, named after the Spanish explorer Juan Bautista de Anza Nieto (1736–88) and the Spanish word 'borrego' for Bighorn sheep. There is an eighteenth-century portrait of Nieto, which shows a man with one of the most impressive beards I have ever seen in my life. It looks, in fact, as if he has an entire Bighorn sheep tucked under his chin. But big beard aside, Nieto made a brilliant military career from fighting Apache Indians in Arizona and then traipsing around California on behalf of the king of Spain to prevent the Russians from trying to invade from the north. His name lives on in this simply stunning desert, which he crossed in 1774 along with 3 padres, 20 soldiers, 11 servants, 35 mules, 65 cattle and 140 horses and then claimed for the Spanish throne.

Today the Anza-Borrego Desert has 500 miles of dirt roads, 12 wilderness areas and miles of hiking trails. It is surrounded by a lot of mountain ranges, including the superbly named Bucksnorts and the Santa Rosas in the north, the Jacumba Mountains to the south and the Vallecito and Pinyon Mountains on its western side. To the east are the Borrego Mountains, which taper into the Carrizo Badlands before falling away into the Salton Trough.

It also boasts a huge and diverse range of indigenous desert plants and animals that include roadrunners, Golden eagles, Kit foxes, Mule deer and Bighorn sheep as well as iguanas, Chuckwalla lizards and the Red Diamond rattlesnake. Perhaps like most people, for me the mental image of a desert was of a lifeless expanse, a dead area of rocks and sand and nothing much else. On closer inspection while on the road, and later doing some homework, I discovered just how much life is sustained in a desert. Plants and animals have found a very successful way to adapt to the desert, despite the extremes in temperature and a distinct lack of rainfall.

Right now, though, for one afternoon I had this entire desert to myself. Well, that's not strictly true because Anne was with me, taking photographs, and once while pulled up at the side of the road we were passed by an immense truck heading straight for San Diego. But that was it. For the next 50 miles we saw nobody – no cars, and not a thing to remind us of twenty-first-century life.

There were some truly impressive aerobatics being performed by a couple of Turkey vultures immediately ahead. Wheeling on the thermal currents rising from the desert floor, these immense birds with wingspans of up to 70 inches were to be constant companions over the next few weeks. Always on the lookout for road-kill or, in my case, incompetent motorcyclists, they looked magnificent until you got close up. Their aerodynamic wings and body are covered in a dense black plumage that stops abruptly at the upper part of the neck and there is then a totally bald red-pink wrinkled head, two sinister-looking eyes and a very sharp hooked beak. They reminded me of my old history teacher, Mrs Griffiths, and she was a pretty fearsome woman too.

My motorcycle, being all black, was heating up nicely in the fiery desert sun. The matt paint was absorbing all the sun's rays while the air-cooled V-twin engine, which relies on the bike being kept moving to remain cool, was slowly cooking the lower part of my body.

I had also learned early on this trip to read the road signs. In a car I tend to ignore the suggested cornering speeds at the side of the road. On a motorcycle they are invaluable. The road surface through the desert was excellent, but it had some odd cambers that threw you off balance in the middle of a corner. I really had to begin concentrating and spend less time admiring the landscape.

The bug population seemed to have increased dramatically and my screen was now awash with debris and the remains of insects. I was having a hard time looking through all the blood and guts that were smeared across it, and I found the only way I could see the road ahead was to stand up a little on my bike's footpegs and peer over the top of the windshield.

I was concentrating so much on the roads that I failed to notice that every time I braked the inside of my right leg was catching the bike's air filter which was scalding hot. It wasn't until I stopped in the evening that I discovered some curious burns to my right calf muscle. In the ensuing weeks on the road I had to ride with my right leg tucked out slightly to try and prevent this, but without much success, and I carry the scars today. Right now, though, in the Anza-Borrego Desert I was in seventh heaven. The road rose, weaving through the desert landscape, and despite the heat I felt comfortable cruising at a steady 60mph, savouring the feeling of being alone on a motorcycle with nothing and nobody ahead as far as the eye could see.

I stopped to take a moment to reflect, pulling into a historical site marked as Box Canyon. This is a significant point in the Anza-Borrego Desert as waves of nineteenth-century immigrants came through here, along with the Butterfield Overland Mail Route, while in 1846 General Keamy led the US Army of the West through here just before the battle of San Pasqual. This was one of the bloodiest conflicts of the Mexican War in California, and ultimately led to Keamy and his army finishing off the Mexican resistance at San Gabriel River and La Masa, thus securing California's future as part of the United States.

A group of Mormons had dug through the shallowest point in the mountains to create the first route, finally completing the work in 1847 to make this one of the first immigrant gateways into Southern California. It was an amazing feat of engineering and must have been exceptionally hard manual work, considering the inhospitable environment and the ever-present bands of marauding Indians. Many of these trails have eroded over time and there's not much to see today, but you can still get an impression of how important this place was in the history of California and the US.

* * * * * *

Time was pressing again, and we needed to cover as much ground as possible if we were to get to Arizona the next day. This desert highway was now leading towards the town of El Centro, some 50 feet below sea level, in the far eastern corner of Southern California. In less than a few hours we'd gone from 4,000 plus feet high on a mountainside to below sea level. Such is the topography of the US.

El Centro lays claim to being the birthplace of pop star Cher. It also grows vast quantities of melons and grapefruit, thanks to irrigation water diverted from the Colorado River, and is the winter home of the US Air Force display team, the Blue Angels. Just as I was considering all that information I spotted two military jets flying side by side. I am no expert, but these guys were certainly travelling fast and they appeared to be almost within touching distance of each other. Midway on the flat horizon both planes suddenly reared up and pointed vertically towards the sky like a couple of rockets, then shot up several thousand feet and out of my sight. It was like having my own personal air display. Earlier in this book I said there were numerous occasions, while I was out there in America's backwaters, when I wondered if any of this really happened. This was such a day.

* * * * * *

The next morning we were heading due east and straight towards Arizona on Interstate Highway 8. The weather was definitely getting hotter by the minute. It was well above 90°F and climbing steadily towards 100°F at only 10.00 in the morning. For a while I'd been surrounded by featureless, scrubby desert brush, which was flat and uninteresting, but suddenly I was thrust into a bizarre landscape of towering white sand dunes which completely surrounded me and the road.

These, to be more precise, were the Algodones Dunes some 42 miles east of El Centro, and at a rest area in the middle of the two-lane highway I rolled to a halt to take a better look at them. This immense natural phenomenon, which stretches along both sides of

Interstate 8 for more than 50 miles, measures just 10 miles across with the dunes reaching 200 feet high in places. It's like being in a child's immense sand pit. The dunes have featured in several Hollywood films, including scenes in the *Star Wars* epics. At any given moment I quite expected Lawrence of Arabia to appear on the horizon leading a band of Bedouin tribesmen.

Perched on the highest sand dune, however, all I could see was a Chevrolet SUV of the US Border Patrol (USBP), with two officers scanning the horizon with binoculars for illegal immigrants coming over the border from nearby Mexico. The Border Patrol was to become an inextricable part of my journey through the US South-West. Many times I had entire stretches of roads and huge empty areas all to myself – with the exception of the Border Patrol.

A few weeks before my arrival in Arizona, the state had created a new law that gave police officers the right to stop anyone and ask for their residency credentials. There were arguments for and against this new rule, with some people condemning the action as draconian while the law's supporters applauded the new measure, saying that it was about time. As I write this, some of the more liberal American states were threatening to boycott Arizona for its new immigration measures while other states were considering following their example. I am not well informed about the US illegal immigration problem, but any place where you can be stopped and your identification checked out just because you look foreign doesn't sit quite right with me.

My own encounters with the US Border Patrol were frequent on this trip, but I found them always to be civil and polite. I lost count of the number of checkpoints we passed through, but every time I received a salute and a wave from the armed young men and women stopping and searching vehicles. Even in the middle of the day, in the searing heat, you might well turn a corner to find a USBP vehicle sitting in the blazing desert with the officers just watching and waiting.

We often passed long convoys of USBP vehicles out in the sticks, and huge car parks in small towns were often filled with vast numbers of USBP trucks and equipment. Never mind the reasoning and the logic behind all this, the thought that kept returning was how much all of this was costing the US taxpayer. And as we headed into Arizona there were occasional glimpses of the 800-mile-long fence that had been built between the US and Mexico to keep the illegal immigrants out. A fence or a wall doesn't work, to my mind. Just ask the East Germans or the Palestinians.

* * * * * *

The Algodones Dunes were bizarre, and they left a deep impression on me. They started abruptly and ended in just the same way, and nobody seemed too certain how or why they were created. Some experts think there is a link to a nearby lake, with desert winds blowing sand from the lakeshore that simply piled up over thousands and thousands of years. It's as if someone had emptied part of Africa's Sahara Desert into a river basin in Southern California.

Between El Centro and Yuma, which was the first town we came to in Arizona on Interstate 8, are 110 miles of empty, baking-hot desert. Yet this was the route the early Spanish explorers and settlers took as they headed out on the flat but forbidding Camino del Diablo, along the banks of the usually dry Gila River. It was also freeway riding at its worst for me. My hands were numb again from a combination of the engine vibration running up through my bike's frame and still holding on to the handlebars too tightly. I couldn't feel my fingers, which made it difficult to use the brake and make turning signals, and I was constantly being buffeted by hot gusts of turbulent air as trucks and cars tore past me. I just hung on to my motorcycle for dear life for the next two hours as we headed towards Yuma and Arizona.

Right behind me was Anne. She had absolutely no problem with freeway bike riding and was running rings around me. If she was frustrated with her scared and pathetically slow husband she didn't show it, instead keeping up a constant conversation via the intercom on things that she had just seen or wanted me to look at as we rode along.

'Are you OK? Would you like to stop?' Anne would often ask me.

'Hgmmff … no … I'm fine,' I would reply, when in fact all I wanted to do was get off the motorcycle and walk away, or even hail a passing cattle truck and go home to bed.

When we eventually got to Yuma we stopped in the old town to take a look and give me time to get some form of circulation back into my hands. The scalding air intake on my bike's engine was making the burn on the inside of my calf worse, too. I came to the conclusion I was slowly cooking myself on my motorcycle plus I was seriously dizzy and dehydrated from the dry desert air and the high temperatures.

The Colorado River marked the crossing from California into Arizona and I have to admit to a sense of disappointment. Instead of a huge rushing torrent some miles across, I was faced with what could best be described as a big murky green stream. The re-routing of the Colorado, the man-made dams further upriver and the huge demands made upon the water supply by the states of California, Nevada and Arizona had reduced the Colorado to nothing more than a slow meandering trickle as it made its way past Yuma and out into the Gulf of California.

The town of Yuma claims to be the hottest town in the US, but this may not be strictly true as whoever was taking the temperature was caught manipulating the figures some years ago. It does, though, have extremely hot summers and mild winters with average July temperatures of 107°F. According to the *Guinness Book of Records*, Yuma is also the sunniest place on earth. Out of a possible 4,050 hours of daylight a year the sun shines there for 90% of the time, and it receives a mere three inches of annual rainfall.

The area's first settlers were the Cocopah and Quechan Native American tribes, who still live close by on reservations. Early Spanish settlers spotted Yuma's potential, as its position was a natural crossing point for the Colorado River. Originally it was called Arizona City yet paid its state taxes to San Diego in California. The town changed its name to Yuma in 1873.

At one point in its past Yuma was a major military outpost, with the US Army Quartermaster Depot (QMD) stationed there. It's easy to see why, as Yuma could easily be supplied from the ocean by steamboats coming up the Gulf of California and then the Colorado River. Back then, in the late nineteenth century, Yuma QMD maintained a six-month supply of ammunition, clothing and food at all times. The place acted as a natural stepping-off point and gave the US Army an instant foothold right in the middle of Indian lands. Today it is hard to believe that steamboats ever made it up the Colorado River. I think even a small dinghy would have problems navigating the low water levels today.

The town had recently renovated the old military QMD buildings as a tourist attraction, and on display in a large riverside warehouse there was proof, in the form of a massive propeller on display, that steamboats once came up the river. There was also a mixture of pioneering tools, some military uniforms, a few covered wagons and not much else. I got the impression that Yuma's only claim to fame today was bickering with nearby rival towns as to which was the hottest place in the US.

Old-town Yuma seemed to consist of a scattering of old buildings and not much else, although there was a prison in town that closed in 1909 but is now open to the public. At one time this place was known as the 'Hellhole of Arizona', where prisoners worked in 110°F heat during the day, breaking rocks – but they were able to relax in the evening with access to a library. Apparently this was the first recreational facility ever introduced into a US prison.

I was standing outside the town's own library in historic downtown Yuma, considering the burns on my legs. This involved me undoing the top of my jeans and then bending over trying to peer down one of the trouser legs. I suppose to any passer-by it might have looked like I was carrying out some sort of personal examination – in public – but it didn't seem to stop people coming up to talk to me. A very weather-beaten old man, pushing a bicycle, approached me. He appeared to have most of his worldly goods in plastic shopping bags and was wearing a Vietnamese-style bamboo conical hat against the heat.

He eyed me for a few seconds, watching me examining my right leg, before saying: 'Hey buddy, got any change you can spare me?' I might have been fiddling about in a public park with my trousers undone, but he was unperturbed. Money from any source was OK. Clearly this man was down on his luck and, judging by his appearance, this had been the case for some time.

I hate being asked for money. It makes me feel very uneasy and, at the same time, guilty.

'I'd like to, but I'm afraid I don't carry any money. My wife looks after all that sort of thing,' I said, sounding like a schoolboy who can't be entrusted with any form of currency in case he ran off and blew it all on chewing gum, hookers and drink.

The old guy looked at me pityingly and shook his head. 'Does she now. Good luck with that,' he said and wandered off, pushing his bicycle and shaking his head, while I did up my trousers.

Yet again I was being astonished by America. The richest nation on earth, yet this was one of countless times I was asked for spare cash in the street by total strangers. I just find it odd that the US, with all its wealth, has such huge extremes between the haves and the have-nots. But then again, I suppose I shouldn't really be surprised. After all, this is a country that advertises on national TV that one in eight Americans does not have enough to eat.

At a gas station in Arizona a couple of days later I was approached by a man who was genuinely excited to see my motorcycle and started telling me about his '78 Harley-Davidson Shovelhead Chopper – how he used to ride it, and rebuild it, and all the things he had done to it. He had even ridden to the famous Sturgis bike rally in South Dakota and told me a few things about what he used to do there. He said he loved the look of my motorcycle and then asked some serious technical questions about it that I couldn't answer.

As he leaned over the shopping trolley he was pushing in order to get a closer look at my bike he said: 'Hey buddy, do you have any spare change? Times are difficult at the moment and I am not going to spend it on beer.'

I came up with the same get-out response I'd used in Yuma and insinuated I was incompetent when it came to money and my wife held all the cash. He said he would wait. Anne was paying for fuel in the garage kiosk and full marks to him, upon her return he did ask her for some change. In good direct American fashion Anne simply said no. He seemed more satisfied with her answer than mine.

* * * * * *

On the road again and my back was killing me. Leaning into the wind put my spine at a curious angle and I began to realise why some of the Harley-Davidson owners on websites complained about the standard solo seat on the Street Bob. It looked good, but after four hours of non-stop riding its wafer-thin padding didn't really work and it was starting to become very uncomfortable.

Through a series of manoeuvres I could inch myself backwards from the seat and sit on my bike's rear mudguard, which elevated my seating position and relieved the numb sensation in my backside. When I found myself doing this at 70mph on the freeway and the motorcycle started to wobble alarmingly, however, I realised I had to find another solution before I fell off and then had to explain to the emergency services and the insurance company why I'd been riding a motorcycle while perched over the rear tyre. Right now, though, Anne and I were heading to the mysteriously named town of Dateland, 25 miles east of Yuma.

The name Dateland made me think of a holiday resort where young couples could find each other and true love. In reality it's a small collection of buildings just off the Interstate 8 freeway. Originally someone had come up with an idea to make milkshakes out of dates here in the desert … and then the rest of Dateland's history becomes a little obscure, until a Canadian couple moved here some years ago and really got stuck into the date thing. They planted more than 300 date trees on nine acres of land, and they supply a small gas station, restaurant and gift shop with dates. You can buy anything you want here as long as it involves dates.

Even after visiting it was still unclear how dates came to be out here, but the area is famous for date milkshakes, date ice cream, date sweets, date cakes and anything else you can do with a date. Maybe it's all thanks to the Second World War air force base that was built nearby, which more than one million young US servicemen passed through before being sent to the European and Pacific theatres of war. Apparently only the best dates – the Medjool variety – are used at Dateland and everyone from the visitors' book seemed to be of the opinion that they did indeed taste very good. I'll leave it to the experts, though, because just the smell of dates makes me feel sick. Anne told me the date ice cream, which to me looked like brown sludge, was very good but not something she would necessarily want to eat again.

* * * * * *

'Hey, how fast you been on that bike of yours?' asked an elderly man who was sitting in the driving seat of his car in the Dateland visitors' centre parking lot. 'Ever managed to get it over 100mph?'

He was in a tatty-looking Buick that had a wheelchair on the back seat, and he was shouting to me from inside his car through an open window. I walked over and said: 'No, never been that fast. I'm frightened that I might lose control and fall off. I think maybe I have got it up to 50mph a few times, but that was pretty scary. I have enough trouble walking, let alone riding a motorcycle.'

My attempt at irony was totally wasted on him. He looked me straight in the eye and then slowly shook his head. 'Well, that's a god-damn shame, then,' he said. 'If I was a little bit younger I'd be out there burning up the road right now. What's the matter with you?'

Indeed, what was the matter with me? Good question – and I didn't really have an answer for him.

CHAPTER THREE

TRAINS, PLANES & GUNS

Trains – Space Age motel – Geronimo – Running out of fuel part 1 –
Fighters and bombers – Shoot-out at the OK Corral – Arizona guns –
Weeping bikers – The Thing – Running out of fuel part 2

One of the most evocative noises in the US is not the wail of a police siren but the hauntingly lonely sound of a freight train's warning tone in the middle of the night. There is a national line that first came through Arizona in 1880 and today there are huge freight trains still passing through the town of Gila Bend almost every hour, hurtling in through the desert and accelerating out again with the clanging of crossing bells and the low bellow of the train's klaxon horn. These immense, sometimes 40-truck-long trains can almost be measured in miles rather than feet, and at night their Cyclops-like headlight beam cuts through the desert darkness, lighting up the track ahead. They evoke images of the Wild West and, yet again, of the immensity of North America.

The soulful sound of those night freight trains reminded me of the Palo Verde derailment that took place some 25 miles from Gila Bend on 9 October 1995, when an Amtrak Sunset Limited train came off the rails. The two locomotives and eight of the 12 carriages were derailed, four of them plunging 15 feet off a bridge into a dry bed. One person was killed and 78 were injured, 12 of them seriously.

Four identical notes were found near the derailment, criticising the ATF and the FBI for the 1993 Waco Siege in which David Koresh and his cult followers died in a stand-off with Texan law enforcement. They were all signed 'Sons of the Gestapo'. The saboteurs clearly knew what they were doing as the wiring on the train tracks had been tampered with, to prevent engineers being forewarned of the problem. The culprits have never been identified, and the FBI now believes that the 'Sons of the Gestapo' was a fictitious group, an invention to conceal the real plan to rob a freight train.

After 1996 this stretch of line was abandoned and the section of track where the derailment took place is now used just for storage. A lonely railway line in the middle of the desert, going nowhere: sounded very evocative to me.

In some of the travel guides I looked at Gila Bend was described, I thought somewhat unfairly, as a nowhere town, nothing more than a suitable point to fill up your car or motorcycle before heading east for the bright lights of Phoenix or Tucson. To be fair, Gila Bend has seen better days. Not much exists of the old town and nothing, as far as I could see, of the Maricopa Indian nation that first settled out here.

The quaint Stouts Hotel on Main Street was now closed; it originally opened in the early 1920s. At one time it was the town's combined barbershop, café, grocery and butcher's store as well as the hotel; it generated its own electricity and had its own air conditioning and ice-making area. That must have been quite something and it's a place I would love to have seen in its glory days. There was a faded sign in the hotel window which said that the big movie stars of the 1930s used to stay there on their way from Hollywood to the cowboy film sets in Tucson. The sign also said that the owners – descendants of the original proprietors – were hoping to reopen the hotel shortly. The sign looked old, tired and dusty – a bit like Gila Bend itself.

But Gila Bend did have those trains, and a lot of them, plus it rivalled Yuma in claiming to be the hottest spot in the country (but had also been accused of messing around with its thermometer readings). It might have been just another hot desert town, but it boasted one of the most magnificent motels I'd ever stayed at in my life – the sensationally named Best Western Space Age Lodge Motel.

From the outside it looked what a demented six-year-old boy growing up in the early 1960s might have designed for a homework project on what a motel might look like in the future. I am not sure when the Space Age Lodge was actually constructed, but it seemed to have been conceived at a time when space travel was in its infancy and comic book superheroes were fuelling young imaginations. It was hideously kitsch and at the same time simply fantastic, with lots of drilled aluminium – for decorative purposes only – absolutely everywhere. There was a huge flying saucer strapped to the roof, an aluminium tripod outside the front of the hotel had another flying saucer mounted on it, and each of the 41 hotel rooms sported an alien spacecraft motif on the door. I felt I'd taken a step back in time, perhaps to 1962, and was in the midst of the US–Soviet space race – and judging by the Space Age Lodge Motel's decor, the US had won that race outright.

Apparently a section of the motel burned down a few years ago, and for some connoisseurs it lost some of its sci-fi fantasy charm when it was rebuilt. But I thought it was the most fantastic-looking motel I'd ever seen as I happily parked my bike and wandered in. Three very large, very round ladies were sitting behind the reception desk, and one of them was wearing a pair of those 'cat's-eye'-shaped spectacles that were so popular in the 1960s. There were also some badly painted images of, I think, Neil Armstrong doing his famous walk on the moon, but Neil appeared to be missing some fingers, and he was surrounded by rockets and spaceships of every description and hue – all dark blue, light blue and retina-damaging neon colours – and a mass of outrageous flames, stars and moons. After the brilliant white light in the desert the artwork in the lobby really hurt my eyes.

But no matter. The motel had a room for the night for us, at a modest price, and also a swimming pool and an in-house restaurant. That was a relief because, apart from an overstocked liquor store and a badly understocked supermarket, there appeared to be nowhere else we could get anything to eat in Gila Bend. As I heard the sound of a passing freight train, which rattled my room so hard it made the lights shake, I couldn't have been happier.

I had promised Anne when I set out on my US travels not to make unkind comments about Americans, merely to observe and not judge, but I had no worries here. The staff in the motel's gift shop and at the Outer Limits Restaurant were all very kind and courteous and I could not fault them on their service. The restaurant was definitely in the rebuilt part of the motel as the wall murals had lost the intensity and weirdness of the reception area, and there were more relaxing moonscapes to sit and stare at while enjoying your meal of an entire half chicken and fries.

The large Native American lady who was the restaurant greeter wore glasses and spent a lot of time staring at her hands while waiting for customers. Every so often she would disappear to be replaced by our flamboyant waiter who wore a lot of jewellery, clearly liked to get his nails painted and looked identical to the lady greeter (except he wore no glasses and was a man). When the chef came out to check on the number of customers he looked weirdly identical to the other two, apart from sporting a chef's uniform. I never saw all three of them together in the same place at the same time. Aliens, maybe?

The intrigue was rounded off nicely the next morning when I checked out and the large lady behind the reception desk looked exactly like all three characters from the restaurant the previous evening. Aliens perhaps – or maybe the Space Age Motel in Gila Bend was run by just one alien that could morph its body into different people that somehow all looked the same. Fun. Trust me. Go there and stay a night.

* * * * * *

Although I knew it would be hot in the Arizona desert I had not appreciated quite how torrid it could get. The heat was magnified by my wearing a full-face helmet, leather jacket, heavy boots and gloves and sitting on an extremely hot motorcycle. The sun was so strong I could see the outline of the Harley-Davidson 'shield' burnt into the back of my hands through the gaps on the back of my gloves. It looked as though I'd had some curious tribal hand tattoos or developed an unusual skin complaint.

We were heading towards Tucson and riding straight into the old stomping ground of Apache war chief Geronimo, one of the most enigmatic Native American leaders. Highway 85 was taking Anne and me straight into the heart of the Sauceda Mountains and even more desert. It's hard to understand how people today make a living, raise families, go to school or even live in such a harsh environment. This land is inhospitable at best and downright ferocious at worst – stark and with very limited vegetation; boiling hot in the day and cold at night. To survive out here with just knives, as Geronimo and his followers did, took a special sort of skill that has long since disappeared.

Born at Turkey Creek in 1829, near Gila Bend, Geronimo was actually a medicine man of the Chiricahua Apache. His name in his native tongue was Goyahkla, which loosely translates to 'one who yawns', and he emerged as one of the most resilient Native American leaders of his generation. For almost all his life, he fought against far superior military forces from Mexico and the US in the Apache Wars, the longest military conflict in US history. In one skirmish with Mexican soldiers, Geronimo repeatedly attacked them armed only with his knife while they shot at him with guns. He was an exceptional and talented guerrilla leader, and it was the Mexican forces that named him Geronimo. Legend has it that his actions and bravado caused the Mexican soldiers to appeal for divine help from St Jerome – or St Jeronimo – and the name stuck, although the history books have never explained why the Mexican military, in the midst of battle, were appealing for help from the patron saint of translators and librarians.

Despite Hollywood's representation of him in Westerns as an Apache chief, Geronimo was not actually a tribal leader. He was, though, an excellent war leader and because of this the Apache warriors chose to follow him and take on the might of the US military and the hordes of incoming settlers. He apparently had the ability to walk without leaving any tracks in the desert, had great telekinetic and telepathy skills, and survived numerous gunshot wounds. From 1858 to 1886 Geronimo was constantly on the run from the US and Mexican armies, as he and his small band of followers hit towns and farms across the Mexican border and throughout Arizona. He could see what was happening to the traditional Native American way of life and was determined to do as much as he could to stop the settlers and the military while he could.

He even famously managed to evade capture when holed up in a cave with a large group of US soldiers waiting immediately outside for him. It just added to the myth that was Geronimo. Eventually he had to concede that the days of the Apache were over and surrendered to Captain Lawton of the 4th US Cavalry and then officially to General Nelson Miles in September 1886 at Skeleton Canyon, Arizona. He and his band of Apache warriors were sent to a prisoner of war camp in Florida, and he also travelled to Oklahoma and Alabama after he was freed. In later life he became something of a celebrity, selling souvenirs and photographs of himself at $1 a time; you can still buy these pictures of him as an old man and he looks freaking scary to me, staring at the camera with a fierce and direct gaze.

Geronimo never returned home to Arizona. He died of pneumonia in 1909 after falling off his horse one winter's night and lying on the ground until next morning when he was found dead: a tough old bird, right until the very end.

Growing up with Western movies and romantic images of proud Apache warriors always getting the better of the US cavalry, I had expected to see something similar on the road or in the small Native American settlements we passed through as we rode south towards the towns of Ajo and Why. Where were the 'noble savages' that I'd seen on TV when I was a kid, the guys who knew how to live out here and survive in this desert environment? All I could see from my motorcycle were fat, disillusioned Apache people who had lost their lands to the white man and in return had been given alcohol, a lot of trans-fats and very little else. They'd also lost the ability and skills to live in there in the way Geronimo's generation had, and today they have little choice but to seek out a living of sorts in this hostile desert wilderness. They have a really tough life.

* * * * * *

We were planning a 200-mile ride, straight through the desert on Highway 86 and then on to Tucson for an overnight halt. I had been paying far too much attention to the landscape and not enough to my bike, however, and had failed to notice I was getting dangerously low on fuel.

The gauge had gone rapidly from an optimistic 150-mile range to just 70 miles in the space of 20 minutes. And I was sure there was at least another 90 miles to ride until I stood any chance of being able to fill up the tank again. Stupid. Stupid. Stupid. I have an unquestioning faith in modern technology and while my Harley-Davidson had not let me down I was beginning to discover that its fuel gauge had some serious estimation problems. I had been too trusting of its abilities. It's always tricky trying to guess how much fuel you have left in a motorcycle tank, and if you take the fuel cap off and peer inside you can't see anything except a black empty hole.

I began playing out scenarios in my head as to what I would actually do when I finally spluttered to a halt, literally miles from anywhere, watched by the opportunistic vultures that were waiting for an easy meal like me. You can die in the desert out there in Arizona and I had, of course, forgotten to pack any water. It was mid-afternoon and the temperature was well into the upper 90s. If I stopped I would use up precious fuel restarting. Despite the intense heat I was starting to break into a cold sweat. I was very concerned.

In situations like this, for some reason only known to myself, I start using the foulest language possible and so I rode the next 60 miles shouting every expletive I could think of until I was hoarse, exhausted and just plain angry with myself. But, as always, Anne was the voice of reason in such circumstances. She suggested that I pull over and she would then go ahead to the nearest fuel station and come back with a gallon tank strapped to her bike to get me going again.

Now I am stubborn. It's an inherent streak that has got me into more trouble than I care to remember. Neither Anne nor I had any idea how far the nearest fuel station was, but I was adamant I was not going to stop. I was determined I would get my bike there even if I had to push all 667lb of it myself. So I kept on going. Kept on cursing and shouting at myself and secretly praying that I wouldn't end up a skeleton at the side of the road with my bones picked clean.

Finally, in the distance, I could just make out the familiar yellow, red and white of a gas station. I had made it. My motorcycle was literally running on fuel vapour as I spluttered into the forecourt. The sense of relief was like a new form of high. I'd never been so pleased to see the Shell symbol in my life. Unfortunately I was not to learn from my mistakes and managed to do the exact same thing a few days later.

* * * * * *

It is a curious thing to go from having an entire US desert road to yourself, with no traffic, pedestrians, intersections or road junctions, just an empty tarmac surface disappearing into the distance, to the rush hour on the outskirts of Tucson. I had been relaxed and was enjoying the ride. Now this sudden traffic was messing with my mind. I had to reacquaint myself with modern life, constantly forcing myself to look round and pay attention to everything that was going on both behind me and in front.

Tucson was not what I had expected. References to it in Country & Western songs had led me to believe it was a small outpost in what was once the Wild, Wild West. Its name was derived from the Spanish name of Tukson which in turn was borrowed from O'odham Indian language meaning '(at the) base of the black (hill)', a reference to an adjacent volcanic mountain. It is, in fact, a very big city. In 2008 the US Census Bureau estimated the metropolitan area population of Tucson at 1,023,320, which ranked it as the 32nd largest city in America. It certainly seemed to be thriving and bore some resemblance to the cities I was used to in California.

But I never got a close look at downtown Tucson because no sooner had we arrived at our motel than we were being whisked away by friends for dinner at their favourite Mexican restaurant. All I saw of the city was a glimpse from the back seat of a massive SUV being driven at ungodly speeds by our friend Jen, who was managing to eat breakfast cereal, talk on her phone and steer this mechanical behemoth through Tucson's early evening traffic.

Jen's young children and husband Erik were waiting patiently for us at the restaurant. I'm no expert on Mexican food, but it was very good and certainly well received after eight hours in the saddle – and it seemed that having a Mariachi trumpet player blowing Mexican folk tunes into your left ear for three minutes at a time was considered to be the height of dinner-table etiquette by the locals.

Erik was an interesting and very bright guy. He'd spent years studying, had a truly impressive list of university degrees and qualifications, and had made a brilliant career in cancer research. Or, to be precise, skin cancer research. He said the biggest hurdle he faced was not the research work or knowing what to do but the infinite form filling and proposals to government departments and charitable foundations to find the money to do the job. Something like 60% of Erik's time was taken up just looking for financial support. I was dumbfounded that someone who was clearly as talented as he was in his chosen field had to spend his valuable time in this way, especially if you think of the very real successes that have been achieved by research into, for instance, leukaemia and some breast cancers.

Our conversation inevitably led to the big question: would there ever be a cure for cancer? Perhaps a silver bullet, which could eradicate this dreadful disease forever?

Erik thought not in our lifetime, as there was so much work that had yet to be done, plus cancer as a disease had a tricky way of altering itself. From my simple perspective it's easy: let people like Erik get on full time with their research work and stop this madness of making them look for money and fill out paperwork. Not that he was complaining, just resigned to the fact that it was all part of the job.

* * * * * *

There was one attraction in Tucson I was keen to see: the Bone Yard. Or to give it its proper title, the Aerospace Maintenance and Regeneration Center. Try saying that after a few beers.

Friends had told me in hushed voices about the astronomical number of US military and civilian aircraft that sit in the Arizona desert either being cannibalised for spares or simply stored in the open until they can be used again or sold to a third world dictator. I was very interested and excited to see this. However, I had not reckoned on having to provide some form of official government ID – which luckily I did have with me – nor did I relish the prospect of being herded on to a bus with a group of like-minded plane spotters which would then be locked for an hour and a half as it drove up and down long corridors of abandoned aircraft.

Fortunately, right next to the Bone Yard was the simply splendid Pima Air and Space Museum with more than 275 exhibits extolling the virtues of man's prowess in the air. It was superb. Better than anything I could have hoped for. I loved the fact the exhibits were split up into categories such as Attack Aircraft, Bombers, Fighter Aircraft, Fire Fighting Aircraft, MiGs and Drones.

Very friendly and knowledgeable people staff the Pima Museum and I thought it was terrific, but there was just too much to take in. Lovingly preserved aircraft from every generation since man first took to the air were all sitting in huge hangars or parked outside in the baking desert sunshine. You could get right up close and touch them. Did I tell you I thought this place was fantastic?

I was taken with two planes in particular. The first was the SR71 Blackbird, which looked like it was in a science fiction movie. I'd never seen anything quite so menacing, so intimidating and yet so bizarre. This was an aircraft that first saw service in 1964 and if my notes serve me correctly it used to leak fuel while it sat on the ground as its aluminium skin was designed to expand with the heat of travelling Mach 2 speeds at 80,000 feet in the sky. Only 32 were ever built at a gazillion dollars apiece, and only 20 survive today as 12 fell out of the sky at some point – but not a single one, the US government is quick to point out, was ever lost to enemy action. I didn't think there could be an enemy anywhere on the planet that could deal with the Blackbird – even when it was sitting still, all black and brooding in an aircraft hangar, it oozed with what a friend of mine nicely calls 'The Fuck Off Factor'.

Then, tucked away in a corner, I was delighted to see a 1940 British Hawker Hurricane in its correct RAF trim. It even had a series of swastikas painted on its side and was displayed in the colours of Wing Commander Robert Stanford Tuck, who was credited with 27 kills (hence the swastikas). I patted the Hurricane affectionately on the nose. This was the plane that had played such a strategic role in the defence of the UK during the Second World War. The American planes in the hangar simply towered over it.

I got nostalgic, too, over a 1943 English Bristol Blenheim bomber, from the same era, that was sitting outside in the desert heat. It was like seeing old friends again.

But the plane that astonished me the most was the B-29 Superfortress with *Sentimental Journey* painted on its nose that sat nonchalantly filling up all the space in the massive Hangar 5. The 1940 B-29 was designed as what the US Army Air Force called a 'Hemisphere Defense Weapon'. It was supposedly capable of carrying 20,000lb of bombs for more than 5,000 miles at 40,000 feet at speeds of up to 400mph. It also introduced pressurised crew compartments to military aircraft, and sported electronic fire-control systems and remote-controlled machine-gun turrets.

Although it was designed as a high-altitude daytime bomber, in practice during the Second World War it actually flew more low-altitude night-time incendiary bombing missions. It was also the plane chosen to drop the atomic bombs on Hiroshima and Nagasaki, to end the Pacific War in 1945. I was not quite sure how I felt, standing there in front of this immaculate B-29 in Arizona. During my career I had been to Japan many times, and Hiroshima in particular, and I'd seen what had happened when the atomic bomb was dropped. Nothing of old-town Hiroshima was left and the startling images on display in the Hiroshima Peace Museum had left an indelible image on my mind.

The actual Hiroshima B-29 bomber – the *Enola Gay* – is not at Pima but is on permanent display at the Smithsonian Institution in Washington DC. 'But it's roped off and you can't get near it as there are people that want to damage it or break it,' explained one of the Pima Museum's helpful guides. 'Someone once threw red paint all over it so it's under constant video surveillance.' I am not condoning the dropping of that bomb on Hiroshima, but I just couldn't get my head around why someone would want to destroy or damage the plane that did it. What on earth does that achieve?

For me the most poignant exhibit was the last one. Near to Pima's B-29 aircraft were a full-size poster of 'Little Boy', the atomic bomb that was dropped on Hiroshima on 6 August 1945, and a similar rendition of the second bomb called 'Fat Man' that was dropped on Nagasaki three days later. 'Little Boy' killed or vaporised approximately 140,000 people living in Hiroshima, caused severe structural damage to buildings in about a one-mile radius from ground zero, made a circle of destruction two miles in diameter and sent out shock waves travelling at the speed of sound, turning buildings into flying shrapnel. This was followed by a fireball of 7,000° Centigrade that turned sand into glass. One Hiroshima victim left only a shadow, permanently etched into the granite stone steps of a bank building. I know, because I have seen it. The bombs were just a little bigger than me and I could not comprehend how something so small could create such devastation. I stood under the Pima Museum B-29 and looked up into the bomb bay area where its deadly cargo was stored, and I was struck by how simple its mechanics were. From a space that measured perhaps 20 feet by 4 feet a bomb scarcely bigger than me had dropped from the sky and changed the world forever.

I lingered for a while at Pima in the 390th Bomb Group Museum – a sort of museum within a museum, and the only one of its kind dedicated to just one bomber group. In July 1943 this Bomb Group (consisting of four squadrons: the 568th, 569th, 570th and 571st) was assigned to Suffolk, in England, as a new base of operations for flying missions to the European continent. Over the next two years they achieved a remarkable record of 301 operational missions, dropping more than 19,000 tons of bombs over Europe before flying their last mission in May 1945. Out of the 3,000 young men who flew with this group, 670 were killed in service and 179 aircraft were lost.

It's a moving and fitting tribute to them and had been very well presented. The statistics and planes, and even a bunkhouse brought over from the Suffolk airbase, were all nicely done, but it was the display of the aircrews' personal effects that really made me stop and stare. Leather flight jackets with painted slogans on the backs, flight gloves, diaries, even mess tins and dog tags – it was this personal touch that made it so much more than just another museum for me.

I could have stayed at Pima all day, but I had my sights firmly set on heading to Tombstone and staying there for a couple of nights. Furthermore, I had found a great route out of Tucson that would take us in a winding loop through the Empire Mountains and the Coronado National Forest on Highway 82 and allow me to brag for years to come that 'I rode into Tombstone'.

* * * * * *

The road to one of the most notorious towns in the Wild West was a gentle morning ride across countryside that boasted ranches and vineyards. Wine from Arizona, who would have thought it? It was terrific, despite spending some ten miles staring at the back of an RV camper as the driver wouldn't pull over to let me pass. My hands still felt numb from the long riding stints, and the burns on my right leg were still there and festering nicely in the heat, but the sun was in the sky and a god was in a heaven somewhere.

Well, not for everyone. As I rounded a corner there were four emergency vehicles parked up, with anxious-looking ambulance and fire service crews milling around. A few hundred yards further on we passed a small bar with several motorcycles parked outside, being circled by a group of sheriff's deputies holding their guns in outstretched hands. Something was going down, but I was in no mood to see how it unfolded. Judging by what was going on at the bar there was still an element of the Wild West alive and kicking.

I had not been prepared for the sensory overload that was about to hit me from visiting Tombstone – or, as it likes to call itself, 'The Town Too Tough To Die'. The guidebooks had warned me about the bikers, RVers (recreational vehicle or motorhome drivers) and busloads of tourists who descended hourly on Tombstone, but maybe we were lucky, because Anne and I had the whole town to ourselves that weekend – with the exception of the Goatheads. This band of men described themselves as a social group with a motorcycle problem and went under the banner Live to Ride – Ride to Bars.

It was hard to know where to start. I immediately opted for the infamous Boothill Cemetery about a half-mile outside Tombstone, and I was expecting lots of lights, music and glitzy razzmatazz to accompany arguably one of the most famous cemeteries in the world. One guidebook went so far as to describe Boothill Cemetery as 'so kitsch that it's a must-see – complete with fake-looking headstones, cute epitaphs and piped-in Willie Nelson music'. But the music wasn't switched on that day and the 300 or so graves and their headstones all looked genuine enough to me.

In the late nineteenth century Tombstone was a very rough and lawless mining town with some 10,000 inhabitants. The town's founder, Ed Schieffelin, had spent 20 years prospecting for gold with little success. He arrived in the area and just south of Tombstone discovered rich silver deposits in the San Pedro Valley. Schieffelin had been warned that this was Apache country and all he would find would be his tombstone. The name for the town stuck.

With money from investors in the East, the Tombstone Mining District and the town itself were established. By 1888 some $30 million worth of silver had been dug out of the area surrounding the town. That was a lot of silver and a lot of money in those days. But the long arm of the law did not quite stretch as far as this small place in southern Arizona, while local politicians and landowners were fighting a continual battle to gain control of the town and the mining rights. In fact, US President Chester A. Arthur once threatened to impose martial law over the entire territory as it was so out of control.

Into this heady cocktail of money, lawlessness, silver mines and politics wandered buffalo hunter, gambler, gold prospector and part-time lawman Wyatt Earp, his brothers Virgil, Morgan and Warren, and Doc Holliday. I had always thought Holliday was a medical doctor until I visited Tombstone, where I discovered he was in fact a dentist. Aside from being best friends with the Earp family, he liked to gamble, raise hell and had a girlfriend called Big Nose Kate who ran the biggest bar in town. The Doc sounds like my sort of guy.

The Earps and Holliday were known in Tombstone as the Dodge City Gang (prior to his arrival in town Earp had been a deputy policeman in the Kansas cattle town) and together they made political friends and enemies. Virgil was appointed town marshal. But differences with the Clanton family, who had a reputation for rowdiness and cattle rustling as well as having a powerful political benefactor, simmered for months before exploding into the famous gunfight at the OK Corral on the night of 26 October 1881. It lasted all of 30 seconds and involved 30 bullets.

But I am getting ahead of myself. I needed to see all of Tombstone and spend some time looking at where this famous gunfight took place. Right now I was content to wander Boothill Cemetery, the final resting place for many of the town's citizens, who all seemed to have met some untimely and unpleasant death. In truth, Boothill Cemetery was perfect and just what I had hoped to find in a former Wild West town. Clearly the rights and wrongs of the OK Corral gunfight were still being argued today, even here, because the graves of Tom McLaury, his brother Frank and friend Billy Clanton stated they were murdered in 1881. This was going to be an interesting story to try and unravel, as Earp, his brothers and Doc Holliday were all arrested for their murder, only to have the charges against them dropped.

There were some classic epitaphs on many of the graves that made me wonder if they were really genuine. Some of them did make me smile, like:

Here lies
George Johnson
Hanged by mistake 1882
He was right
We was wrong
But we strung him up
And now he's gone

Or my favourite:

Here Lies
Lester Moore
Four slugs
From a .44
No Les
No more

Boothill Cemetery seemed a fitting place to be buried whether you'd been hanged, murdered, stabbed in town or just killed by Indians. It sits on a small hill above a dry riverbed – you can just make out Tombstone in the distance – while in front of the cemetery is a wide-open desert plain with a spectacular backdrop of the Dragoon Mountains. The epitaphs also showed that all these deaths had occurred in a very short space of time. Nearly everyone here was buried between 1879 and 1882. There are some later, more modern graves, but the funeral business clearly reached its peak in the early 1880s. That lawless time may have been short-lived, but a lot of people lost their lives and the Earp family were credited with the deaths of no fewer than 21 outlaws. Quite an impressive tally, even for those days.

* * * * * *

I heard the jangling sound of spurs before I spotted the wearer. I should have been expecting it but I really wasn't. As I turned a corner to walk down East Allen Street – the main thoroughfare of Tombstone – there he stood. Six feet and more of cowboy in boots and spurs, long black rancher coat, hat, gun and a truly impressive moustache. Instead of giving me the impression that I had stepped back in time I was merely confused as to what the heck he was doing. It was 90°F in the shade and he looked like he was going to a fancy dress party. But of course this was all for the tourists. Locals are either paid or choose to dress up in the style of 1881 – the momentous year of the OK Corral shoot-out. In fact the whole town seemed to have entirely built itself around this 30-second event, which actually happened in a stabling yard for horses.

Let's cut to the chase. On 9 October 1881, US marshal Virgil Earp had been informed by the town's sheriff, John Behan, that the Clanton brothers, Billy and Ike (who ran away before the confrontation), and their associates, Tom and Frank McLaury, were looking for him. The sheriff said they were unarmed but he was unsure of their motives. Virgil called in his brothers Wyatt and Morgan and they were joined by their friend Doc Holliday. They then went looking for the Clantons, finally finding them in the OK Corral.

I'll leave it to an eyewitness, R. F. Coleman, whose account was faithfully reported at the time in the town's splendidly named newspaper, the *Tombstone Epitaph*. Much to my delight the paper is still in operation today, and its offices are well worth a visit to buy facsimile copies of the newspapers that were printed the day after the OK Corral gunfight.

Mr Coleman later told a courtroom murder trial about how the Earps and Holliday appeared:

I was going along to Fly's Photographic Gallery, when I heard Virg. Earp say, 'Give up your arms or throw up your arms.' There was some reply made by Frank McLowry (*sic*), but at the same moment there were two shots fired simultaneously by Doc Holliday and Frank McLowry, when the firing became general, over 30 shots being fired.

Tom McLowry fell first, but raised and fired again before he died. Bill Clanton fell next, and raised to fire again when Mr Fly took his revolver from him. Frank McLowry ran a few rods and fell. Morgan Earp was shot through and fell. Doc Holliday was hit in the left hip, but kept on firing. Virgil Earp was hit in the third or fourth fire in the leg which staggered him, but he kept up his effective work.

Wyatt Earp stood up and fired in rapid succession, as cool as a cucumber, and was not hit. Doc Holliday was as calm as if it was target practice, and fired rapidly. After the firing was over sheriff Behan went up to Wyatt Earp and said: 'I will have to arrest you.' Wyatt replied: 'I won't be arrested today. I am right here and am not going away. You have deceived me; you told me these men were disarmed. I went to disarm them.'

Wyatt Earp was the only one to escape unscathed. Two months later, in Tombstone, his brother Virgil was shot again in the arm while crossing Allen Street late at night and crippled for life. His assailant was never caught. Then in March 1882 the younger Earp brother, Warren, was shot and killed by another unknown assailant in Hatch's Saloon, also on Allen Street, while playing pool. The Earp family obviously had a few enemies. Wyatt himself left Arizona shortly afterwards and went on to live to the age of 81, trying his hand at gold prospecting and running a gambling saloon before finally dying in 1929 in Los Angeles. He and his brothers and Doc Holliday have left a legacy that the town of Tombstone is still, quite rightly, milking for all it's worth today.

I soon spotted another man in period costume, but there was something definitely sinister about him. He twirled a walking cane, had a pencil-thin moustache and seemed to be constantly darting up and down Allen Street, in and out of the tourist shops and bars. He seemed to appear wherever I went, and eventually I confronted him one night in the Longhorn Restaurant after I'd already seen him in two of the bars we'd visited. (The Longhorn Restaurant, incidentally, served half a side of cow which they called a steak.)

His name was Stephen and, to his chagrin, I hadn't realised he was in fact playing the part of Doc Holliday, hence his walking cane and tiny moustache. Stephen told me he ran the OK Corral site just down the street and he dressed as the Doc every day. There were gunfights organised daily at 2.30pm and twice on Saturdays at the original OK Corral site, or you could sit and watch *Tombstone Historama* (what a great made-up word), a video with a voiceover from actor Vincent Price narrating the dramatic turn of events that had made the town of Tombstone so notorious. (Vincent Price is the famous English actor who made his name playing Dracula in 1960s horror films.)

For some reason Stephen adopted a very authentic English accent when he spoke to me. He explained that the re-enactment business was good and he liked what he did. Getting paid to dress as Doc Holliday has to be one of the more peculiar vocations in life. 'I have just had dinner with the lead singer of some English heavy metal thrash band which is why I probably sound English to you. Maybe I have picked up on the accent,' he explained. It couldn't get more surreal than this. Dracula film actors doing voiceovers for history films, grown men engaging in shoot-outs every day at the OK Corral, and the lead singer of a heavy metal band dining out in downtown Tombstone with a man whose job it was to dress as a nineteenth-century vigilante lawman.

And it got weirder. Big Nose Kate's saloon and bar, named after Doc Holliday's girlfriend (although the pictures I saw of her showed a woman with a very pretty nose), turned out to be a great place to sit and watch people. The original had been burned down and rebuilt at some time – as had much of Tombstone – but it still managed to convey an authentic Western flavour and I loved it. A huge mahogany bar ran the entire length of the saloon and the waitresses were dressed in what looked like distinctly uncomfortable basques. There was a ton of Western and motorcycle paraphernalia on the walls, although perhaps the oddest item was an English policeman's helmet sitting in a Perspex box above the bar.

Most of the tourists had gone home long since and Big Nose Kate's had become the favoured watering hole of that group of motorcycling enthusiasts I mentioned earlier. The Goatheads claim on their website that they are just a group of guys who like bikes and riding, but they looked like an outlaw motorcycle club and were being watched nervously by the bar manager. He was in full cowboy dress with the biggest revolver I had ever seen strapped to his thigh. It must have had a barrel at least 18 inches long and his fingers were hovering around the trigger.

Arizona is an 'open weapon' state. Providing you meet the legal requirements, you are entitled to carry a gun strapped to your side, but it must be in full view for everyone to see. On my way to Big Nose Kate's bar I'd called into the Tombstone Trading Company just off Allen Street to see what was needed to purchase a gun in town. The Tombstone Trading Company is a federally licensed firearms dealership and claims to have the largest inventory of handguns in the state of Arizona, so it seemed to be the perfect place to find out more.

'If I wanted to buy a gun today, could I?' I asked hopefully of the man standing behind a glass counter that was stacked right to the top with firearms.

'Sure. We just need some form of ID and your social security number and the computer will do the rest. Providing you check out you're good to go and can leave here with the gun of your choice,' he explained.

That astonished me. For $250 or less I could leave the store with a working firearm and ammunition strapped to my side. Gun buying in Arizona appeared as easy as getting a loaf of bread or a pint of milk in the local supermarket.

The previous day I had seen a tall, angry-looking man arguing over the price of cigarettes with the teenage sales assistant in a gas-station kiosk. The teenager looked very scary, with several pounds of carpentry nails stuck in his face. I assumed this was a fashionable 'piercing' statement and not the result of an accident with a nail gun at a nearby construction site. This metallic look was nicely rounded off by the lad's earrings, which were the size of large coat buttons and had distended his earlobes so they flapped lightly against his brightly coloured neck tattoo. He looked like a tribesman from the Amazon rainforest who had somehow been transported to work at the Chevron gas station on the outskirts of Tombstone. He was just missing a blowpipe.

What he couldn't see, though, was that every time he argued about the latest price of cigarettes with Mr Angry, the man's hand would reach and touch the butt of his revolver as if he was thinking about shooting the kid before reaching across and taking the cigarettes he so clearly needed. Thankfully it all ended amicably enough and, as the man left after paying for his cigarettes, Teenage Metal Face confided to me: 'Jeez, he's always in here arguing. One of these days I will let him have it.'

But back to Big Nose Kate's saloon and the Goatheads, who had been drinking all afternoon and had just ordered 50 shots of tequila. It took the harassed barmaid about five minutes to fill all the glasses and then place them on a pair of enormous trays. The band had stopped playing Country & Western music and in unison all 50 immense, and in some cases extremely immense men shuffled to their feet to listen to a muffled speech about a man called Ernie. I think Ernie had just died. Certainly something sad had happened to him. With a shout of his name the Goatheads all simultaneously downed their tequilas and then sat down. As they did I saw that several of these big burly bikers were openly weeping. I can tell you, it sometimes gets kind of weird out there in America.

* * * * * *

I am a sucker for the unusual and the US has it by the bucketload. Whether it's the World's Largest Ball of Twine, the World's Largest Baked Potato or the World's Largest Killer Bee, I have to go and see these peculiar monuments scattered around the country. Some have a vague historical tie to the local community or are promoting a local company's wares. If you live in an area where peanut farming is the staple industry, for example, why not create a 30-foot peanut, put it in a field and pull in passing tourists to take photographs? Some act as great advertising promotions for famous brands (and even not so famous brands). In general, though, I think these wonderfully outsized creations are simply designed to attract road trippers on long boring journeys across the US into some small town to gawp and then spend a few dollars before they move on. I hope America never stops doing it, because it works for me.

With that in mind, I simply could not turn down an offer to see *The Thing – What Is It?* It was enticingly advertised on huge blue and yellow hoardings all along Interstate Highway 10, heading east out of Arizona. For 32 miles I rode, getting increasingly excited as the signs counted down the miles, until I eventually reached *The Thing*. It was housed in a nondescript service station off the freeway. I parked my motorcycle and wandered inside. After a quick chat a lady behind the cash till relieved me of $1, and then pointed vaguely at two closed wooden doors at the back of the shop. This, apparently, was where *The Thing* lived.

It was the best $1 I have ever spent, or will probably ever spend, in my life. In fact, they could have charged me $100 and I would still have been very happy, because this was the greatest museum of completely and utterly useless items I have ever visited. And I have been to some unusual museums in my time.

After the wooden doors slammed behind me I started to follow a concrete path that had weird three-toed footprints painted on it, as if some massive lizard had been running amok with a can of green paint. I understood that I needed to keep an eye on these footprints as they would lead me to *The Thing*. Before I had got very far, however, I became distracted. There was a series of broken vehicles on display and in the middle of them all was a 1960s Rolls-Royce, with a sign that announced to visitors that this was a car once used by Adolf Hitler. And sure enough, in the back was a hideously ugly wax mannequin of Hitler complete with toothbrush moustache. He had melted a bit in the heat of the Arizona desert, and he was slumped a little forward so his head was pressed against the window. But if you screwed up your eyes enough you could just about see a similarity between this model and the mad despot responsible for trying to create the 1,000-year Nazi Reich in Germany and causing the outbreak of the Second World War. Never mind the fact that the Rolls-Royce was made some 15 years after the dictator had died in his bunker in Berlin. It was also right-hand drive and even had a large chrome GB (Great Britain) plate mounted on the back. But I believed in it.

Then things got even better. The next exhibit was a full-sized Spanish inquisition torture chamber with all of the six characters carved out of wood and hand painted. There was the torturer, complete with obligatory black hood, and a semi-nude woman screaming while he approached her with what looked like branding irons – or it could have been salad tongs. A man in this astonishing diorama was chained to the cell walls, and he too was about to have something very horrible done to him. The other figures were also in various states of undress and all ready to be impaled or stretched. It was either the work of a genius or someone who had some serious mental health issues and had far too much time on their hands. And access to a lot of woodworking tools.

Everywhere I looked were things that appeared to have been salvaged from other people's rubbish bins and then put on display. There was, I think, an American history section as there was a wagon, some saddles and a huge collection of vaguely Western ranch-type tools. The centrepiece was a hideous former shop mannequin, posed awkwardly in a rocking chair and dressed as an Indian, with a badly fitting wig. His trouser fly buttons were undone, his shoes had been taken off and cast to one side, and he was missing a limb. There was no explanation this time and I guess the audience was left to make its own mind up as to exactly what it was all about.

Behind me were large glass display cases filled with broken china, kitchen implements from the 1950s and an eighteenth-century matchlock rifle that the placard claimed was priceless as it was the only one of its kind ever made. I am sure I'd seen several such replicas in junk shops all over the world, but I was in no mood to argue with the owners of this museum. It was all too wonderful.

And so it went on for another 20 minutes. An astonishingly eclectic collection of the most amazingly worthless trash had been put on display for my pleasure and all for the princely sum of $1. My enthusiasm for everything that had preceded it meant that I only gave a cursory glance to *The Thing*. It turned out to be a sort of mummified body in a stone coffin with a Perspex lid. You could peer in to see a lot of dust and just make out a few bone-shaped objects all wrapped in what looked like a dirty hospital bandage. It looked like some type of mummy from an ancient civilisation high in the Peruvian Andes, except that I had a feeling it might have been made quite recently in someone's back garden. The museum owners were right: it was a *Thing*. But it wasn't nearly as good as some of the other things they had so thoughtfully put out on display in their museum, just for me.

I stood blinking in the bright Arizona sunshine, wondering if I had really just seen all of that. I would have willingly paid another $1 to go and do it all again. But Anne and I needed to be in New Mexico tomorrow and ahead lay several hundred miles of highway motorcycling.

* * * * * *

I am ashamed to say I knew nothing about the state of New Mexico before I went there, apart from where it was. I had never visited or paid any real attention to this state, which has huge oil and gas reserves and a rich Native American and Spanish history. It is also one of the least populated states in the US, with just 16 people to the square mile. Compare that to the New York metropolitan area with its 6,270 square miles and 2,842 people in each one of those miles and you get some idea of how empty New Mexico actually is.

It is also immense, with a landmass of 121,412 square miles and a total population of 2,009,000 people (according to the 2009 census). If you compare a tiny country like the UK (93,278,000 square miles and a massive and growing 61,383,000 population in 2008) you may understand why we Brits are sometimes accused of 'being a little uptight'. New Mexico, on the other hand, is a vast empty space with very few people.

To get there we had almost 100 miles of Arizona still to cross and I was aiming to reach Bisbee before lunch, prior to crossing the Arizona–New Mexico border on Highway 80 close to the appropriately named town of Rodeo.

Every morning, when I swung a leg over the motorcycle, was like the start of a new adventure. It may sound a bit of a cliché, but I found the thought of the miles ahead and what I might find there a very exciting prospect. I had grown in confidence on the bike and now, with close to 2,800 miles on the odometer, it was feeling a lot more comfortable to ride. Something had gelled. I wouldn't go so far as to say I was at one with my bike, but I definitely had a better understanding of how to ride it. Consequently, I had relaxed my grip on the handlebars and was starting to lose the numb sensation in my hands so that I found I could actually steer and ride better. Who would have thought it?

Pulling into Bisbee in the far eastern corner of Arizona my right leg was hurting like hell, but the attraction of this old mining town, which boasted almost 200 miles of tunnels dug into the surrounding Mule Mountains, made me forget the pain for a while. Bisbee was founded in 1880 after vast copper reserves were found there together with the by-product of that mining: some truly impressive turquoise stone. Those early miners also found cuprite, aragonite, wulfenite, malachite, azurite and possibly even kryptonite, but it was copper that placed this town on the map for a good 70 years. Good evidence of this remains even today as, just south of Bisbee, there is an immense open-cast pit that is several hundred feet deep. It is a massive scar in the ground and testimony to the lengths to which mining corporations will go to extract minerals. Peering over the edge directly down into the Lavender Pit, as it's called, you can see a large pool of iridescent brown liquid right at the very bottom.

A fellow motorcyclist had parked next to me at the Lavender Pit visitors' car park and was curious about the helmet intercom system that Anne and I were using.

'What sort of range do you get out of that?' he asked.

'About half a mile, if I'm lucky. It's actually really useful to keep in touch with my wife as we ride,' I said.

'I've thought about a system like that too, as my girlfriend here rides on the back of my bike. I would have to remove her microphone, though, as she never stops talking,' he said, eyeing a large angry-looking woman who was standing right behind him. Rather you than me, I thought.

Mining left Bisbee in the 1950s and by all accounts most of the town left too. But somehow it has survived. In the 1990s it was rediscovered by the 'Baby Boomer' generation who moved here in their droves, attracted by the cheap property prices and the all-year-round good weather. Bisbee's fortunes may be on the way up as well, as there are plans to start mining again. One of the world's largest mining organisations, Freeport-McMoRan Copper & Gold, began some preliminary excavation work in 2007 and are still exploring, so copper mining could return to the town. I got the feeling, however, that there was some form of collective breath-holding from the town's residents. The newcomers to Bisbee were going to be against any form of mining, yet the older residents, I am sure, would welcome the jobs and prosperity. Time will tell, but Bisbee has managed to survive a lot so far. I really liked the place.

* * * * * *

After a quick look at a map, Anne and I had decided to head north-east on Highway 80 and through the tiny town of Douglas that sits right above the border between the US and Mexico. It was flaming hot and there was, again, literally nobody about on yet another fabulous desert road, although this one had corners. It was fast, too, and we were making good progress in our plan to get to New Mexico by that evening.

Just ahead I could see a tall stone tower standing by the side of the road, with a gravel lay-by in front, so I pulled off, parked my bike and wandered over to read the metal inscription plate bolted on to it:

Near here Geronimo last Apache chieftain and Nachite surrendered
On Sept 6th 1886 to General Nelson A. Miles US Army.
Lieutenant Chas. B. Gatewood with Kieta and Martine Apache
Scouts risked their lives to enter
the camp of the hostiles to present terms of surrender
offered to them by General Miles.
After two days, Gatewood received the consent of Geronimo
and Nachite to surrender.
The surrender of Geronimo in Skeleton Canyon on that historic day
Forever ended Indian warfare in the United States.

This was a pretty big deal, the last time any Native American defied the US government in open warfare, yet all that marked this singularly important historical event was a simple tower in the middle of nowhere alongside a nowhere highway. It was a dusty, lonely and very quiet place but a poignant tribute to the last stand-off by Native Americans against the settlers. It was also a place to stop and think a bit about what once was and is no more.

A few miles later, and a little further down the road, Anne was determined to take a picture of the Arizona–Mexico border marker. We had flown past it at 60mph and she was keen to turn around. We swung the bikes around and parked up. But then I heard Anne squeal over our helmet intercom system. She had parked her motorcycle on the side of the road, pulled the kickstand down into gravel, and the bike had leant to one side and fallen over. It was now lying on its right side.

Running back up the road in helmet, leather jacket, gloves and boots in 90°F desert heat makes you break into a mild sweat. Trying to lift 670lb of Harley-Davidson back on to two wheels, plus all the weight of Anne's luggage, makes you really sweat. I had been told by Mac precisely how to pick up a motorcycle after you have dropped it on the ground. It involved a lot of bending of the knees (never the back) and easing the bike up, and he'd made it look easy. After several minutes of swearing and grunting we finally got Anne's bike on to two wheels and then on to its kickstand. I was so hot I felt someone had poured a bucket of water all over me. Sweat was literally pouring down my back and I had a torrent running down my face. I also knew I had lifted the bike totally incorrectly as my spine was twingeing slightly, but I was more than a little astonished at myself and what I could apparently do in an emergency – admittedly with Anne's help. Normally I have trouble just lifting a fork to my mouth.

The dash warning lights on Anne's bike were continuously flashing 'engine tip'. We knew, damn it. We'd been there. Fortunately there was no damage and it was a case of switching the ignition on and off a few times. We were soon safely back on the road again for a further 40 miles of some astounding desert riding. Except for one small problem. My motorcycle was telling me I had 25 miles left until the tank ran dry. Shit, I had done it again. I had ridden my bike into an empty wilderness without bothering to check my fuel range. I couldn't turn round, as Douglas was at least 50 miles behind us and there was no way I would ever make it there. Soon it would be evening and dark, for night comes quickly in the desert. Lordsburg in New Mexico, which was our evening's destination, seemed the only hope but I silently prayed to the god of motorcyclists that I would find a fuel station somewhere, anywhere, along the way.

Riding fast on a bike in the American desert is fun. Riding slowly to conserve fuel is unmitigated hell. You want to go quicker to get to the gas station, but if you do you'll use up more fuel. It's a sort of 'heads you lose, tails you lose' situation. I was getting very concerned because we'd not seen anybody for ages. Nobody lived out here and even the US Border Patrol had stopped popping up from behind the desert brush. Furthermore, it was a Sunday. Anyone who had any sense was at home with their feet up.

My loud swearing started again and continued for the next hour and a half as we crawled through the Pedregosa Mountains, sometimes reaching the heady speed of 30 mph. I was hot, worried and trying to work out a plan of what to do when my bike finally ran out of fuel. Then, ahead, I saw a tall sign for a gas station. My heart leapt. But as we got closer it sank right back down into my boots. It was abandoned.

'We have to get on the freeway again now,' said Anne into the intercom. 'I'm sure we'll find a service station there.'

Fantastic. Not only did I have to get back on to one of my least favourite roads, I was also having to ride at speeds no faster than a running chicken. The Harley-Davidson gauge was now joining in the debacle by flashing 'low on fuel'. It had given up even estimating how much was left in the tank.

The first sign I saw on the freeway from the *very* slow lane was 21 miles to the nearest gas station. My mathematics have never been good, but half an hour previously I'd had an optimistic estimate of 25 miles from the Harley-Davidson fuel gauge. I knew I had ridden close to 35 miles. How was this bike still running? I was crawling at near-walking speed by now, Sunday afternoon traffic whizzing by with curious people no doubt wondering why I was going so slowly, and as I started to turn a corner the bike began to splutter and cough.

Just as I had resigned myself to spending the afternoon on the hard shoulder waiting for a tow truck or a gang of neo-Nazi militia to come by and kill me, I saw the service station sign and freewheeled on to its forecourt. Somebody was looking out for me that day – again. I promised myself there and then never to run out of fuel again...

As I got off the bike my foot hit a small round metal object. I bent down to get a closer look. It was a spent 9mm Luger pistol shell casing lying on the ground. Welcome to New Mexico.

CHAPTER FOUR

JUST DESERTS & FIREWORKS

*Fireworks and explosives – Billy the Kid – Snow and ice – Mining engines
– Green ivy and grey gravy – Joshua trees – Lawnmowers in the desert –
Ortega Highway*

After a long day's ride I was never sure what we were going to find waiting for us at the motels that we'd randomly picked the evening before. Sometimes they were packed with people attending business conventions, or families on the road and passing through, or on occasions absolutely empty with only Anne and me staying there.

As we pulled into our New Mexico motel in the Hidalgo Desert there were only two other vehicles in the parking lot. That was the good sign and meant we would definitely get a bed for the night. The bad sign was a cloud of grey smoke that was pouring out of a portable barbecue six rooms along from ours. Three very big men and one large tattooed lady were having a late afternoon party, drinking tequila from a bottle and cooking large slabs of unidentifiable meat on the grill while playing rap music very loudly. This had been going on for much of the day judging by the heap of empty beer cans and spirit bottles lying next to them. They had watched us pull in and park the bikes up, and a short time later one of the men wandered over to offer us some skirt steak. In return, we had to bring our own alcohol. I politely declined as I had seen a glorious shop over the road from the motel that I felt compelled to go and visit.

It was called Border Line Fireworks, a tinder-dry wooden building crammed from floor to ceiling with every kind of incendiary device known to man. Everywhere you looked there were boxes and boxes of fireworks piled up on each other; shelves of fireworks; tables of fireworks; single fireworks; bags of fireworks – fireworks as far as the eye could see. It was a pyromaniac's idea of heaven. In California, like many other states, there are strict government controls on the type of fireworks that can be bought and sold. Some states are even stricter, permitting you to light only tiny amounts of explosives that sort of fizz and then immediately go out. And you can only light them on public holidays like Independence Day on the Fourth of July.

New Mexico, I was learning, had no such problem with fireworks – clearly the bigger the better. The cheerful owner, who was originally from California, said he had customers coming from all over the country to buy his incendiary items. This was firework selling on an industrial level, the like of which I had never seen before. I asked him if he was ever worried about working in such an explosive sort of place.

'You know what, we've never had a problem. We smoke in here and the air is so thick with gunpowder that sometimes you can even see it floating around, but you need a lot of it in one place for it to ignite,' he said. To my eye there appeared to be more than a lot of gunpowder in this shop. There seemed to be a ton of the stuff, liberally sprinkled everywhere. I could see it on the shelves and swirling around in the air where the sun shone through the windows. But the owner seemed happy enough and he said business was really good.

The top seller, apparently, was a $25 firework that seemed to promise explosions that would punch your kidneys out, light up the night sky, burn all your neighbours' houses down and then require you to be immediately taken to jail – at least according to the illustration on the outside of the box. It was the size of a small military mortar round. In fact that might have been exactly what it was, because outside the store there was a huge banner advertising 'Artillery Shells: Buy One Get One Free'. I was seriously tempted, even though it would have been illegal to let it off in the garden back home in California, but the real problem was where to store 3lb of potentially unstable incendiary device on my motorcycle. I wistfully put it back on the shelf. Another time perhaps. At least I now knew where to come the next time I felt the urge to blow up the neighbourhood.

* * * * * *

I wanted to head north, deeper into New Mexico, and start the long haul up into the Mongolian Mountains that frame the western edge of the state. From what I could make out on the map the climb was pretty steep, at some 8,000 feet above sea level, culminating in the Apache-Sitgreaves National Forest and back over the border into Arizona and the town of Alpine.

Anne and I stopped briefly in Silver City so I could look around, while she decided to go off to look at interesting things to photograph. I was amused by the astonishingly high 18-inch kerbs to the sidewalks – either they'd been built to allow riders easier access to their horses or because the nearby Mimbres River was constantly flooding. It was hard to tell because there was nobody around to ask. The town claims to have a population of more than 10,000 people but they were all out the day I called by.

Most of the shops were closed or closing down and it was only later, when I did some research with the local history society, that I was able to discover the kerbs *had* been put there to avoid flooding. When Silver City had first been set up as a mining town it was constructed in the path of rainwater run-off, so every time it rained heavily – which was, of course, rare in the desert – an immense wave of water would literally charge through it. It apparently got so bad in 1895 that a small river ran through Silver City for weeks, forcing the citizens to rethink the whole layout of their town. What was once Main Street became a 55-foot deep ditch and the businesses fronting on to Main Street simply made their back doors their front doors and then life carried on as usual. Confused? I still am.

Silver City, like many mining towns in the late nineteenth century, also had a high rate of lawlessness and violent crime. A certain Sheriff Harvey Whitehill arrived in 1874 and gained some control over the unruly element who had been living it up there. I mention Sheriff Whitehill as he became the first US lawman to arrest the legendary outlaw Billy the Kid, then known as Kid Antrim, who was living in Silver City and working as a dishwasher in the town's hotel. Whitehill apparently incarcerated Billy for stealing cheese and described him as 'a likeable kid whose thieving was more out of necessity than criminality'. Billy the Kid went on to earn notoriety as an infamous outlaw and the killer of 20 men. More informed sources think his murderous tally was probably down to four men, but nevertheless I feel this is a good rule to live by – never, ever, piss off the dishwasher and if he wants your cheese let him have it.

Silver City is still a mining town today. In 2006 the Chino and Tyrone mines that you pass before you get to Silver City itself dug 127,000 tons of copper out of the ground, and more than 1,200 people are employed there. However, the clock is ticking as the mining company expects the copper to run out within the next 25 years. What would become of Silver City in the next few years, I wondered, as we headed off and out of town.

* * * * * *

Highway 180 was fast and smooth as it wound through pine forests, and the scenery seemed to change at every point the higher we climbed. We had gone from baking hot desert to cool forest glades in a matter of miles.

I was hungry, but there seemed few places to stop and grab some lunch. Out of desperation I pulled into a parking lot with a drab-looking building that said it served food. Called the Adobe Café, it was actually to prove a great decision as it served the best meal I had experienced so far on the trip. A sign above the counter stated: 'If you are looking for fast food McDonalds is 60 miles down the road ... if you are looking for good food, welcome!' Everything they sold had been made at the café and the staff were friendly and helpful – it was a great shop, but empty of customers. Where the hell was everyone? Time and again, out in America's quiet places, I felt I had the entire country to myself.

Well, not entirely this time. In the afternoon sunshine, as we came out of the Adobe Café, I could see a man's large bottom clothed in blue jeans lying alongside my motorcycle, and it appeared to be talking directly to me. I couldn't see its head. The bottom said something along the lines of: 'I hope you don't mind, but I wanted to look at your bike as I see Harley-Davidson is still using the swinging gudgeon pin transaxle cross-member.'

Of course I had absolutely no idea what he was talking about and, as a head had not yet appeared, I waited to see what would happen next. There followed a series of grunts and whistles and then the bottom moved into an upright position and a man with an enormous beard and shaved head appeared on his knees.

'Hi,' he said. 'It's amazing that they're still using that system. I remember them on old bikes of the 1950s and 1960s. What's it like to ride? Does the terminal actuator make any difference?'

These impressive engineering terms sounded to me more like medical conditions than anything to do with motorcycles, but he seemed satisfied when I just nodded and smiled, and said I didn't know. He heaved himself upright and added: 'It's a great day for a ride. I wish I could come with you. Maybe next time, eh?' Then he waddled off into the café for possibly his second lunch.

* * * * * *

Up to this point the ride into the mountains had been just great – no traffic, good roads and for the first time in a long while I actually felt confident riding a motorcycle. But, as always, I spoke too soon. High up the side of a lonely mountain, construction workers were repaving the road. We sat and waited a good ten minutes as traffic was brought down the mountain behind a sweeper vehicle and then it was our turn to go up. But the two-lane carriageway had been reduced to just one and that had been liberally covered with about two inches of loose gravel. That was probably why the man controlling the STOP sign had looked so smug as I rode past.

Nothing had prepared me for keeping a fully laden bike upright on a surface that felt like I was moving over rolling marbles. Go too fast and you fall off. Go too slow and you fall over. Somehow you have to balance the throttle at a smooth and even speed – and on no account use the brakes because the chances are you'll take a tumble. Throw into this equation the downhill sections where you gain momentum at an alarming rate as you cannot use the brakes, a few very tight hairpin corners at the bottom of the steep incline and an incompetent bike rider like myself and there's the recipe for utter disaster.

The road works went on and on. After five miles my eyes were hurting from staring so hard at the road ahead, my arms were aching from trying to keep the bike steady and my hands had gone numb again from gripping on to the handlebars. My adrenal gland was working overtime. I may well have emptied it.

Behind me was a long line of traffic, for the cars and trucks couldn't pass even if they had wanted to. They could, though, sit back and enjoy the spectacle of me and my motorcycle plunging over the side of the mountain to hit the valley floor and exploding like a New Mexico firework. I may be exaggerating a bit, but it was downright scary for few miles and, of course, involved a lot of swearing from me. Even Anne was struggling a little as she had to contend with the wake of gravel stones that my rear tyre was kicking out. Every so often I would hear her squeal as a stone pinged off her crash helmet or bounced off her bike.

In all this drama I had failed to notice that we had gone from the 90°F heat of the New Mexico desert to the distinctly chilly 62° of Alpine, but I quickly understood how the town had got its name. It was bloody cold, and even though it was late May there was still evidence of the past winter's snow on the ground. With a population of just 256, Alpine sits at the eastern end of the White Mountains. I could see why the first European settlers came up with the name Alpine as it was very reminiscent of landscapes I'd seen in Switzerland, with rolling grasslands, tall pine forests, craggy mountains and deep, dark lakes. It's a popular hiking and fishing resort, and good for whatever else you might want to do in the great American outdoors, like wrestling bears. But there was absolutely nobody about. Again. Perhaps they'd all decided to stay indoors. Even the bear was probably curled up in the warm somewhere.

* * * * * *

'What on earth brings you here?' asked the bemused motel receptionist in the next town of Eagar (population 4,126), when we went to check in. She seemed incredulous that people wanted to come and stay in her town, which mystified me as she was working in the business of selling overnight lodging to passing strangers. She did, though, hand me a small pamphlet: 'The current town mayor is Kim Holaway. The largest ski resort in Arizona is only a 30-minute drive from Eagar. The town of Eagar is located in a beautiful valley right below the White Mountains.' Maybe if I'd studied it better words such as 'ski resort', 'valley' and 'White Mountains' might have set alarm bells ringing, but all I did was amble across the motel's quiet car park to the nearby supermarket to buy something to eat.

The next morning was grey and cool, but not unpleasant, and I hoped we could cross most of Arizona that day before getting back into California, a leg of 215 miles. We were on the outer limits of the Fort Apache Indian Reservation, home to 12,000 people according to the 2008 Census of the Apache Nation. Some of them ran the local casino and the Sunrise Ski Resort, but more than half actually lived a life well below the US poverty level.

We climbed quickly into the White Mountains and I could hear my ears popping with the sudden changes in elevation. We passed a tourist sign directing people to Mount Baldy Peak at 11,403 feet. It was also getting much colder and a stiff breeze had picked up through the pine trees, forcing me to ride my motorcycle at an uncomfortable angle as I tried to compensate for the sudden and sharp gusts of mountain wind that hit me hard every time I came to an open clearing alongside the road. For the next 82 miles I had to stop every 15 minutes to try and get some circulation back into my hands, legs and feet. I was only wearing my leather jacket, jeans and a T-shirt and I was nearly frozen. My hands had started to go a fetching shade of blue, my feet were so cold they could have fallen off for all I knew, and I had lost any sense of feeling in my face. The wind chill factor must have been close to freezing and plummeting. To say I wasn't enjoying the ride through the White Mountains would be something of an understatement: I was hating it.

At one point we came upon a ski lift with its chairs swinging in the icy wind. As I rounded the next corner there was a mass of compacted dirty snow, built up two feet high, beside the road. The winter season might have been over months before and the skiers had all gone home, but even in late May there were huge blocks of ice sitting in the shadows on the verges and under the trees. There were a few White Mountain Apaches milling around broken-down houses in the small towns we rode through, but nobody else was stupid enough to be up this high and so badly equipped for riding a bike in icy weather.

And so it went on. I discovered the faster I went the better I was able to deal with the very strong cross-winds, which were making my back hurt like hell because my helmet was constantly being forced back. But in going faster I went into potentially icy corners far more quickly than I wanted or needed to. I was then stamping on the rear brake pedal to slow the bike to a more cautious speed and that was making the back tyre slew out, which unnerved me even more than the weather. I kept cursing myself for being stupid enough to ride up here in the White Mountains, but I couldn't go back as we had already come too far plus there was nowhere to pull over and stop for a while, so I opted for the English maxim of 'keep calm and carry on'. It was a real shame because the scenery of forest clearings and wide expanses of mountain lakes was absolutely beautiful. I just didn't see much of it.

Just when I thought I couldn't cope any longer we started to drop rapidly back down into the Arizona desert. It was bizarre, like a lot of America's topography. In the space of an hour we had gone from freezing to death on an ice-cold mountain ridge to cooking ourselves yet again in a blazing hot desert.

* * * * *

I really wanted to return to Jerome, one of my favourite small mining towns in the Southwest. It's perched high up in the National Park and when I'd visited a few years ago I'd loved the place. It looked down on its luck and many of the shops were closed, but it did have one amazing attraction that I have visited on no fewer than five occasions.

This time, as I joined the small two-lane road that winds up the hills into Jerome, I was overtaken by a fleet of ten men who were each on a quad bike – those four-wheeled vehicles with a motorcycle engine that are controlled by handlebars and have a propensity to fall over a lot and catapult their rider into the scenery. These were road-registered quad bikes and they were going like the clappers as they tore past me, a very odd sight as they bounced and lurched around the hairpin bends ahead of me, heading for Jerome.

Tucked just outside Jerome were the abandoned Gold King Ghost Town and Mine, both owned by an intriguing man who looked and dressed like one of the original nineteenth-century miners. He didn't say very much or tell you his name. Last time I'd seen him he was doing some blacksmithing work in the open air, surrounded by what looked like charred firewood. It turned out that the previous day he had accidentally burnt his entire blacksmith's shop down but he was carrying on regardless, working in the open. I admired his spirit.

He had amassed an amazing collection of old trash, vehicles, machinery, buildings and just general Western crap, but his *pièce de résistance* was an immense single-cylinder 10,000 cubic inch mining engine which he had brought to Arizona all the way from Illinois on the back of a very large lorry. For the very reasonable sum of $5 he was willing to start this massive industrial engine, which he affectionately called Big Bertha. It involved twiddling lots of knobs and pulling levers and chains before he got on to an ancient red tractor with a pulley running off the rear axle. This was needed to prime Big Bertha, apparently, and after five minutes of the tractor running the engine suddenly awoke and fired into life.

With slow piston strokes the open exhaust sounded like an artillery cannon being fired, and the explosive noise bounced around the valley until it almost made my ears bleed. This went on for a full ten minutes: the residents of Jerome, down below, must curse the mine owner every time a passing visitor offers him money to start his engine up. To my mind it was, and is, a deeply satisfying experience and money very well spent.

This time I was delighted to see that there was a new air of prosperity in Jerome. Shops had opened, the restaurants had been refurbished, and it was busy with visitors. Good for them. I do like this town.

Leaving Jerome there is the very challenging Highway 89 that has exactly 159 tight corners. (I know this because you can buy a T-shirt in town that says as much.) It's an amazing ride that really focuses the attention, because on one side there's a continuous slab of rock face while on the other there's a sheer drop down into distant valley floors. I erred on the side of caution and stuck to the speed limit, despite often having a large truck riding my rear wheel. I made it through all 159 corners, although I counted 163. I do like my T-shirt slogans to be accurate.

Highway 89 goes straight over Arizona's Black Hills before dropping abruptly into the blisteringly hot Chino Valley. Back in the dry desert heat again it was dusty and very warm, but this was a fast route that would take us all the way to the town of Parker, and another overnight halt, before arriving at Palm Springs in California. It was, though, starting to get seriously hot with outside thermometers in passing towns showing readings of well over 100°F.

* * * * * *

The next morning as I pulled out of the motel to join the morning traffic in Parker, a white pick-up truck pulled right in front of me so I couldn't move. The passenger window was down and a man was leaning across an immense woman and shouting something at me. At first I thought I had done something to offend him, as he appeared very agitated. But then I realised what he was saying sounded like utter gibberish – granted I was wearing a full-face crash helmet with the intercom system close to my ears – because it sounded like: 'Green ivy? Ya know where it is? The grey gravy, where is it?'

I was thoroughly confused and leaned a little closer (but not too close, as the woman was looking decidedly unhappy and as though she might bite me). Fortunately Anne had picked up on this somewhat one-sided conversation and she laughingly told me: 'He's looking for the local DMV (Department of Motor Vehicles) office and wants to know if you know where it is.'

Of course, that made perfect sense ... I told him I was a stranger here myself. With a shake of his head he accelerated away on the wrong side of the road, towards oncoming traffic, with the fierce-looking woman still staring at me through the open truck window. It was another interesting start to the day.

* * * * * *

Time and time again, while Anne and I were on our long-distance trips, I'd ask myself the same question. *What the heck do people do out here?* There are countless random small towns, sometimes no more than a cluster of buildings with an occasional store or a gas station. What can people do out in these remote and inhospitable parts of America? Clearly there is an attraction for some.

One friend had disparagingly said that they were perfect places for methamphetamine makers to come and live. You can apparently buy all the ingredients you need for this highly addictive hallucinogenic drug from your local grocery store. Cook it all up in your trailer or outhouse and, providing you don't blow yourself up, which I understand is one of the many downsides of the meth production process, you then have a great time. Or not. The police will probably turn up and arrest you and impound the meth, and as it has household drain cleaner among its many and diverse ingredients, it will probably also kill you.

To my mind it must be an extremely lonely life in such places. With or without meth. Nothing much ever happens, although I can sort of understand the attraction of the solitude, the immense open spaces and the magnificent scenery. I guess that occasionally, for excitement, you could get into your truck and head into town to shout at complete strangers on motorcycles about ivy and gravy.

* * * * * *

Riding a bike always exposes you to the elements. I hate rain, snow and ice, but sometimes extreme heat is almost as bad and it can sometimes become a tremendous effort just to concentrate on riding. As we headed into the Joshua Tree National Park I was getting increasingly hot and flustered and began to question, again, why the heck I was doing this.

For those old enough to remember, Irish rock band U2 had an international success with the *Joshua Tree* album. It had an enigmatic picture of one of these trees on the album's front cover – and some pretty good songs, too. I have always been curious about them, thanks in part to Bono and the gang. The Joshua Tree or *Yucca brevifolia* only grows in the wild at altitudes of between 1,300 and 5,900 feet and is indigenous to just this area. Personally I always think a Joshua Tree looks like it is dying, but mature specimens in the desert grow to at least 20 feet high and frame the horizon everywhere you look.

The Joshua Tree National Park is immense, covering 789,745 acres and including parts of two deserts – the higher Mojave and the lower Colorado – at 3,000 feet above sea level. Each has a different look and feel, and both have very different plants and wildlife. However, huge rocks and boulders are littered across both of them, looking as if some giant child has been playing a crude form of marbles and just scattered his toys all over the place. These rocks were formed more than 100 million years ago from cooling magma beneath the earth's surface, and wind erosion has carved them into the really peculiar shapes they are today.

Again I was astonished. We seemed to have these two deserts and the National Park entirely to ourselves – apart from a man who had set up camp for the weekend behind an immense boulder and another man on a cross-country record attempt on a ride-on lawnmower. I told you it was going to get weird again.

The camper was clearly a professional. He had a double-sided trailer complete with its own air-conditioning unit; he had roped off his part of the desert with a series of American flag bunting strips; he had his dog tied up; and for enjoyment there was a big beer keg and an enormous barbecue. There was even a satellite dish on the trailer roof. It looked like he was moving into the Joshua Tree National Park for the rest of his life.

And then … after 50 miles on empty desert roads, having seen nothing and nobody, I could just make out something ahead moving very slowly and coming straight towards us. It appeared to be being followed by a big truck and trailer with flashing orange lights. I felt I was beginning to hallucinate.

Anne said she thought it was someone riding a sit-on lawnmower. I thought she was joking and told her so.

'No, seriously. I can see a man on a mower and he's being followed by a huge truck. I think it's some sort of promotion. God bless America,' said Anne. I think she was being ironic but I wasn't sure.

As this odd procession drew closer I could see a very pale man sitting on the ride-on lawnmower, which was travelling at all of 5mph. The truck behind was clearly his support vehicle and it had emblazoned across its side the word 'craftsmanacrossamerica'. This long word with no gaps took some time to decipher before I understood what it was all about. To promote the durability of Craftsman ride-on lawnmowers the company had decided to get someone – this poor sap we were watching – to drive across the entire US on one of their products. I shook my head as he passed by and called out to him 'Why?' He simply shrugged his shoulders in a 'because we can' sort of way.

I understood what Craftsman was getting out of the deal but for the life of me I could not think of anything more miserable for the guy actually doing it. He was being cooked alive at 5mph on what must have been the longest journey of his life. If it had been me I would have waited until nobody was looking and then loaded the infernal mower on the back of the truck and driven a few hundred miles before offloading it again. Nobody would have known.

* * * * * *

It was still getting hotter and hotter and as we came into Palm Springs the temperature soared to 105°F. It's hard to explain how exhausting it is to ride a big air-cooled bike in desert heat, and when you're also very tired after eight hours of riding it gets to the point where you often just want to get off and walk away. Heat and fatigue are not a good combination on a motorcycle. The entire bike felt hot, I felt even hotter, and at every traffic light the engine and exhaust heat intensified, swirling baking air around me. By the time we reached our motel I was dehydrated, dizzy, thoroughly pissed off and drenched in sweat – not the best appearance to present in a motel reception when you want one of their rooms for the night.

Palm Springs is an odd sort of place. It has a constantly warm all-year-round temperature and has attracted the rich and famous for years. I say it's odd because it appears to be entirely man made. You ride for miles through the barren desert landscapes of the Coachella Valley and suddenly you're presented with lush green lawns and a very pleasant 1950s-style town with some outstanding mid-twentieth-century architecture – but it's in the middle of absolutely nowhere.

Located in a desert valley, Palm Springs is surrounded on all sides by mountain ranges: the San Bernardino Mountains to the north, the Santa Rosa Mountains to the south and the San Jacinto Mountains to the west. With an average of 354 days of sunshine and only five inches of rain a year it has, for some people, the ideal climate.

Elvis Presley had a home here, as did Frank Sinatra and many other famous entertainers from the 1950s and 1960s. Palm Springs is within easy striking distance of Los Angeles, but apart from the neatness of the place and the terrific weather I couldn't see the fascination that so many people (42,000 and growing, at the last count) had for this town. It's nice, it's hot and it's out there in the desert – that's the best that I could come up with.

The Cauhilla tribe lived here for hundreds of year before the settlers came through and they used to call the place 'Se Khi' or boiling springs, which it certainly was on 13 July 1985 when a night-time low of 105°F was recorded – the hottest low ever known in the western hemisphere. The Cauhilla are still there, and although the tribe now consists of no more than around 300 people they still own 32,000 acres of land in the valley and almost 6,000 acres within Palm Springs. I am not sure they got a fair deal really, as it was their land to begin with.

Palm Springs still attracts the rich and famous today and has also gained an enviable reputation for holding arts and music festivals. It's all very worthy and nice, but the most exciting things for me were the immense wind turbines generating electricity that sit outside the city limits. They're like weird alien sculptures whirring slowly in the brilliant desert sunshine.

* * * * * *

The Ortega Highway, or Highway 74, lay ahead. This would be the route to take Anne and me back into Southern California. It's a great road, climbing high into the mountains and with a fabulous lookout point halfway up towards Lake Elsinore in Riverside County. But it is a fantastic road in a car, and *definitely not* a fantastic road on a motorcycle, as I'd scarily found out with my first Harley-Davidson, as described in the first chapter of this book.

The Ortega Highway was originally created in 1917 with men using just shovels and mules to clear the dirt to make a 30-mile trail over the hills that separate the coast of Orange County from the inland town of Riverside. Today's road was built between 1929 and 1933 and is a major attraction for motorcycle riders who come from all over to test themselves on the challenging corners, adverse cambers, sudden turns, hills and deep drops of this demanding stretch of tarmac. It had become so notoriously dangerous that it was decided a few years ago to do something about it. There was some road widening and resurfacing done and a few more crash barriers were put up, with the end result being an even faster road.

Just the thought of riding the Ortega Highway made my mouth go dry, but we had no choice. We had to ride along it unless we took a 200-mile detour; it was quite simply the quickest way home. But Anne, who had taken to motorcycle riding like a natural within weeks of buying her bike a few years ago, was very scared of it too. Growing up in California she had been along this 40-mile route many times in a car and hated it.

Oncoming traffic was often in your lane as people tried to steer their massive trucks around the tight hairpin bends, while hard-charging sports bikes would get right up your rear bumper searching for a way past as they whipped around corners. There were sheer drops on both sides of the road, too, often at the same place: go over the edge here and you stood a chance of never being seen again.

Anne is a far better and braver motorcyclist than I will ever be. She has a natural poise and is able to hustle her bike at a smooth, fast rate with absolutely no problem, but even she felt uneasy about taking the Ortega Highway back to our home in Orange County. After a few minutes of deep breathing, standing beside her bike, she finally agreed she would give it a try, providing we could keep the intercom open on our helmets and I could talk her up and down. I admired my wife's bravado and was touched by her faith in me, because I was just as scared as she was. I was again relying on that old maxim that hadn't always served me so well in the past: *it seemed like a good idea at the time*.

The deal was that we would pull over whenever we could if faster traffic came up behind us, we would stop whenever she wanted to, and together we would maintain a sensible speed of no more than 45mph. I could hear Anne's anxious breathing in my headphones so I tried to keep up a running commentary on how well she was doing, telling her that the road was not as bad as we'd thought, although actually I remained unconvinced and thought it was the road from hell.

Anne was making good progress, however, and after about ten miles she suddenly announced over the intercom: 'You know what? This is nowhere near as bad as I thought it would be. In fact, we've ridden far scarier roads in the past few days. I can do this.' And soon, judging by her increasing cornering speed and the fact she was now riding within 18 inches of my rear wheel, she had clearly overcome her fear of the Ortega Highway. My job was done. Now all I had to do was make sure that I didn't fall off.

There is a popular bikers' bar called Hell's Kitchen about halfway along the Ortega Highway where we pulled in and stopped. I pushed my bike's kickstand down and parked right under an enormous sign in the car park that proclaimed in large capital letters: 'NO MATTER WHAT OBAMA SAY'S AMERICAN'S ARE THE WORLDS GREATEST PEOPLE!'

Bad punctuation aside, this was my first indication that not everyone was that encouraged by the country's new president. Obama clearly had some work to do out here on the Ortega Highway. Outside Hell's Kitchen were some very shiny motorcycles and a group of what some people, perhaps unkindly, refer to as 'weekend warriors' – motorcycle enthusiasts who go out for a short ride at the weekend and then go home and clean their bikes. It was at this point in my travels, after more than 3,200 miles through Arizona to New Mexico and back to California, that I realised I wasn't part of their gang any more.

CHAPTER FIVE

UFOs & LONESOME ROADS

Fighting cats – Bike modifications – California driving –
Burning down McDonalds – Nevada brothels – Gambling and mining –
Motel feeding frenzies

We'd covered a total of about 3,500 miles on our first big trip, through Arizona and New Mexico. I had been very lucky so far. I'd not been hurt, or run over, or even fallen off (apart from when I was learning to ride back in the Irvine car park and once, for some inexplicable reason, while standing completely still in my driveway; I think I forgot to put my feet down). Nor had I become one of the NHTSA's horrendous motorcycle statistics, and I'd even managed to navigate myself home along the notorious Ortega Highway.

But I had to stop riding for ten days when I came off second best in a dog and cat fight, stepping in to prevent a friend's cat killing the next-door neighbour's dog. The cat showed how much it resented my actions by sinking its teeth into my left hand. At first the bite was just a little bit painful, but in a matter of hours an infection in the two puncture marks on the back of my hand caused my lower arm to turn into a throbbing swollen limb, which grew to Popeye cartoon proportions. It went sort of smooth and shiny and reduced any hand movement to a feeble waving of the tips of my fingers. I definitely couldn't get a motorcycle glove over the hand – it wouldn't go past the first joint of my fingers – so, feeling very sorry for myself, I went and stared at a map of the US to work out where the heck we were going to head for next.

The problem with living in California is that to get anywhere else in the US you have to ride for at least a day even to get out of the state. I'd created a small office in our garage and felt that by sitting next to my motorcycle I'd draw inspiration from it, as well as from the map I had nailed to the wall.

Oregon to the north promised rain, and even in June northern California had fog and drizzle and could be very much like England in the summer. Nevada seemed to me like a very good option, and perhaps we could go on into Utah and Wyoming – basically wherever the road would take us. It looked easy on the map, but what I had not properly estimated were the huge distances we would need to cover. At the time I thought this would be a good ten days' riding, at most. As it turned out it was closer to four weeks and the best part of 4,500 miles through some of the loneliest towns and emptiest roads I have ever seen.

* * * * * *

It had taken nearly two days to clean my motorcycle after our first big trip. When I'd taken Street Bob's saddle off and looked underneath the frame I realised I'd somehow managed to accumulate a mass grave of dead bees and other unidentifiable body parts. At least the bike no longer smelled of burning insects when I rode it.

I also tried to check that everything was working correctly before we headed off for Nevada and beyond. This basically consisted of fiddling with things and seeing if they fell off. If they didn't I was satisfied that my bike was good to go. I studied the wiring box that sat beneath the saddle and wondered if I should do anything to it – electricity fascinates me but I have absolutely no idea how it works. Perhaps I should check the connections and see which ones came loose or might give me a shock? But then I had visions of my motorcycle catching fire in the middle of nowhere because of what I'd done to it in my misguided enthusiasm and I decided it was best to leave it all well alone.

The one thing I could not find a solution for were the bike's standard 'mini-ape' handlebars. On our previous long trip the riding position had killed my arms, and for some unfathomable reason whenever I rode on interstate freeways there was such bad vibration that my hands and arms went completely numb so I could barely tell if I was touching the indicator buttons or squeezing the brakes.

I had read somewhere on the internet that by taking off a few bolts and moving things around I might find a more comfortable riding position so, armed with a small Allen key, I started undoing a few things, thinking how easy this was going to be. When the entire top end above the bike's forks fell backwards with the mirrors resting on the tank and the indicators pointing at the sky I realised I was out of my depth. Again. I had created a motorcycle that looked as if it was controlled by a handle from a baby's pram. Furthermore, if I adopted this interesting steering rake, I would have to lie stomach down on the bike's fuel tank with my legs stretched out behind me, unable to reach the rear brake or gear shifter.

I also appeared to have an extra bolt that did not fit anything and what looked to be a very important cable was now pressed hard up against the fuel tank. It was a mess. What had taken me four minutes to take to pieces took the best part of two hours to put back together again and even now I am not sure what that extra bolt was for. But I still carry it around in my pocket today, just in case I should ever need it.

I had got the art of packing for trips down to a better format, however. Gone were the carpentry tools and I was now going to rely on plastic ties if anything broke or fell off, plus a large pocketknife and a flashlight.

* * * * * *

It was time to head out of California and north-east to Nevada, but there was something missing this time. I had learned a lot from riding through the US on our previous trip, but there is a rhythm you get into when you ride a motorcycle and mine was definitely absent the day we set off. I felt exposed, nervous and downright unsure as I rode in light Sunday morning traffic on Highway 91. I kept slowing down, dropping from the legal freeway speed limit of 65mph to 55mph, and then to 45mph, and speeding up again. I was really struggling and began to have serious doubts about making it out of California and beyond.

I pulled off and sat down on the kerb outside a gas station to take stock. I had invested too much time and effort in this planned series of rides to give up now. After all, I had survived one long motorcycle trip already, and also ridden around Southern California since, taking everything Orange County's traffic and its roads could throw at me from ever more congested freeways, where it can sometimes take as long as an hour to travel the 15 miles to work, to mums driving formidable Hummers on the school run, tough-looking Mexicans in ageing Toyota pick-ups, always equipped with the compulsory heavy-duty garden machinery rolling around in the back, and random road-rage shootings on Interstate 5, which the LAPD put down to people having a bad day.

When there are road-rage shootings on the Californian freeways it's an unwritten law among fellow motorists not to have any eye contact with the driver in the car or truck next to you. You have to get used to living in a world where the guy alongside you could, at any moment, shoot out your tyres, windows or brains just because, in a moment of crass stupidity, you'd forgotten to use your indicator when turning left or gesticulated at someone in a car talking obliviously on their mobile phone while wandering all over the road in front of your bike.

Anne was sympathetic, but confused by my sudden panic. She gave me some quiet advice, reminding me that a lot of people are armed in California and it's best to ignore their anti-social behaviour, and she also tried the tactful approach of asking: 'Do you want to follow me on the freeway and we'll just keep to the slow lane?' It was kind of her, but I knew what I had to do: conquer my fears, saddle up and push on. I told myself I could do this, and ten minutes later we were on the road again. We had to get out of California via the San Bernardino Pass on Highway 215 and reach the town of Barstow before nightfall.

* * * * * *

I had chosen to do very little riding at night on our previous trip. Motorcycle riding is tough enough during daylight hours in America and I just knew I would be tempting fate by riding after dark. This decision always added additional pressure to our journeys as I needed to ensure I was at least within striking distance of that night's motel before the sun went down. On occasions it made me ride a lot faster than I should have.

With the afternoon sun starting to lower in the sky, I started my bike up and headed off for Interstate 15, the freeway which climbs quickly and cuts dramatically via a pass through the San Bernardino Mountains to the northern tip of California's Mojave Desert. You face a five-lane road on both sides of this freeway, which encourages people to overtake slower-moving traffic, such as me, on both sides. I was back to my pet hate of 18-wheeler trucks driving at well over the speed limit. It was Freeway Hell all over again and I simply could not wait for it all to be over and turn off for the town of Barstow.

Barstow is a strange place that had once been an important railway junction in the late nineteenth and early twentieth centuries, supplying the flourishing Californian and West Coast communities. I had always wanted to visit it because apparently it had some great railway architecture, including the impressive Casa del Desierto that was built in 1911 as a hotel and railway station and now houses the Western America Railroad Museum. Massive goods trains still rumble through Barstow today and you can take a train to anywhere in the US from the Desierto, but the huge station has been unmanned since 1973.

As we discovered, the Casa del Desierto is a truly lovely railway building, described in the guidebooks as a mixture of Spanish Renaissance and Classic Revivalist style. It had been very well restored and was certainly worth a visit. Inside was totally empty, but the Rail Museum, built alongside, had some interesting artefacts including a small room dedicated to the nails used on railways across the US. The collection consisted of literally thousands and thousands of nails that someone must have taken a lifetime to amass. They all looked exactly the same to me, mounted in their wooden boxes, with the one exception that the year each nail was made had been stamped on every head. I was truly impressed by someone's dedication to something quite so obscure.

As ever, small town America confused me. Much of Barstow was run down and shops were closing, but there was a huge amount of traffic coming and going to Las Vegas, which is a three-hour drive up the freeway. Barstow's Main Street was nearly empty, with just a few people wandering around, and they seemed busy not doing very much at all.

A woman approached me, asking for spare change. She was pushing a child's pushchair that had a large can of household paint in it. She also looked like she'd just taken a lot of illegal substances. I could barely make out what she was saying as she stood in front of me, swaying slightly and gripping tightly to the pushchair handles to maintain her balance.

'Spar some shaansh, sir?' she asked, looking at me with madly wide eyes that looked as if they had been made up with paint from the tin she was pushing around town.

'Yes, possibly, but it might rain later,' I said in my best English accent, pretending to ignore what she had asked me. I tried to avert my gaze and stare into the empty shop window of what had once been a ladies' outfitters.

'Nah, shaansh,' she continued. 'Got anything that you cown let me have?'

I continued staring at the window hoping she would go away, and eventually she did, staggering across the road towards someone who looked a better prospect. But she did look back at me to say something that I did understand: 'Whattsa matter with you? Don't ya unnerstand English?'

There were some interesting murals in Barstow, which seems to be another feature of America's small towns. If times are tough in a small US town then the thinking seems to be that the remedy would be to paint a large colourful mural to cheer the townsfolk up, or spend a lot of cash and renovate an historic building. The net result is usually an incongruous mixture of vivid wall paintings depicting a place's past history – normally settlers, horses and Indians and a lot of covered wagons stare at you amid a sea of rundown houses, closing shops, disillusioned people and empty streets.

In the tourist literature Barstow promised an open air cinema showing two films a day (it was closed when I rode past) and an opportunity to go spelunking in nearby lava caves. I had no idea what spelunking entailed and why precisely you would need to do it in caves, and can only assume it might lead to pushing a child's pushchair with a can of paint in it. What I did find fascinating and amusing was the description of a big fire in Barstow in 1986. I had envisaged the entire centre of the town wiped out in one of the many blazes that small desert towns in the US seem habitually to suffer from. But this was far better.

In September of that year the McDonald's restaurant, which at the time allegedly sold more fast food meals than any other McDonald's outlet in the US, was subjected to an inferno thanks to an 80-year-old customer using its drive-through window. Not only did Mr James Bradey burn the restaurant down, he also lost his car and all his worldly possessions. The local paper – the *Desert Dispatch* – recorded the events of that day as follows:

James Bradey was on his way to live with his daughter when he stopped for breakfast at the Barstow Station McDonald's. He suspected something was wrong with his car after he bought some gasoline and stopped at McDonald's.

'I noticed the car just wasn't starting right. When I pulled up to the [McDonald's] window it was smoking real bad,' Bradey said.

The car burst into flames at about 7.00am at the drive-through window at the restaurant. Bradey first tried to put out the fire with his hands, a McDonald's worker said.

Bradey then tried to rescue some of his possessions. This amounted to an out-of-state cheque and his toiletries. The fire destroyed 9,000 square feet of the restaurant and was so intense the fire crew chief evacuated his 15-strong team and 25 customers that were inside; 70 firemen and 16 engines eventually brought the blaze under control at 8.50am.

Although some of the restaurant was saved, its reputation as the biggest selling McDonald's restaurant in the US was lost forever and some say was claimed by another outlet in Chicago. I am still mystified how Barstow, with a slender population of 20,000 people, could have generated so much customer traffic. Were the residents of Barstow each having a McDonald's meal up to three times a day in 1986? The *Desert Dispatch* doesn't say what happened to Mr Bradey after the fire either, except that a passing sympathetic Marine Corps sergeant took him away to call his insurance company.

I'd been adamant from the outset that I did not want to visit big cities and towns, but after getting off the freeway the map told me the logical place to head for would be Las Vegas in Nevada. A number of things that seem to me to be wrong with western civilisation are embodied in Las Vegas – the excess, the money and the unsavoury characters you are likely to meet are just a few at the top of my list. I had been there many times before on business but never, ever, for pleasure, and I'd always been shocked by the many sad-looking people trying to have 'fun'. I recall going to bed at night, passing lost souls working the slot machines, only to get up in the morning and find these same people still playing the next day, in exactly the same place and looking completely worn down.

There are no windows in any of Las Vegas's buildings. You don't know what time of day it is and there are constant streams of people arriving to have a good time and party. I once shared an elevator in a Las Vegas hotel with a couple: the girl was on her knees and appeared to be talking intimately to the crotch of the gentleman she was with – except no actual words passed between them. I studied every single floor level light on the elevator display panel before getting off at the 32nd, not daring to look round behind me. The man, though, did say goodnight to me.

The only option if I wanted to avoid Las Vegas and get into Nevada proper was to head north from California, skirting the eastern boundary of Death Valley, then take the empty roads in the middle of the state with the objective of eventually getting to Utah.

* * * * * *

Nevada is America's seventh largest state and covers the area from the Mojave Desert in the south to the Great Basin in the north. It is also the driest place in the US and surprisingly (or maybe not) it's estimated that more than 86% of the land is owned by the US government for civilian and military use. It was also, I was shortly to find out, very sparsely populated indeed because 85% of Nevada's 2.6 million residents live in either Las Vegas or Reno. Aside from gambling, and easy marriage and divorce laws, Nevada also permits legalised brothels in eight out of its 16 counties. This was a place I had to see.

It was a very odd route into western Nevada. Taking Highway 127 at the town of Baker we headed almost due north on 60 miles of two-lane roads, immediately climbing up a range of mountains and then coming down the other side to a large plateau. The first time this happened I was surprised to find such a huge plain waiting for me on the other side of the mountain with absolutely nobody about apart from, literally, just a farm or two. By the fifth time this happened I was beginning to get very bored.

The road was dead straight, flat and featureless and it just went on for miles and miles, climbing up tall brown mountain ranges and then dropping down into the vacant plains below. You end up riding as if you are in some kind of weird vacuum, where everybody and everything has left and there is nothing to see but rocks, desert and scrub. Every so often, to break the monotony, I would ride in the left-hand lane as if I was in England and then swerve back to the right, and then speed up to 100mph and slow back down again. It didn't really help with the ennui, though, and I couldn't help feeling this was the most barren and empty place in the world.

Occasionally we saw a small ranch or farm, but with the exception of a surprised-looking cow that clearly hadn't seen a human for years, let alone one on a motorcycle, we rode for almost three hours without seeing another living soul. It was also getting very, very hot as this was the route that wound past the eastern edge of the infamous Death Valley.

* * * * * *

Death Valley was well known to me from my years in the automotive industry, as many car manufacturers go out there to test and develop their latest models in the extreme conditions. Spying photographers working for international car magazines make a lot of money by hiding behind a cactus or a boulder and taking sneak pictures of the next Ford, Toyota or even the occasional Aston Martin. However, the car companies have got wise to this and in recent years have started to disguise their prototypes with startling blocks of cardboard and black and white zebra paint to break up the new model's lines. The consequence has been a series of blurry photographs of forthcoming cars rushing through the scorching desert of Death Valley which look like they have been designed by a four-year-old kid. The magazines are still happy to pay big bucks for these pictures, though, despite the fact that the cars always look the same and the reader can't tell whether they are looking at a Hyundai hatchback or Bentley's latest luxury saloon.

Death Valley is the lowest and driest place in North America at 282 feet below sea level, and just 76 miles to the east the land rises to 14,505 feet at Mount Whitney, the highest summit in the US (apart from Alaska). Death Valley is also incredibly hot for most of the year. In fact, the highest temperature ever recorded there, at Furnace Creek in 1913, was 136°F, or in new money 57.8°C. In those sorts of temperatures, of course, car manufacturers can test their latest products until they break, explode, melt or bits fall off, or possibly all four.

I had driven through Death Valley some years previously as a very naïve young man in a bright red convertible Mazda MX-5 and nearly cooked myself alive. I had been loaned this great little Japanese sports car for six weeks while working on a press launch and liked everything about it apart from the huge amount of attention it caused wherever I drove it. It had just been launched and everyone in the US was going crazy for it, with people flying across America to Mazda dealerships to buy what some had described as the new MGB sports car. It was selling for thousands of dollars over list price. America had what the newspaper *US Today* reported at the time as *MX-5 Fever*.

I soon got tired of answering questions from over-zealous

Californians at intersections and in car parks, shopping malls and gas stations about how much it cost and where you could buy one, so one weekend I took off for the east side of California with absolutely no idea where I was going. I dreamed about achieving another ambition of mine, to drive a convertible around California for a few hundred miles and never put the top up. After 400 miles and eight hours in blistering heat, and feeling distinctly unwell, I passed a sign that simply stated 'Now Leaving Death Valley'. I had no idea I had been through this flaming hot desert, apart from the fact that everything I touched inside the MX-5 was scalding hot, my head was on fire and my face resembled a tomato that had been beaten with a large blunt instrument. I was lucky not to have suffered severe sunstroke.

So I had, unintentionally, already been to Death Valley, and I had absolutely no desire to repeat the experience on a motorcycle.

* * * * * *

Anne and I stopped for lunch in a small place called Shoshone that had a gas station, a small museum and, despite the impressive collection of flies buzzing in its window, a great diner with really good food. Time and again in rural areas we found that if you made a point of staying away from the fast food chains you could always find good, basic, home-cooked food to eat that was both filling and cheap.

Which is why I found it amusing that an elderly English couple who'd arrived at the Shoshone diner shortly after us turned their noses up at the menu and asked the waitress if they could perhaps have a cup of tea. The wife was complaining to her husband: 'There's nothing but fatty foods for sale at these sort of places. Just look at the people eating here – and there are no fresh vegetables or anything worth eating.' He looked embarrassed and coughed loudly rather than replying to his wife. Here I was, a long way from home in California, a long way from the country of my birth, in an isolated town in Nevada, with two fellow countrymen keeping the moaning spirit of middle England alive by asking where on earth they could get a decent cup of tea and complaining about the food and the locals. As we English say, I was gobsmacked.

My gob was further smacked about 30 miles out of Shoshone when we came across an opera house in the middle of nowhere. To be fair, there was a small sprinkling of abandoned buildings loosely tied together to form a community once called Amargosa. Who the hell, I thought, drives all the way out here, close to Death Valley, to watch opera in the Nevada desert?

This opera house cum theatre was no spur of the moment thing, though. Back in 1967 a lady by the name of Marta Becket discovered a theatre that had been abandoned after the Pacific Coast Borax mining company had left town. Between 1923 and 1925 Pacific Coast had constructed a series of adobe buildings to house offices, a store, a 23-room hotel, dining rooms and employee headquarters.

In 1968 Marta began running and developing the theatre and painting murals, as she put it, 'to re-create an entire audience on the walls, filled with characters that might have attended an opera back in the sixteenth century'. It took her four years to complete the murals and when she had finished Marta apparently looked at the building's ceiling and spent the next two years on scaffolding and painting a sky, complete with cherubs, clouds and the four winds in each corner. It's still a working theatre and opera house today.

The Amargosa Opera House was closed when we passed by, but Marta had a musical season planned for 2010 entitled 'If These Walls Could Talk'. I wish I could have found an excuse to go and see this spectacular. It sounded like fun.

Just 500 yards up the road was a T-junction with a sign that simply said 'Death Valley', pointing off vaguely towards a low range of dusty brown hills. I pulled over and rested to watch for a bit. In the space of two minutes three cars pulled up behind me, turned left, and headed off into the hottest place in the US. A minute later two of them had clearly had a change of heart as they came charging back and shot off the way they had just come. It seemed a pity to have come so far just to turn round, and it was not even very hot – only around a piffling 106°F that day.

* * * * * *

I was minding my own business cruising along the highway and taking in the scenery. As I was constantly to learn, this is a big mistake on a motorcycle because the moment you break your concentration something stupid happens to you. In this case it was a small bronze Pontiac car on the opposite side of the road that had crept up behind a big rig truck. The road was dead straight for about three miles and I had watched the car's progress as it had gained on the truck before tucking right up behind it. As I drew closer to both of them the Pontiac driver suddenly pulled out from behind the truck right into my lane and drove straight towards me.

My instant reaction was to scream like a girl, very loudly into my helmet, and steer my motorcycle rapidly to the right. As the car drew level between the truck and me I raised my left hand in the universally understood middle-finger salute. The look on the very large man's face behind the windscreen was a blend of confusion and real annoyance. I immediately congratulated myself on this narrow escape and then spent the next 15 miles worrying that he had in fact turned his car around and was now coming back to get me because he was offended by my giving him the finger.

Fortunately a few minutes later I was distracted by an enormous billboard sign by the side of the road inviting me to sample the delights of the Shady Lady Ranch 'for the tired traveller'. It was an incongruous sight – a solitary and immense billboard in a field advertising a brothel – and what was even odder was that it was being studied by a black and white cow, no doubt reading about the delights of the Shady Lady Ranch and wondering which bus to take to get there.

Prostitution is legal in Nevada and clearly the Shady Lady Ranch was very proud of the fact that for the past seven years it had been voted the best small brothel in the state. That's clearly quite an achievement in anyone's book, but I am still not clear on who precisely does the judging for the *Good Brothel Guide to Nevada*. What

MOJAVE DESERT, CALIFORNIA–NEVADA BORDER: *A long straight road through an empty desert – this was what I had been dreaming about. But after 200 miles it could get a little boring.*

ENTERING JULIAN: *First stop on my travels and time to consider what the next few thousand miles were going to involve.*

ALGODONES SAND DUNES: *The origins of this bizarre landscape continue to cause arguments among the experts. The dunes have famously appeared in many Hollywood films, including 'Star Wars'.*

ENOUGH: *I hate this. Whose stupid idea was it to ride around the US through inhospitable wilderness and baking hot deserts?*

PACIFIC COAST HIGHWAY, CALIFORNIA: *There were spectacular moments too, of course – lots of them. Here, surfing is taken to a new level. A few hundred yards out to sea were a whole group of people kite surfing, an extraordinary sight to watch.*

SPACE AGE MOTEL, GILA BEND, ARIZONA: *If you like your overnight accommodation to be more sci-fi than wi-fi this is the place for you.*

GILA BEND, ARIZONA: *Retina-hurting paintings are everywhere in the Space Age Lodge Motel. This is what confronts you at breakfast time.*

SAUCEDA MOUNTAINS, ARIZONA: *Nobody about apart from the ubiquitous Border Patrol and a couple of US Air Force military jets practising loops and turns in the desert sky.*

PIMA AIR AND SPACE MUSEUM, TUCSON, ARIZONA: *A 1968 Douglas B-26K built for special operations in the Vietnam War. Just sitting in the desert heat.*

SONOITA, ARIZONA: *Just a few miles away from achieving a lifetime goal I could boast about – riding into Tombstone, scene of the famous gunfight at the OK Corral.*

BOOTHILL CEMETERY, TOMBSTONE, ARIZONA: *In 1881 Wyatt Earp, his brothers and Doc Holliday killed Billy Clanton, Tom McLaury and Frank McLaury at the famous OK Corral gunfight. They were accused of murder but all charges were dropped. Clearly the Clanton and McLaury families disagreed with the verdict.*

BIG NOSE KATE'S BAR, TOMBSTONE, ARIZONA: *The Goathead Motorcycle Club salute a fallen comrade.*

TOMBSTONE, ARIZONA: *Taking a break from playing to the crowds. Many of the locals dress up in nineteenth-century Western clothing and twice a day the famous OK Corral shoot-out is re-enacted for visitors.*

OK CORRAL, TOMBSTONE, ARIZONA: *On 26 October 1881 Wyatt Earp, his brothers Virgil and Morgan, and their friend Doc Holliday made history in just 30 seconds with 30 shots that left three men dead and turned Earp into a Wild West legend.*

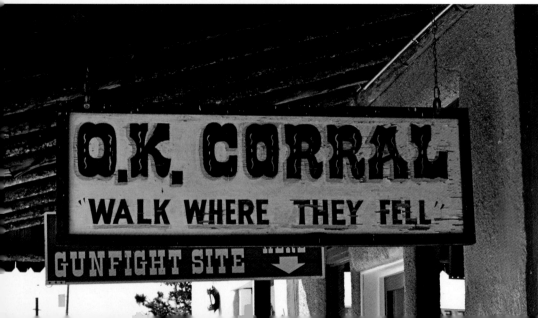

HIGHWAY 10, ARIZONA: *The Thing was the best museum I have ever been to – and all for just $1.*

THE THING, HIGHWAY 10, ARIZONA: *This museum had a sensationally eclectic collection of oddities. Adolf Hitler lurked in a Rolls-Royce round the corner alongside a full-sized hand-painted Spanish inquisition torture chamber.*

LORDSBURG, NEW MEXICO: *The banner says it all. This was the largest fireworks shop I had ever seen.*

JOSHUA TREE NATIONAL PARK, CALIFORNIA: *You couldn't make this up: the guy was driving across the US on a lawnmower at 5mph – and it was 102°F in the shade.*

JOSHUA TREE NATIONAL PARK, CALIFORNIA: *Hanging out in the desert under a Joshua tree.*

MOJAVE DESERT, CALIFORNIA–NEVADA BORDER: *Just remembered what I don't like about desert riding – it gets very hot.*

TONOPAH STATION CASINO, TONOPAH, NEVADA: *I thought I'd try my luck at the gambling machines and walked away a $1.21 winner.*

My unquestioning faith in technology meant I trusted the fuel gauge on my Harley-Davidson – but I did run out of fuel in Nevada's Egan Mountains.

HIGHWAY 6, CONFUSION MOUNTAINS, UTAH: *The wet weather was behind me in Nevada, but two hours of sand storms lay ahead.*

DELTA, UTAH: *Time to study the map, recover from the sand storm and rest my paralysed left leg. I thought I'd suffered a stroke, but actually I'd got tar on the sole of my boot which had then become welded to the footpeg.*

FLAMING GORGE NATIONAL RECREATION AREA AND RESERVOIR, UTAH–WYOMING BORDER: *Some 207,000 acres of land and a 92-mile reservoir that was built in 1956. The dam I rode over holds back more than 3,788,000 acre-feet of water.*

HIGHWAY 28, SINKS CANYON, WYOMING: *Deep valleys and green grass contrast beautifully with the bright red rocks and a wide open sky. I liked this state very much indeed.*

DUBOIS, WYOMING: *The coffee was good but I couldn't work out why it was called a 'Coffee Haus'. Dubois is also home to the Bighorn Sheep Center which describes itself as 'high, wild and on the edge'.*

HIGHWAY 26, ROCKY MOUNTAINS, WYOMING: *Wow! Wow! And wow again! This utterly astonishing and beautiful road led me right up into the Rocky Mountains.*

MURPHY, IDAHO: *There are plenty of good places to eat in the US if you stay away from fast food chains, but there are limits.*

SIERRA NEVADA MOUNTAINS, CALIFORNIA: *Nothing had prepared me for the outstanding beauty of these mountains or one of the best motorcycle rides of my life.*

GOLDEN GATE BRIDGE, SAN FRANCISCO, CALIFORNIA: *Another dream achieved despite the bridge being shrouded in fog and drizzle so I couldn't see a damn thing. I was charged $6 for the privilege of going south over the bridge, but it's free to go north.*

the Shady Lady brothel did explain on its website, which I looked up when Anne was out at work one day, was:

> *Today in the State of Nevada, Legal Brothels still exist, and are still very important to those men who feel the need for out of home sexual experiences. Perhaps the romantic lure of the Old West is why houses of prostitution are still so popular and frequently visited, especially to the many visitors that come to Nevada each year. They love to check out the latest houses to see what's new and different. For the tourist there couldn't be a safer way to have sex than in a Legal Brothel. The girls are checked weekly by a Doctor and many safeguards are in place to prevent any medical problems for the girls and their clients.*

Apparently for $200 you get 40 minutes with the girl of your choice, although there appeared to be only three of them listed on their very informative website. Interested couples can pay $700 for an hour with a girl, or if you really want to push the boat out you can stay overnight for $2,000. I hope that makes the matter entirely clear for anyone who has questions. With Anne keeping me in check on this trip there was absolutely no way she was going to agree for me to have an *out of home sexual experience*. It was probably just as well as the road to the Shady Lady Ranch looked like it had seen better days and the gates were very definitely padlocked and closed. I am simply recording it on these pages for the reader's interest.

* * * * * *

It was going to be a long ride of more than 300 miles to get to the old mining town of Tonopah, and while the desert roads were empty of traffic and people I had not reckoned on dealing with dust devils. These are like mini-tornadoes created by rising heat off the desert floor and they throw a spiralling plume of dust sometimes as high as 100 feet into the air. I could see two of them on the horizon and as I got closer one of them started to move from my right and then shot across the road in front of my bike. I had no option but to ride through it. There was dust and sand swirling in front of me, maybe as high as 60 feet, and it was certainly a good 30 feet wide. It felt very odd to be riding a motorcycle straight into what looked like a moving, twisting cloud of brown fog.

I could cope with the sand and vegetation being thrown around, but I had not expected the strength of the wind that was moving it all about. Great gusts hit me hard in the chest, making my bike pull violently first to the right and then back the left. It took only a matter of seconds to ride through, but it scared the crap out of me. I slowed to watch over my shoulder as the dust devil meandered off to the other side of the road and then across the flat plateau beyond, picking up loose leaves, small sticks and sand and throwing them up in the air in a plume of brown mist as it went. I had just ridden through a mini-tornado. I tell you, it's weird out there in the Nevada desert.

* * * * * *

It was nearly as weird as my first visit to a rural Nevada casino in the town of Tonopah. It was very dark inside and just for a second I thought I had been stuffed into a time machine and the clock had been rolled back to 1974. There was shag pile carpet on the floor and even up some of the walls, stuffed animal heads leered at me from the walls, people were smoking and drinking and all of them were pushing money into slot machines. I couldn't remember the last time I had been able to sit in a place where you could sit and smoke at a bar, and the amazing décor of velvet curtains, huge TV screens and the smell of complimentary popcorn burning away in the corner just added to the whole 1970s experience. The men all seemed to be dressed in baseball caps, jeans and heavy duty working boots. And so were the women.

There was a cacophony of sounds as Country & Western music was being piped in through the antiquated stereo speakers which in turn battled for dominance with an enormous TV screening the news, while above it all were the electronic blips and music of the gambling machines. This was no time-travel experience, however, just the Tonopah Station – a casino, hotel and RV (recreational vehicle) park that I had wandered into. Nevada makes a huge amount of money in taxes and income from legalised gambling and this tiny town, despite being down on its luck, had a thriving casino that seemed to attract locals and tourists alike.

I thought I would try my luck at the slot machines and pushed a $1 bill into the first machine I came to. It had a mass of flashing ancient Egyptian icons – similar to those found on the walls inside the pyramids – but Nefertem, the god of the lotus and the eternal sunrise, appeared to be offering a basket full of fries and a burger, while Anubis, the deity in charge of the ancient Egyptian afterlife, was definitely holding a police baton and a multi-coloured shopping bag.

Nothing happened for a second while the machine digested my dollar, then some electronic pseudo-Arabic music started blaring, lights started flashing and the reels took on a life of their own. I kept jabbing buttons, hoping to make the horrible noise and epilepsy-inducing lights stop, but it seemed my solitary dollar had bought me 100 chances of winning the jackpot so I just kept on prodding random buttons. Then a loud klaxon sounded. The top of my slot machine had a white strobe light that started flashing and a robotic voice announced I was a winner.

I couldn't work out what I had won, but a group of middle-aged women who up to now had ignored me scurried to look over my shoulder.

'You've won, honey,' drawled one of them while she puffed on her cigarette. 'Let's see what you've got. I have been playing for over an hour and I've not won a damn thing. This could be real exciting … oh dear.'

In less than ten seconds I went from elation, due to their excitement, to downright disappointment and embarrassment. My good fortune amounted to $1.21 in winnings, not the shiny new Chevrolet or the $250,000 jackpot that was advertised on the top of the slot machine. My fellow gamblers slunk away to try their luck elsewhere, and a weary-looking casino worker wandered over to check out the huge fortune I had amassed.

'Just $1.21, right. You want to cash in?' she said.

'Yes please,' I mumbled and stared at my shoes, trying to avoid eye contact. She wandered off, jangling a huge bunch of keys, went to a cupboard and then to a locked office, opened a safe and took out a $1 bill from a huge wad of notes, plus some change, locked the safe, locked the office, came back and handed over my winnings.

'Don't spend it all at once, honey,' she said. I think she may have been being sarcastic, but perhaps I was the only person in the place who was actually going to walk out of there that evening having successfully beaten the system. Time for a drink, I thought.

'What do people actually do in this town?' I asked Anthony, the cheerful casino barman.

He stopped for a second and raised one eyebrow. 'I'm new here myself,' he replied. 'I moved here just four months ago from Utah with my wife as she wanted to get back to be with her family. There's still a lot of mining done around here and of course there's this place. That's it really.' I got the feeling that Anthony was not that impressed with Tonopah.

The town was created in 1900 after the discovery of gold and silver. Legend has it that the town's founder, Jim Butler, went looking for a lost donkey in the area. When Butler found the animal he picked up a nearby rock to throw at it (a drastic thing to do, but maybe that's the way they round up lost donkeys in Nevada) and discovered the rock he was holding was very heavy and contained a huge amount of silver. I like legends like this.

Mr Butler had actually stumbled upon the second-richest silver strike ever recorded in Nevada and it was not long before Butler Town was a thriving community. Over the years, though, the town changed its name and it eventually ended up being called Tonopah, the Shoshone Native American word for 'hot spring'. Even today there are mineshafts all around the town and silver mining still going on, although on a much smaller scale than in the town's heyday. The mines are close to being worked out now, which would explain why the town, despite having some magnificent early twentieth-century buildings, looked neglected and as if it was teetering on the edge of going out of business and shutting down completely.

The town does have a strong military presence, as the US Air Force's notorious F117 Nighthawk, otherwise known as the Stealth Bomber, was developed and flown here from Nellis Air Force Base just up the road. There is even a dramatic stone monument in the centre of town, next to the fire station, to record the fact that these planes were flown in and around here in the 1980s and 1990s.

* * * * * *

Even more interesting, from my point of view, was the Tonopah Missile Test Range or Area 52. Being a military installation, not too much is known about what actually goes on there. The entrance was marked by wooden gates and a large, and I assume unarmed, intergalactic missile was just lying on its side in the desert dust. The US Military uses the area for launching research rockets designed to take measurements and perform scientific experiments during sub-orbital flights some 30 to 1,000 miles above the surface of the earth. NASA also has a presence here, sending the Terrier MK70 missile up into space to test the payload-carrying capacities of space rockets.

So basically there is a lot of military ordnance going up into the sky in and around Tonopah, along with experimental planes and missiles. All these activities are top secret, and of course no civilian is ever allowed in. This in turn has led to some fantastic conspiracy theories. With the backdrop of the huge Nevada night skies and remote desert landscapes there have been countless 'alien' sightings and suggestions of extraterrestrial activity from over-optimistic people with nothing else to do.

There have been even more 'alien' sightings at another top-secret military base, imaginatively called Area 51, just a little further down the road from the Tonopah Missile Range. Area 51 is off Highway 375 to the east of Tonopah and many travellers on this road have reported UFOs shooting across the sky. So many, in fact, that in 1996 the state of Nevada decided to cash in and renamed the road the Extraterrestrial Highway. Today people from all around the world come to this remote, empty place and sit out under the desert night sky, hoping to catch a glimpse of a spaceship, or an alien, or something not of this world.

The US Federal Government does concede that the US Air Force has 'an operating location' in Area 51 but does not provide any further information. The base's primary purpose is thought to be the development of experimental aircraft and weapons systems, and the presence of this twenty-first-century military hardware has probably increased the number of UFO sightings. I certainly didn't witness any UFO activity while I was out there, nor did I spend time with any of the alien watchers who are convinced that Nevada is being regularly visited by life forms from another galaxy, but I was fascinated to learn of a turn of events around Highway 375 that had come to a head in 1989.

A certain Mr Bob Lazar claimed in a Las Vegas KLAS TV station interview that he had worked on alien spaceships in Area 51 and had seen flying saucer test flights in the nearby Tikaboo Valley. He went on to tell the TV audience that he had been inside many of the flying saucers and had seen briefing documents. Apparently they were all powered by the splendidly named Ununpentium – an atomic-based fuel that, he said, gave alien spacecraft the ability to defy gravity. He then went into full confessional mode and described how he had seen nine different alien space discs and understood how they all worked as he had seen the owners' manuals.

Mr Lazar's story faltered a bit when many of the educational and research establishments that he claimed he worked for said they had never heard of him. His response was that this was just a US government conspiracy designed to discredit him, and that officials had destroyed his education and qualification records.

His accounts of alien activity out there on Highway 375 prompted even more UFO sightings from other wannabes, and then a frenzy of TV and newspaper reports about other like-minded people who claimed to have had similar experiences. Then things calmed down a bit, at least until 2006, when Bob Lazar again claimed the media's attention with the news that he had been selling minuscule amounts of radioactive polonium similar to that used recently to kill the Russian secret agent, Alexander Litvinenko, in London.

Mr Lazar was last heard of in 2007 when he and his wife were charged with violating the Federal Hazardous Substances Act for selling restricted chemicals across state lines via the internet. He was fined $7,500 and entered into a consent decree forbidding his company from ever selling 'firework-related chemicals' again.

Basically, I felt that Bob Lazar sounded far more entertaining than anything else that is alleged to have happened out there on Highway 375 – flying saucer manuals, poisoned Russian spies and selling illegal firework material made him sound an interesting sort of guy.

* * * * * *

Not far on from the Extraterrestrial Highway is the aptly named town of Goldfield. I liked it immediately because it called itself 'an almost ghost town'. Founded in 1902 after huge quantities of gold ore were discovered nearby, it grew to be one of the largest cities in Nevada at the beginning of the twentieth century and at one time boasted three newspapers, five banks, a mining stock exchange and a population of 35,000. When the gold ran out eight years after it was first discovered so did Goldfield's luck, and as we passed through the town's occupants seemed to consist of a dog with three legs and two old men who looked as though they both needed a good bath.

It did have some interesting old mining buildings, though, and a scrapyard on the edge of town was strangely full of wrecked black and white police cars. There was also the Goldfield Hotel that in its prime, in 1908, cost $300,000 to build, and had four storeys and 154 rooms with telephones, electric lights and heated steam. I'm not sure what the heated steam did, but it seems to have impressed everyone back then. The hotel also boasted a gold-leaf ceiling in the lobby, and apparently some of Europe's finest chefs were brought over to cook for the constant flow of celebrities who came through town and then realised the gold was running out and moved on.

Once it had run out for good the Goldfield Hotel started to change hands rather rapidly. One owner even sank two mineshafts under the hotel in a desperate bid to find more of that elusive gold, but eventually it was turned over to the US Military in the Second World War and then, when the army left in 1945, the Goldfield Hotel closed its doors for good. It is claimed to be the most haunted hotel in the state. It's a great-looking building, though, even if it is empty; I am pretty sure you could buy it if you wanted to.

* * * * * *

Anne and I had decided to strike out for the eastern tip of Nevada and were now moving quickly along a deserted Highway 6 towards Ely. My motorcycle was cruising at a steady 65mph and I was starting really to get to grips with it. For the first time in some weeks I was actually relaxed and enjoying the riding. With hundreds of miles of deserted roads this was an ideal opportunity to try and get my act together and ride as well as I could. But I was filthy.

I couldn't see out of my helmet visor as it was covered in dead bugs, and from the knees downwards my jeans had accumulated the carcasses of literally hundreds of small insects. They looked like some mad seamstress has decorated them in vivid hues of red and yellow. Every time I stopped the bike to take a rest I got a whiff of insect barbecue rising off the hot engine and exhaust pipes.

Each morning on these trips my heart would beat a little faster as I stepped over the saddle and fired the bike up. I tried always to start off with the mantra in my head taught me by my robotic motorcycle instructor, Mac: 'Today I am going to ride to the best of my ability. Nothing else.' The problem is that I was easily distracted by the fantastic landscapes, the empty roads and the ever-changing scenery that unfolded around me and all my good intentions were quickly forgotten.

Now, though, I was actually facing a new problem. Every few miles there were bright yellow roadside warning signs stating: CAUTION DEER CAUTION ELK CAUTION STOCK RANGE. I'd read some real horror stories about motorcyclists and deer in the US. Deer apparently have a built-in self-destruct button, because every time a bike passes they simply have to fling themselves at both motorcycle and rider. An adult Mule deer can weigh several hundred pounds and an accelerating motorcycle and rider weigh even more. It was going to hurt a lot for everyone concerned if deer started randomly jumping out at me from the Nevada countryside.

I'd seriously considered fitting a deer alarm to my machine. It sort of works along the same lines as a dog whistle. You attach one to the frame of your motorcycle so air is forced through it and it emits a high-pitched noise that is only audible to deer ears and apparently warns them. But I'd also read stories where the reverse had happened and the alarm had encouraged even more deer to throw themselves at motorcyclists, so I was in something of a quandary.

Suddenly, as I rounded a corner, there was a massive Mule deer standing on what looked like his grass launching pad. He had watched me come up the valley and now, with his nose twitching, I was convinced he was waiting to jump straight at me. He had what looked like an entire tree on his head – that would be his antlers – and I was certain he was about to cross the 200 yards to the road and clear the fence. As it turns out he merely stood and watched me pass by. Clearly I was no prize in the Mule deer world.

All this concentration on suicidal wild animals meant I'd not been paying attention to my motorcycle's fuel gauge, yet again, and things were looking pretty grim. I started swearing, as usual, when I worked out there were about 30 miles to go before we reached the town of Ely. Coming down the White Pine Mountain Range the road was curling away ahead of me into the valley and I was trying desperately to work out if I could coast to the next town. Was it all downhill?

I finally had to come to a halt just before the start of some major road works. Running out of fuel in the middle of this construction area would make me feel even more stupid than I did already. Anne agreed to ride ahead, buy a fuel can, somehow strap it to the rear fender of her bike and come back for her idiot husband. But as I sat back to wait I realised I'd parked on the apex of a downhill bend with massive 18-wheel trucks thundering by. There was nowhere to go, no space to move the bike as the edge of the road fell away to a deep, dark valley several hundred feet below me. For the next 45 minutes I studied maps and paced up and down, waiting for Anne's return. In all that time not a single person stopped to ask if I was OK or needed some help.

When Anne returned with a gallon of fuel in a plastic can tied to the back of her bike I managed to spill most of it over my bike's tank and on to the exhaust. That made me dance around like a demented person waiting for my bike to burst into flames, a bit like a gardener I once knew who checked the fuel tank of his lawnmower with a cigarette still in his mouth and wondered why he lost all his eyebrows and most of his hair. (I learnt later, though, that you need a flash point like a match or a spark to set fuel alight.)

I fired the bike up and within five miles came to the fuel station that Anne had managed to reach earlier. It took almost 3.4 gallons to fill the tank up so I *was* running on fuel vapour coming down that hill. Right now all I wanted to do was head for the motel and get off the damned motorcycle. The town of Ely was just up the road and that's where we stopped for the night.

* * * * * *

After checking into the Ely motel we stumbled into the nearby Silver State Diner just before it closed for the day and ordered two fantastic pulled pork sandwiches. It was good food again but amazingly indifferent service from the very bored waitress, who clearly wanted nothing to do with dirty, tired motorcyclists.

The Silver State Diner was clearly popular with the Ely locals, though, as many of them had placed photographs of themselves on the walls showing off an astonishing range of hunting trophies. There were lots of pictures of big bearded men holding up the floppy heads of dead deer and other assorted wildlife while grinning at the camera – the men, not the animals. One picture in particular caught my eye: an enormous man was standing in the snow hugging what looked like a gigantic lion around the waist. The dead cat's paws hung limply on the hunter's shoulders and together the lion and the man looked as if they were stuck in some kind of grotesque dance.

There was an amazing collection of weapons photographed in the pictures as well, everything from sporting rifles with impressive telescope-sized sights to what, to my untrained eye, looked like ex-military automatic machine guns taken straight off a tank and then adapted for deer hunting. In a few of the photos some of the braver hunters appeared to be relying on bows and arrows to kill things.

The helpful town guidebook for Ely told us that the town's name rhymed with freely, just in case we were wondering. It was also once a stagecoach stopping post and a place where the short-lived Pony Express mail service changed horses in the nineteenth century. Much of the town's early prosperity was based on copper mining and there was the usual collection of nice, solid stone, early twentieth-century buildings put up when the town's fortunes were on a high, and then a series of crap ones when things were not so good, particularly, it seemed, in the 1970s. Photos showed some very odd architecture from the 1980s that had needed to be pulled down immediately and rebuilt.

Most of the easily accessible copper had been pulled out of the ground around Ely by the late 1960s and life in the town came to an abrupt halt. The mines closed and people left in their droves. Then someone discovered a process called cyanide leeching and Ely's fortunes returned, albeit temporarily. This is a way of extracting gold from low-grade rock or the piles of stone left over from the town's previous copper-mining activity. Not being very well versed about mining techniques I felt anything that involved using old mining rubble and cyanide couldn't be good for the people doing it or the environment in general, but since 2005 there has been a growth in international demand for copper and full-time mining had come back to Ely. The ore was being mined deep underground, transported to Seattle on the US west coast, and then shipped to Japan for smelting.

To me, though, the town of Ely looked as though it was yet another place on pause. Businesses were closing and nothing much was happening on Main Street. Someone had bravely opened a Basque restaurant, although it was currently closed and shuttered up, and the only place doing any real form of business was the historic Nevada Hotel and Casino.

Once the tallest building in Nevada, when it opened in the 1920s, it had the usual slot machines, card and roulette tables, a restaurant and even its own version of the Hollywood Walk of Fame with a series of bronze plaques placed around on the pavement outside the building. They featured a bizarre collection of entertainers' names from stage and screen, many of whom I had never heard of but who had apparently stayed at the Nevada Hotel at some time and therefore got their names preserved for eternity on the concrete outside.

The Nevada Hotel had a fantastically eclectic collection of stuff liberally scattered around its rooms in dark corners, on the walls and beside the gaming machines. The hotel claimed to have the largest collection of moose, elk, deer, wapiti, wildebeest and dik-dik heads, antlers and horns of any hotel west of the Mississippi. Everywhere you walked inside the hotel you were followed by the glassy-eyed stare of dead animals' heads. I felt it just needed a few human heads to make this impressive collection complete.

There was a fabulous 1947 Indian motorcycle parked next to the hotel's restaurant. A notice stated emphatically that it was not the same Indian model that New Zealander Burt Monro rode when trying to set land speed records at Bonneville, in Utah, in the 1960s, but the hotel did say it reflected Munro's opinion on life, which was printed on a card for all to read: 'You live more in five minutes flat out on a bike like this than most people do in a lifetime.'

* * * * * *

Maybe it was the luck of the draw, or perhaps just our choice of overnight accommodation when we were on the road, but at almost every motel we stayed at Anne and I were the youngest guests. Our fellow travellers were predominantly aged over 75 and consequently, as seems to happen when you get older, they were always up very early in the morning. Either that or they knew about the Breakfast Feeding Frenzy that we were to experience at every single motel on our trip.

One of the attractions about any good motel in the US is the offer of free breakfast in the mornings. Of course it's not really free, as it's included in the price of your motel room, and sometimes it's nothing more than cereal and toast and some hot brown water they optimistically call coffee. But I like the fact that it is offered as free.

One motel we stayed at in Arizona had developed an extraordinarily complicated system for its guests that involved collecting as many points as you could to qualify for eggs, bacon, orange juice and coffee. Even the waitress didn't really understand how the process worked and I watched as she awarded different points for different breakfast items to different people. By the time she and I had worked out my points it turned out I was entitled to half a waffle, one egg (possibly boiled or maybe scrambled), 65 sausages and 18 pieces of toast providing I ate at a separate table outside the restaurant wearing a straw hat.

The Breakfast Feeding Frenzy happens like this. A collection of perhaps eight or nine elderly married couples will be present, all dressed in identical leisure suits. Ideally one of the men will be deaf and unable to understand what his wife is explaining about the breakfast menu. He will also announce to everyone that he does not like bacon and ask why there is no granola while simultaneously swallowing a large quantity of brightly coloured pills that have been thoughtfully lined up on the tabletop by his wife.

Another elderly gentleman will be trying to understand the intricacies of the waffle machine, which consists of a piping hot, circular, cast-iron griddle standing on the motel's breakfast bar. You are supposed to pour a vanilla-coloured liquid with the viscosity of engine oil into this machine and it will then start making waffles. The elderly waffle operator will always stand in front of it for a good five minutes and spin it aimlessly until it makes a strange bleeping noise, but in my experience he is nearly always disappointed with what comes out of this machine. The waffle looks like a bright yellow flip-flop with an intricate tribal tattoo burned into it, and it appears to be totally inedible. The old guy will nevertheless pour copious amounts of maple syrup on to it and then suck or chew noisily for a good few minutes before finally giving up and going in search of something he can actually eat.

While this is going on there will be a gathering of elderly ladies, some with blue hair, standing guard over the solitary motel toaster watching it cook their piece of bread. They will not move for anyone and heaven forbid that you come between them and the jelly preserve or try and reach for a glass of orange juice.

A constant ballet seems to take place as people try to get past each other. Many of them will still be half asleep as they press toaster buttons, squeeze bagels and keep an eye out for the waffle-making machine becoming vacant. And all the time there is a hum of disjointed conversations about how well they slept, where they are going today and why the front of their trousers is caught in the waffle machine.

If you are fortunate enough to stumble across something from the buffet they have not spotted this provokes a flurry of activity as they stagger up from their chairs to see what new treasure you have found and what they may have missed out on. It's enough to make your head swim first thing in the morning and yet it was a scene that was replayed endlessly while we were on the road, a show that never ceased to entertain and amuse us. I would honestly pay good money to watch it again and again. It's that good.

CHAPTER SIX

DUST & DINOSAURS

Dust storms – Suffering a stroke – Capital punishment –
Butch Cassidy and the Sundance Kid – Dinosaurs – Posting bricks –
Raccoon encounter – Bears – Flaming Gorge

Every morning, waking up in a new town out in the sticks, I would check the day's weather forecast. I don't mind riding when it's cold, of course prefer it when it's warm, but I categorically hate riding when it rains. Water gets everywhere – it's a truly miserable experience. The bike handles differently and the constant spray thrown up from other vehicles makes it almost impossible to see.

The weather was not looking good for the next leg of our journey towards the eastern edge of Nevada and into Utah. The ever-smiling weather forecaster on the local TV news station seemed excited and pleased as he delivered news of 56mph winds, thunderstorms and torrential rain, and we left Ely with dark clouds swirling behind us in the Schell Creek Mountains. I was hoping Anne and I could run ahead of this weather front and planned to keep going towards a small V-shaped area of blue sky I could just see on the horizon. The wind began picking up, however, and the bike started swaying when, every so often, a gust would hit me, causing it to swerve alarmingly into the centre of the road.

With Ely behind us we picked up Highway 6 again. It's known as the 'loneliest road in the world' but also has the official and impressive title of 'Grand Army of the Republic Highway'. Try saying that when you're being hit by winds of 50mph or more and need to keep a motorcycle upright. Highway 6 is more than 3,000 miles in length and goes across 13 US states, starting in California and ending up in Massachusetts, making it the second longest road in North America.

It was completely empty of any form of traffic as we rode along, and I decided only an idiot Englishman like me would be out on a motorcycle on this stretch of the road in the back of beyond with severe storm warnings being broadcast across the state. In his cult 1957 travel novel *On the Road* American author Jack Kerouac and his companion Sal Paradise actually considered hitchhiking to Nevada on Highway 6 but were told by a fellow traveller 'there's no traffic passing through 6'. Jack was advised he would be better off going via Pittsburgh and the Pennsylvania Turnpike; I wish this well-informed man had told me the same thing, as I was starting to get very concerned.

Highway 6 descends into the Snake River Valley and then crosses the Snake River Mountain Range at the Sacramento Pass, just north of Nevada's second-highest mountain, Wheeler Peak at 7,563 feet. We'd been on the road for more than two hours now and had seen nobody – no people or cars – and all the while I kept glancing into my rear-view mirrors to see massive black thunderclouds gathering quickly behind Anne and me. I felt as if we were trying to outrun a fast-moving storm and hoped if we could get across the state line into Utah we might miss the worst of it.

At Baker on the Nevada–Utah border there was a small Mormon community and a gas station beside the road. I stopped to refuel: there was no way I was going to risk being stuck out there in a thunderstorm with an empty fuel tank. It was the last place I would be able to get petrol before the next town, which was almost 100 miles inside Utah.

I was also pleased to discover that this was an interesting stopping-off point. There was a casino and restaurant and a shop selling weird Native American souvenirs that seemed to consist of a lot of dead animal parts and feathers. While slugging back my fourth cup of coffee of the morning I tried my luck once more on the gaming machines and went through the rigmarole of flashing lights and buzzers, spinning wheels and electronic music. Within seconds I had an instant return on my investment: the winner's light came on and I had to explain to the casino staff, as I had in Tonopah, that yes, I would like to cash in all my winnings of $2.12.

The same procedure as before was followed, with a cashier called Pat wandering between locked doors and moneyboxes, padlocks and keys before she finally returned and wearily handed me the amount in small change. This time, though, she made me sign for it. In duplicate. And as she handed over my cash she eyed me for a moment and then said: 'Are you riding a motorcycle today?'

I have lost count of the number of times I have been asked the question 'Are you riding a motorcycle?' in the US, when I am standing before the person in full motorcycle riding gear. The sarcastic English streak in me always wanted to reply in the way I wished I could have done to Pat – 'No, I am an exceptionally nervous passenger and the only way you will ever get me to ride in a car is for me to wear a leather jacket, big boots, gloves and a crash helmet' – but of course I didn't have the gumption, and took the lower road with her. She was much larger than me anyway, and she had tough look in her eye. I just nodded and mumbled and said that I hoped the weather was going to hold out for me.

Pat's reply was perhaps unexpected: 'The weather ain't nothing. What you have to look out for is the 26-mile mark out there on the highway. That's where they always go down on their bikes. It's very dangerous, real twisty, and it's also annoying for the emergency services as it's midway in the county and it can take a long time for them to get to you and then scrape you off the road.'

Thanking her for these words of wisdom and encouragement, I sidled out just as three Harley-Davidsons rolled into the parking lot outside the casino. They were coming from the Utah direction, which was where we were heading – a couple of guys and a woman, and they looked more than a little tired.

'Man, it's crazy out there,' said Rob, a serious-looking man who told me he'd been riding motorcycles for almost 35 years. 'I have never seen anything like it. There is a massive dust storm coming up from Utah. The highway to there is under construction in places and there are rock falls all over the road and the corners are bitches. Hey, Steve, come over here and tell this English guy what just happened to you.'

Rob beckoned over his travelling buddy and the man's wife. Steve looked white around the gills and told me, in a really quiet voice, 'Well, it was really weird. One minute I was on the road and the next thing I'd been hit by a gust of sand and wind that pushed the whole bike and me over to the other lane and nearly down the side of a deep cliff.'

Steve's wife, standing behind him, nodded gravely, backing up her husband's story. She said she thought Steve was going to be launched over the side by the wind and all three of them had decided enough was enough and they'd call in at this gas station to wait out the storm.

'I wouldn't go back out there just now,' added Steve. 'Who knows what could happen to you?'

Who knows indeed? Pat, the casino lady, had been adamant I was going to fall off my motorcycle at a point exactly 26 miles after leaving the gas station while Rob and Steve had predicted I'd be blown off the road and into a crevasse. I, on the other hand, needed to get to Utah for the night and, as always in my life, those nine words came back to haunt me: *it seemed like a good idea at the time.*

* * * * * *

It was time to saddle up once more and see what was really around the next corner. To be fair to Rob and Steve, there was a lot of rock debris in the road, as they had warned me, and there was some road construction going on, but there were no workers about as they had clearly paid attention to the TV's bad weather reports. The sky over the gas station had been completely black, and now I could no longer see the mountains behind as they were lost in clouds of heavy rain. What little blue sky was left was immediately ahead of me on Highway 6, in the direction we needed to go.

We hadn't seen anyone for nearly half an hour when we hit Pat's famous 26-mile mark on the road, but I was somewhat disappointed. Yes, there was a sharp right-hand bend with an adverse camber; there may even have been grooves in the tarmac surface where motorcycle footpegs had dug in before spinning wildly out of control and smashing their riders against the massive yellow rock outcrops that butted on to the road. But it was no more dramatic than some of the bends I had experienced in the past two weeks and I began to hope that maybe we would be able to make it into Utah without any real problem.

Highway 6 dropped us down from the Confusion Mountain Range on to a flat low plain. In the distance, perhaps ten miles ahead, I could just make out what I thought was mist or fog, although it appeared to be moving very quickly, covering most of the horizon and coming straight towards me. The sky began rapidly getting darker and I thought the rain had finally caught up with us, but it was also getting hotter and there was a strong wind whipping up the roadside vegetation. Suddenly we went from daylight to murky twilight, as if we had been enveloped in some kind of fog.

I couldn't see more than ten feet ahead of me with the bike's headlight on full beam so I slowed down to a miserable 25mph, with the bike rocking from side to side. As my eyes became accustomed to the gloom I realised we were right on the edge of a dust storm. Something amazing had happened to the weather – two warm fronts perhaps meeting a cold front – but now all of western Utah was being covered in a fine sandy dust as the strong storm blew through. And I was riding right through it on the loneliest road in the world.

It felt like being in the middle of a giant vacuum cleaner, and soon both the bike and I were covered in layers of gritty dust. I couldn't see out of my helmet's visor properly and I was breathing in lungful after lungful of air that tasted like mud.

'Can you actually see anything?' Anne asked me over the intercom. She was riding right behind me, following my bike's tail lights.

'A little bit. Maybe a few feet ahead but not much, and it's getting worse,' I replied, trying to sound confident but secretly hating every second.

Every ten minutes or so the swirling winds would stop briefly and we'd have glimpses of what looked like a lunar landscape. Everything – trees, bushes, rocks, fences, gates – was covered in brownish-white sand. Then the curtain would drop again and we were back to riding through swirling brown fog unable to see anything and constantly trying to work out which way the road was going.

We still had more than 40 miles to go until we hit the first town in Utah. The light was really making things look most odd. Sometimes the sun would come streaming through and I could make out the edges of the road a little better, and then it was as if someone had switched the vacuum cleaner back on and the dust and sand would whirl around again in weird shapes and patterns. We passed a sign hung on a farm gate that announced this was Bob's Taxidermy and Coffee Shop. Who on earth would ever come out here on this road to get something stuffed and then have a cup of coffee with Bob? Actually, the way I was feeling about riding at that moment, I would have welcomed Bob with open arms no matter what he tried to do to me. Heck, I would even have drunk his coffee.

Then unbelievably, from out of nowhere, a human figure appeared, standing in the middle of the road holding up a large STOP sign. A road construction crew was actually out mending the road, and the man didn't even look too concerned about the crazy weather as he waved at us to slow down and stop. That gave me a chance to sit back for a few minutes and gather my thoughts. It was clear we had to press on, but my entire body was aching from the stress of this ride, my head was pounding from the concentration, and I really wanted a drink of water.

After ten minutes a small convoy of traffic led by a construction work pilot vehicle came into sight, passed us and disappeared into the twilight-like gloom. Anne and I were alone again. The man with the STOP sign waved us on and we spent the next five miles following the pilot vehicle while trying to keep our bikes off the mounds of gravel and in the tyre tracks of the vehicles that had gone before.

I tried to make myself more comfortable in the saddle and move my body around a bit, but I was suddenly struck with absolutely abject terror because I couldn't move my left leg at all. It felt like an enormous weight was pulling it down. It was exactly the same sort of fear I'd experienced as a kid when a local farmer told me not to eat the grain seeds that he had been planting in the field behind our house as they were covered in highly toxic pesticide. I remember the sensation of chewing the seeds very slowly as he told me this. My eyes must have been huge circles. And when he had finished telling me about all the different types of death I might experience if I ever ate any of his seeds again I promptly threw up in a hedge.

My initial self-diagnosis was that I had suffered a stroke all down my left side, from the waist down. Granted my medical knowledge was sparse, at best. I am the man that walked around for an entire day, drove his car and took the dog for a walk, after misjudging a step on a ladder and falling downstairs that morning, fracturing my ankle in three places.

The dust clouds were getting thicker, however, and I knew this was neither the time nor the place to stop, no matter what ailment I had been struck down with. I consoled myself with the thought that even though I might have had a stroke I had not yet passed out, wet myself or started dribbling. I started to talk to myself, to see if my speech was slurred, but I couldn't hear anything over the whistling wind of the sand storm and the noise of the motorcycle engine. Maybe this was just a minor stroke? I didn't want to alarm Anne by telling her over our intercom system that her husband might be dying; I felt she had more than enough to contend with already.

No matter what I tried to do over the next 20 minutes I could not lift my left foot. It felt like someone had tied a lump of lead to it. My mind was racing. All this riding and concentration must have caused a blood vessel to burst in my brain. Would I ever be able to walk again? How the hell would we get the bikes back home? I could just make out the distant shape of houses and an abandoned gas station, its broken doors flapping in the wind, and I seized the opportunity to get off the road and come to a stop beside the rusting petrol pumps and find out what the heck was going on with my leg.

With a huge effort I managed to yank my boot off the bike's footpeg. There appeared to be something like a large lump of black chewing gum stuck to the sole. I had managed to stand in molten tarmac from the road construction work we had passed and that, coupled with the heat coming off my motorcycle's engine, had effectively welded my left foot to the bike.

The relief was intense. To Anne's astonishment, and the occupants of a couple of passing cars, I performed a Michael Jackson-style Moon Walk dance, moving rapidly backwards, to drag the sticky tar off the bottom of my boot.

* * * * * *

I didn't know a lot about Utah. I knew its name was derived from the Native American Ute tribe, who used to live there before the settlers came in 1847, with the literal translation meaning 'people of the mountains'. I was sort of aware of Salt Lake City and the immense 30,000-acre salt flats at Bonneville, where crazy people do even crazier things in super-fast cars and motorcycles, all in the name of breaking land speed records – like Burt Monro, riding an Indian bike similar to the one we'd seen in the Nevada Hotel in Ely.

I knew there was a large Mormon community throughout the state, with experts estimating that around 58% of the population were members of the Church of Jesus Christ of Latter-day Saints. The church's spiritual leader, Brigham Young, and the first band of Mormon pioneers came to Salt Lake Valley in July 1847 and stayed. Over the next 22 years it is estimated that more than 70,000 pioneers crossed the plains of the Mid-West to settle in Utah. I choose to know very little about any religion, but the discovery that the Mormons had been here a long time and had fought continual battles with the US government over their beliefs was interesting. The most prominent of these is that the Mormon faith permits polygamous marriages. The Mormons also have some splendid churches in Utah, all of them crowned with what looks like a golden statue of a boy blowing a trumpet on the very pinnacle of every steeple. Aside from that, I am going to leave all Mormon matters there in Utah.

I thought that most of the state would be just like northern Nevada

– an empty desert of nothing – but as it turned out it was a fabulous place. True, nearly 80% of the population live in an area known as the Wasatch Front around Salt Lake City, leaving vast expanses of the state nearly uninhabited. After leaving the dust storm behind we travelled along a winding road that followed the course of the meandering Sevier River, a tranquil, green, lush valley of farmsteads. This was not what I had expected at all. The sun was out as we passed through small sleepy-looking towns in the Juab Valley. There was a feeling of prosperity and order here and for the next two hours I felt relaxed and happy. There was little traffic and great scenery. It was a very nice place to ride through on a motorcycle.

The motel at Nephi was empty and the manager greeted us like long-lost friends. He explained that he'd been having trouble with his electronic locks and consequently spent the next ten minutes jamming an assortment of plastic key cards into every one of his motel-room doors until he finally found one that worked.

The dust storm that I thought we had left behind was now moving up the valley straight towards the front of the motel, and although it hadn't brought any sand with it, it was really windy. The motel manager said he'd lived in Nephi for ten years and had never seen weather like it. He wasn't kidding, either. It wasn't until my motorcycle began rocking from side to side on its kickstand and the plastic corrugated roof on the motel's indoor swimming pool started banging and slapping around that I could see I was back in the middle of the storm that had followed me around all day.

* * * * * *

It was a very odd sort of day altogether, with the TV news that evening all of a buzz with the story of double murderer Ronnie Lee Gardner who would be shot by firing squad at 12.20 the following morning, the first prisoner in 14 years to be executed this way in Utah. By all accounts Gardner was not a nice person at all. He had killed two men, his first victim a barman in Salt Lake City whom Gardner encountered while on the run after escaping from prison in 1984. The second person he murdered was a lawyer he'd shot in the eye during a botched escape attempt from a courtroom.

Other than Oklahoma, Utah was the only state that lists the firing squad as a possible means of execution, allowing condemned prisoners the choice between a bullet or a lethal injection. In recent years Utah had stopped offering death-row prisoners the right to choose, but because Gardner was convicted before this amendment he was allowed to opt for the firing squad. How peculiar, I thought, that as a condemned man you can choose how you would like to die.

Gardner's execution was to be carried out in a specially designed chamber inside Utah state prison. The next morning I learned that he was taken there shortly after midnight, having spent his final hours sleeping, watching the *Lord of the Rings* film trilogy and reading the thriller *Divine Justice*. He was strapped to a black chair with a metal tray placed beneath it to collect his blood, and had a hood placed over his head and a white circular target pinned to his chest to mark his heart, the precise location of which had been identified earlier by a prison doctor.

Five local police officers, chosen for their skill as marksmen and kept anonymous to minimise the risk of any reprisals, were ushered into the chamber and lined up behind a brick wall at the other end of the room, about 25 feet away from Gardner. The officers were handed .30-calibre rifles, the muzzles of which they inserted through gaps in the wall to aim at the condemned man. Four of the rifles were loaded with a single live bullet. The fifth rifle contained an 'ineffective' round which, unlike a blank, gives the same recoil as a live bullet. That way none of the five executioners knew whether they had delivered the fatal shot. Some people described it as a fair and just way to die while others thought the whole episode was simply organised murder.

With that debate raging in my mind we saddled up for a hectic ride to the town of Helper, aiming to get to the Utah–Wyoming border some 327 miles away that evening. It was going to be a long day.

* * * * * *

We'd only been out on the road a short time before I needed to stop for coffee and another glance at the map. The route seemed fairly straightforward, taking Highway 6 to just before the town of Helper and then the twisting Highway 191, which would run us up some 9,469 feet past Gray Head Peak Mountain. It looked like a fabulous ride and I was really looking forward to it.

I was always surprised by the number of times I met friendly strangers who wanted to stop and chat, out there in the middle of nowhere. They always seemed to be interested in a California-registered motorcycle and its English rider, and always wanted to know what I thought of their town. You can often learn a lot from someone with local knowledge, but time and again, aside from the usual chitchat, I would be given warnings about heavy traffic and inclement weather, or detailed and particularly gory descriptions of motorcycle crashes they had witnessed or a friend had just suffered.

The nice couple Anne and I met in Mount Pleasant lived up to all these expectations. After discussing the niceties of my motorcycle they asked me where I was heading, and when I told them Highway 191 their faces took on a look of grave concern.

'You do know there will be at least three feet of snow up there if the road is even open,' said the man. 'The road and views are spectacular but there'll be a ton of snow. It occasionally clears for the summer once the plough has been through, but it'll be freezing and not a good place to ride your motorcycle. You should find another way.'

I was somewhat confused. Highway 191 is a road on the eastern section of Utah; granted it runs through the Ashley National Forest and is more than 6,000 feet above sea level but this was mid-June, which in my book is summer time. Winter and snow should have been long gone.

'Yep, you'd better think of another route,' said the man's wife. 'That road was blocked two weeks ago with really heavy snow and there's no way you're going to get through today.'

I decided to ignore the couple's helpful advice and take it in the spirit that was intended. They were not trying to mislead us; they were just concerned about our safety. Anyway, I soon had enough to contend with, what with the fast, sweeping curves of Highway 6 climbing straight up the side of a mountain and into the Uinta National Forest. It was a great road, smooth and fast with four-lane carriageways, but there was a lot of traffic, including my bugbear: massive 18-wheel truck rigs heading east towards Colorado.

I am not being critical of truck drivers because it must be a heck of a job driving long, boring distances against the clock, but the speed and size of these monstrous vehicles made me cringe every time they roared by. The air turbulence as they passed moved my bike across the road, sometimes into another lane, and I am sure there were many occasions when the truck driver simply didn't see me or even know I was there. It was terrifying the way they gathered speed down a mountain highway and then charged to literally within 15 feet of my rear tyre – it's an extremely threatening sight in a bike's mirrors.

It was time for a fuel break at the town of Helper before backtracking a few miles and facing the snow blizzards we'd been warned about on Highway 191. Helper was also the only place to buy fuel for the next hundred miles and I thought it might be a good idea to fill up if I was going to be digging myself out of snowdrifts later that day. As I sat outside the gas station shop, drinking yet another coffee, a man on a three-wheeled vehicle that sounded like it was going to explode into a thousand pieces circled the forecourt twice. He was a bizarre sight – long, flowing white hair, enormous motorcycle goggles and a beard that was blowing up and back on to his face. He roared past me, dived down a side alley and was gone in a blur of loud exhaust noise. A quietly spoken man called Dave, on a big Honda touring motorcycle, joined me. He said he was on a solo mission, riding across the US in just six weeks to raise money for charity. His wife and mother-in-law were running behind him in a car and he got to see them every other day when they stopped for the night. It sounded to me like a perfect recipe for marriage, knowing your spouse and her mother would be waiting for you at the end of a long day of motorcycle riding.

Jake, the guy on the trike, told us his Scorpion was a great machine and handled way better than any motorcycle he'd ever ridden. He was a fund of information about the town of Helper, and he also knew all about New York, Alaska, the entire Middle East and a whole series of places that I had never even heard of. He appeared to have lived everywhere, and with my limited mathematical calculations I estimated that if even half of the places he listed were towns he'd actually lived in, he could only have been at each one for about two weeks. Jake was also an expert on an abandoned coal-mining town just outside Helper and began to regale us with peculiar mining stories before suddenly stopping short and saying: 'Hell, why do I need to tell you all of this when I can take you there and show it all to you? There's not much left of the buildings, but there are some cool abandoned mineshafts worth going down, and it's only about five minutes away.'

I declined politely, but mild-mannered Dave was somehow coerced into going along. The last I saw of him he was mumbling something about hoping he would see his wife and mother-in-law that night, as he followed Jake and his trike off into the distance. It takes some bravado to go off with a complete stranger to look inside abandoned mines. I had a feeling Dave and Jake might be down there for quite some time.

Helper was apparently a regular hangout for the infamous outlaw Butch Cassidy and his Wild Bunch Gang. Hollywood immortalised Cassidy, whose real name was Robert LeRoy Parker, and his sidekick Harry Longabaugh, otherwise known as the Sundance Kid, in the 1969 film starring Paul Newman and Robert Redford. From what I have read about Butch and the Kid they don't seem to have been particularly pleasant people. There are some great early photographs of them, though, and I have to admit that Butch, in his Wyoming prison picture, had a certain twinkle in his eye. He and his Wild Bunch Gang robbed many banks and also killed a few people who tried to stop them, and their story ended intriguingly in Bolivia where he and the Kid are both supposed to have died in a hail of gunfire, confronting government forces after robbing yet another bank. Exactly like they did in the film.

However, some people say they both escaped and lived out their lives back in the US. There are some supposedly reliable accounts from Butch's doctor, a lady by the name of Red Fenwick, who told a Denver newspaper reporter in the 1950s that she continued to treat Butch Cassidy years after he was supposed to have died in South America. Either way, Butch and the Sundance Kid were in the Helper area in April 1897. They'd come down from Wyoming to rob the railway offices of the Pleasant Valley Coal Company in nearby Castle Gate of $7,000 worth of gold bullion.

Cassidy and his gang seemed to show up everywhere we passed in the next few days – they'd criss-crossed Utah and Wyoming in a trail of robberies, hideouts and generally bad behaviour – with many places claiming that Butch once lived there for a few days, or had hidden in fields nearby, or just held up their banks. It seemed to be a matter of pride to have been a town where Butch Cassidy and his band of like-minded followers robbed and shot people and generally caused chaos.

* * * * * *

Highway 191 runs straight up into Ashley National Forest, an immense area of land that encompasses 1,384,132 acres and rises from 6,000 feet to more than 13,000 feet above sea level. This would explain why it suddenly got very cold, although fortunately there was no snow on the ground as promised by the nice couple we had met back in Mount Pleasant. At Indian Creek Pass – the highest point on Highway 191 – you are more than 9,100 feet up and there are some magnificent views of forested mountain slopes and deep rugged canyons that stretch for miles towards the horizon.

This highway was also a fantastic road. It looped up past great slabs of rock that were jutting out into the road. There was no guardrail so if you misjudged a corner chances are you were going to go right over the side. It's odd to see the tops of trees peeking over the edge of the road, their trunks and roots hundreds of feet below. There was hardly any traffic, except for thundering great trucks, with trailers, coming down the mountainside to the cement works at Helper.

Everywhere I looked I saw truly magnificent canyons, all shooting off at different angles. Some were wooded and some were hundreds of feet deep with rivers and streams running through. There was also a distinct difference in the vegetation. On the lower levels I was surrounded by slopes of Pinyon pine and juniper running down to the valley floor where the Duchesne River was meandering, but as we began to climb the trees all changed and it wasn't long before we were riding past Ponderosa pine, Douglas fir, White fir and Englemann spruce. I couldn't tell you which was which, though.

Tall red rock formations started to appear as we dropped down into the Indian Canyon River Valley. I stopped for a moment when I caught sight of some strange black dots on the skyline that were moving very fast around the top of the canyon. At first I thought they were a colony of bats, but then I realised it was a nesting site for literally thousands and thousands of swallows. They were moving together in an immense black cloud as they swooped and wheeled over my head, racing towards the slow-moving river and then back to their nests in the rocks. It was an amazing sight.

Duchesne is a small town, but it was worth stopping there to grab some lunch because there was another great diner on Main Street. The place has no major claims to fame except that there is an ongoing debate about a grave in the town's cemetery that is marked as being one William Long but could, in fact, be that of Harry Longabaugh – that outlaw the Sundance Kid again. Recent research has again suggested the Kid did not die in Bolivia in 1908 with his friend Butch Cassidy but came back here, to a farm three miles from Duchesne, to live out a quiet and peaceful life until his death in 1936. I shall await the results of this investigation with interest.

Something that always makes me want to laugh is the sight of men in cowboy hats. This place was full of them. Big, tall working men were kitted out in huge straw cowboy hats, big boots and enormous belt buckles: it just seemed so incongruous in the twenty-first century. As a kid I had dressed up as a cowboy, but only for birthday parties. Here in America, the birthplace of the cowboy, they dress up like one every day for work. Some of the guys were plumbers or construction workers according to the company logos on their shirts, and it seemed odd that they didn't even take their hats off to eat in the diner. All I could see was a mass of nodding hats as they settled down for lunch and to talk about the morning's work.

Duchesne seemed to be yet another very quiet place, and apart from the diner there was not a soul about. A few trucks were meandering along Main Street but all the shops looked like they'd seen better times. Anne and I rode out of town on the road that followed the Duchesne River, leading us into quiet farmland and past small houses. We were heading, in a straight 60-mile run east, for a motel at Vernal – home of Utah's famous dinosaurs and the town's bank that was built by mail-order bricks. This I had to see.

* * * * * *

The motel receptionist at Vernal was clearly confused. 'I'm not sure about any of that,' she said, taking a few steps backwards from the reception desk. I had simply asked her where I could see dinosaurs and if the town's bank was open. Riding into Vernal I had seen three immense concrete full-scale dinosaurs locked in a battle to the death immediately next door to the motel, and I wondered how on earth she could claim not to know what the crazy Englishman was talking about. Maybe I was hallucinating again.

'Oh those,' she said when I mentioned the dinosaur fight next door. 'They were for Dinoland, but that's closed now.' Before I had a chance to ask anything further she quickly added: 'But they have moved everything except those big dinosaur statues just a block down the road to the new museum. I don't know about the bank, though. Maybe best if you walk down Main Street.' And then, as if she suddenly remembered something she had to tell me, she added: 'We also have an awesome huge free breakfast here at the motel. You can't miss that. It's really good and it's free.' She turned out to be right about that. It was immense – perhaps big enough for a dinosaur – and, as she said, it was awesome.

The Utah Field House of the Natural History State Park Museum turned out to be a must-see museum for anyone wanting a glimpse into the past of a US state that seems literally to have been built on the bones of dinosaurs, while some 30 miles east of Vernal, on the south-east flank of the Uinta Mountain Range, was the Dinosaur National Monument. So many dinosaur remains have been found there, and continue to be found, that people flock from around the world to look at it. Some even try and steal the fossils.

There's a quarry at the National Monument where you used to be able to see layer upon layer of dinosaurs preserved in the bedrock, but sadly it closed four years ago as the visitor building was found to be unstable. It's unclear when it will open again. I like to think that in millions of years' time archaeologists will be confused by a twentieth-century visitor building buried among the dinosaur bones.

The land in this corner of Utah is known as the Morrison Formation and comprises sandstone and conglomerate alluvium from riverbeds that is estimated to be some 150 million years old. Dinosaurs and other animals were presumably washed into the area when a river flooded and the sediment built up over the years. This sediment became rock and due to geophysical activity was pushed upwards to form the Uinta Mountains.

It wasn't until 1909 that anybody really knew what this all meant. Earl Douglass, an early twentieth-century palaeontologist working for the Carnegie Museum, excavated literally thousands of fossils in the area, recorded them and promptly shipped them off to Pittsburgh for further research. What started out as an 80-acre site of dinosaur bones has grown into a 200,000-acre national park covering parts of Utah and the neighbouring state of Colorado. In 1915 President Woodrow Wilson proclaimed the 'dinosaur beds' as a national monument.

The Utah Field House Museum at Vernal opened in 2004 and it's very well presented, informative without preaching, so anyone (like me) whose hazy grasp of pre-history imagines a world that was ruled by angry giant lizards will be pleasantly surprised. The museum gave me a much better insight, and there were some fabulous exhibits and explanations about how the dinosaurs came to be found there, what life may have been like then, what the dinosaurs looked like and even what some of them may have sounded like. And if you're wondering about that point they sounded to me precisely like a moose having its knackers slammed in a door. I was particularly taken with the immense Tyrannosaurus Rex that stands just outside the museum, glowering at passing traffic with his huge open mouth, eight million teeth and tiny, floppy front forelegs. He was *awesome* too.

* * * * * *

I like any man who beats the system. In this case I am referring to a certain Mr William Coltharp, who found a loophole in the US Postal Service rules and managed to build an entire bank by getting the 80,000 bricks he needed mailed directly to him in Vernal.

In 1913 the USPS launched the Parcel Post Service, which was designed to allow people to send packages to one another. This was ideal for many Americans living in rural areas as they could now use their local post office as a delivery service and get packages sent through the mail. It was also inexpensive.

In 1916 William Coltharp had been tasked with building the Bank of Vernal on the town's Main Street. He was clearly a man who knew his own mind and he wanted a particular brick façade on his new bank, but the type of brick he favoured was made several hundred miles to the west by the Salt Lake Brick Company, and he needed a lot of them. It was going to quadruple his costs if he shipped them the conventional way, in a horse and cart, so he had the bricks packaged into blocks and then had 40 of them, weighing in at 2,000lb, mailed to him every day via the US Postal Service. These brick shipments were transported from Salt Lake to Mack in Colorado by rail, then transferred to the town of Watson via a narrow-gauge railway, then moved by wagon freight through the steep mountain roads leading to Vernal. Coltharp's 286 packages of bricks each travelled more than 420 miles at the standard cost of a USPS parcel.

As the post office became overwhelmed by the sheer volume of bricks coming through every day, the USPS bosses began to question their mailing regulations. From then on nobody in the US was allowed to mail packages that weighed more than 200lb, and to show that it meant business the USPS issued a clarification of its new rule: 'It is not the intent of the United States Postal Service that buildings be shipped through the mail.'

Coltharp, however, was allowed by the USPS to finish his bank and so beat the system. When it was finished there were no doubt wild celebrations among the postmen of Vernal who'd had the onerous task of delivering his brick parcels. I was delighted to see that Coltharp's bank was still in operation in Vernal and was now called the First National Bank of Zion. I patted a few bricks on the bank's façade on his behalf.

* * * * * *

Some psychiatrists may have a proper term for some of my lesser idiosyncrasies, which might be considered a form of mild paranoia, or perhaps OCD (Obsessive-Compulsive Disorder). Whatever it is I suffer from, I have to lock things up and make sure things are always secure. It can take me several attempts to leave my house or my motel room, as I always believe I have not locked up properly. I like windows to be locked too and have what some may regard as astonishing numbers of padlocks on everything. I feel like a jailer on occasions, as I walk around our house with a huge ring of keys.

I've only experienced theft twice in my life. On the first of those occasions someone stole a particularly resplendent hanging basket of flowers from outside my house. It was hardly a matter of life and death but I overreacted and felt I'd been violated. The second time some man walked into my office while I was out at lunch and helped himself to my passport, cheque book, credit cards and driving licence before proceeding to go up the road and empty all my bank accounts. He even used my passport as evidence of his identity, although I can categorically state that I am not a six foot three West Indian with dreadlocks. (He was caught on the bank's video surveillance cameras and was apparently a familiar face to the local police.)

I know I have been very fortunate compared to friends and family who have had things far more valuable than mine stolen, but something always makes me want to lock, double lock and check all the time, which is probably why I went through a peculiar ritual of securing the motorcycles every night while travelling through America's backwaters. I had brought along two steel cables and two padlocks to tie Anne's and my bikes together each night as they sat outside our motel room. I would thread the large steel cable through the front wheels and then padlock it to the second cable through both bikes' engine-guards. It looked pretty stupid and was probably about as effective in safeguarding our motorcycles as if I had covered them in brown paper, but while we were on the road it gave me peace of mind at night. It probably gave any potential motorcycle thief a good laugh too.

Of course I knew the bikes were insured and that if someone really wanted to take them all they had to do was turn up with a few strong friends and lift them straight off the car-park tarmac and on to the bed of a pick-up truck. I had read this happens a lot in America.

According to the National Insurance Crime Bureau (NICB), 60,763 motorcycles were stolen across the US in 2008. The top five favourite marques that the thieves target are Suzuki, Kawasaki, Honda, Yamaha and, of course, Harley-Davidson. Motorcycle thieves are also seasonal workers, according to the NICB, barely bothering to take bikes in January or February but reaching a thieving crescendo in June and July.

So when I heard the first rattle of metal against metal outside my

Vernal motel room at midnight I sat up and took notice. The noise got louder and sounded like chain linking being dragged across the parking lot. I stumbled out of bed and peered from behind the curtain to see what was going on. Both bikes were exactly were we had left them and there was nobody about. Thinking I had imagined it, I got back into bed and tried to get back to sleep.

But then I heard the clanking noise again. There was definitely somebody out there and, what was more, they were doing something to the motorcycles. This time I opened the door and stepped outside. Nothing. Not a soul. A couple of minutes passed and I returned to bed. This midnight jaunting went on for the next 20 minutes. Clank. I get out of bed. Nothing. Back to bed. Clank, and then rustling. I take another look outside. Nothing. More clanking and what sounded like somebody biting something.

After riding 322 miles that day I was tired and decidedly grumpy and even if the bike thieves were armed and had 15 friends manhandling my motorcycle into the back of their pick-up I was at least going to say something to them about waking their victims up before waving goodbye to my bike.

Clang, clang, rattle, crash. This time I was determined to confront them and flung open the door. Absolute silence. Then an almighty bang caused me to leap into the air and spin around. There was a small face peering at me from the top of the rubbish bin that stood beneath our motel room window. The face even had a robber mask and what looked like tiny fingers clutching a chicken bone. A raccoon had somehow managed to squeeze itself into the bin and had got stuck. Every time it tried to get out the lid slammed down, which would explain the intermittent metal clanking noises I had been hearing for the past hour.

I was desperate for some sleep, and I was standing in my underpants, bare feet crunching on discarded fast food chicken bones from the raccoon's midnight feast. I tentatively kicked the trash bin over and it rolled out into the parking lot, no doubt giving the raccoon the ride of its life. Bin and spinning raccoon finally came to a halt next to a parked car and the hairy thief shot off into the night, just as another motel guest checked into the room next door. He didn't say a word. His face said it all.

* * * * * *

The next morning I noticed how dirty my motorcycle had become. I had just travelled some 2,700 miles and ridden through a massive variety of landscape, from high desert to mountain ranges and wide-open prairies, along single lane roads and empty highways, and I'd experienced some amazing diversity in the weather. My motorcycle finally looked like it had been ridden. There were limbs, wings, heads and thoraxes of a huge range of North American insect life sprinkled across it. The rear end of a massive field grasshopper was stuck in the fins of the oil cooler, while the head of a very large hornet peeked impassively from the bike's battery cover.

Before setting off on the trips for this book I would have worried for ages if there were the slightest speck of dirt on my bike. Now I didn't really care any more. The bike was filthy and I liked the way it looked. It was no longer a Garage Queen, though its rider could probably still learn a thing or two.

My confidence on the bike was at an all-time high when I was out on the open road. Mile after mile of straight roads stretching ahead through empty places were an absolute breeze and a pleasure, embodying to my mind what motorcycle riding is all about. There was a constant sense of freedom that I had never experienced in any other walk of life; not even the expensive Ferraris or Aston Martins that I'd driven ever came close to the way a motorcycle made me feel.

It wasn't even a question of speed – I have paid the price for driving too fast in a car both in court fines and in personal injury. A good steady 70mph on my bike was more than sufficient, giving me the opportunity to focus on riding the machine well and concentrating on the road ahead, which cleared my mind. But every time I returned from the vast open spaces of the US to more populated areas my brain went into overload. I couldn't cope with the traffic signals, the other vehicles, or pedestrians and intersections. It completely fazed me, after eight hours on open roads, to be thrust back into everyday town traffic and have to locate the nearest motel. I forgot to look over my shoulder when overtaking, became a nervous twitchy mess and went back to riding like a beginner.

There is an unwritten rule among the Harley-Davidson fraternity that you wave as you pass each other. It's a simple gesture, raising your left arm in acknowledgement of a fellow rider, but in town it would become positively arduous. With another Harley coming towards me in heavy traffic I would always struggle to control the bike at slow speeds in order to respond to his wave – I wouldn't want to be considered rude or ignore him – but I would then find myself forgetting that I needed to use the clutch to change gear, leapfrogging up the road with the engine making loud revving noises and generally looking pretty insane.

* * * * * *

The great thing about not having a concrete route plan and having an appalling sense of direction meant that I was always full of truly fantastic ideas of where Anne and I should go each day. Every morning we would discuss the day ahead, and talk about where I was thinking of leading us. Anne looked very pensive when I announced we would be in Denver, Colorado that evening. She took the map off me, turned it round the right way and suggested that maybe I should consider Wyoming as it was nearer and at least there was a road leading into that state. Unlike the intermittent trail with 'unmade road' highlighted in red that wound through distant mountains, which I was considering as the best way for us to get to Denver.

So Wyoming it was. We left Vernal and took Highway 191 due north, which promised a straight run into the Equality State. That's Wyoming's official name, but I prefer its unofficial title of the Cowboy State or just Big Wyoming. To get there we had to go through the

Flaming Gorge National Recreation Area, which I was told by people in Vernal was one of the best open spaces in the US.

North-east of Highway 191 is the infamous Brown Park, a low-lying isolated valley which the Green River runs through. For hundreds of years it was an area frequented and inhabited by the Comanche, Ute and Shoshone Indian tribes, but with the influx of settlers in the late 1800s it became a notorious hangout for desperados and outlaws. Tucked away in this corner of Utah it was in close proximity to both Wyoming and Colorado, and had been home to a variety of Western villains. Butch Cassidy and his Wild Bunch Gang, along with many other infamous career criminals, were said to have lived there at some time. They were welcome in Brown Park, it was said, as long as no crimes were committed. The region has never had any formal town of any description, or any type of law-enforcement presence. According to local lore there was just one occasion when the Vernal sheriff ventured out to Brown Park, but he beat a hasty retreat when his life was threatened.

There were no such problems for us. The road was magnificent as we climbed up high into the mountains, passing campsites and hiking trails, before starting a long drop down into the lush valleys of the Green River. Highway 191 wound down in a series of loops to the Flaming Gorge reservoir and recreation site. The townspeople of Vernal were right. This was a fantastic national park. But there was one slight drawback. We were constantly being reminded by bright yellow signs to be on the lookout for wild animals. There were signs for deer and elk and even for bear. I was curious about the Black bear in this area. This was the land of the hunter and, on occasions, their prey was the Black bear, one of the smaller species of bear to be found in North America, weighing in at a measly 320lb compared to the massive 1,200lb Grizzly.

There are numerous stories about bear and human interaction in the US National Parks, some apocryphal, some hearsay and some just plain untrue. But while on the road I had learned from the TV news of a man in Alaska who'd spent a lot of time studying and following bears. A week before he set out to look for a Grizzly a hiker had been attacked by one and had been very lucky to escape with his life. The bear expert knew about this incident but still wanted to learn more and he returned close to where the first attack had taken place. The Grizzly was waiting, and it attacked and killed him. I was certain there was a moral there somewhere.

The Black bear population in the US is healthy but needs to be kept in check every so often by hunters armed with a wide range of weapons. I had checked the bear-hunting season before setting out on our trip and successfully managed to miss all the open days when I could have gone out into the woods to kill a bear. I did ask one hunter whom I met what happened to the bear after it was killed. He told me that most people just had their pictures taken with the corpse for posterity, or had parts of the bear sent to the local taxidermy company. But some people also ate the meat.

He had tried it once, he said, but found it was strong tasting and very fatty, and he wouldn't recommend it. He also warned me about buying bear repellent. This is something that campers and hikers can purchase from sporting shops in the US; you can douse yourself with an aerosol spray that is supposed to give off an unpleasant odour that is unattractive to bears and then they won't attack you. The hunter told me, however, that the consequences were often unexpected, with hikers being pursued through the woods by excited bears as the scent had proved to be utterly irresistible to them. I liked that mental image a lot.

* * * * * *

Flaming Gorge covers an area of some 207,000 acres of land and straddles the state line between Utah and Wyoming. In the middle is a reservoir that was created in 1956 and holds an immense amount of water fed by the Green River; the reservoir alone comprises more than 42,020 acres and it is over 92 miles long.

All these enormous numbers made me smile. The total area of all 14 national parks in the United Kingdom is 7,842 square miles, with the largest being the Cairngorms National Park in Scotland covering 1,467 square miles. The largest of the 58 national parks in the US is the Wrangell-St Elias National Park and Preserve in Alaska, covering a mammoth 800,000 acres of wilderness. And unlike national parks in the US, many British parks are populated, with much of the land in private ownership.

The name Flaming Gorge made me smile, too. I once had a very camp acquaintance who went by the name of Flaming George, and it was difficult for me to disassociate this middle-aged man who liked to dress up in women's clothing at weekends from an area of such outstanding beauty as Flaming Gorge.

This region around the northern edge of the Uinta Mountains was largely undiscovered until 1869 when former soldier, museum geologist and explorer John Wesley Powell mounted a series of expeditions along the Green River, taking him into the area we were now riding through, and then down the Colorado River. George Bradley, a member of Powell's expedition team, recorded his first impressions of the Green River in his diary at the time:

Just below [Henry's Fork, Wyoming] we entered the mouth of the first canyon and encamped amid cottonwood trees surrounded by bluffs 1,200 feet high and on one side nearly perpendicular. It is the grandest scenery I have found in the mountains and I am delighted with it. … The river winds like a serpent through … nearly perpendicular cliffs … but instead of rapids it is deep and calm as a lake.

It appears Powell was equally impressed with the dramatic scenery of the area, and he named it Flaming Gorge on account of the massive orange rockfaces that line the edges of the Green River.

In 1956 construction began on a dam at Flaming Gorge as part of the Colorado River Storage Project. This dam is about three miles downstream from Ashley Falls and was completed in 1963. The resulting reservoir fast became a major tourist attraction and recreation area for fishermen and people with all sorts of boats and watercraft. The fish stocks in the reservoir are legendary, with anglers pulling out 30lb lake trout on a regular basis, although the Utah record actually stands at 51lb 8oz. That is as heavy as a six-year-old child.

The dam is a great piece of engineering and if you like large blocks of 1950s concrete it is exceptionally well done. Standing 600 feet high, it holds back more than 3,788,000 acre-footage of water. I was unfamiliar with the US term acre-foot, but it is commonly used to measure volume capacities of American reservoirs and large lakes. In case you are still curious, just one acre-foot measures 66 feet by 660 feet by a foot high, equivalent to 271,328 gallons, which means the Flaming Gorge Dam is holding back … a flaming lot of water.

The dam was clearly visible from Highway 191 as we descended into the valley. The clear expanse of water with the huge orange cliffs surrounding it, which is where Powell took his inspiration to name the place Flaming Gorge, was astonishingly beautiful.

We emerged from a shady deep canyon on one side of the dam into brilliant sunlight, with the sparkling reservoir water laid out before us. The small two-lane road crossed a small bridge, then ran directly on to the top of the dam. There was an expanse of blue reservoir water to the left and a huge drop to the right, where the dam falls away to the valley floor below, and in a matter of seconds we were over it, following the road that hugs the massive orange cliffs and leaving this enchanted area. It was a great riding moment and one that I will never forget.

If you have the inclination there are even guided tours of the Flaming Gorge dam, but I didn't have the time to spend being dragged around in large groups of people 'oohing' and 'aahing' at water being pushed through a concrete wall. I did, though, enjoy watching a small family of four who had pulled up in their minivan at the dam's car park. They got out, wandered over to the water's edge and discussed among themselves how they were going to launch their boat from this point.

'But we gotta be careful if we do it here,' warned the man, who looked to be the father figure and therefore in charge of the day's boating activity. 'We have to stay away from the dam as you can get sucked into one of the pipes that runs through it and then spat out the other side.' His children look suitably wide-eyed. They had obviously not bargained for that option on their boating holiday.

CHAPTER SEVEN

LANDING IN LANDER

Wyoming and Lander – Voices from beyond the grave – Street party –
The white man – Launderettes – Eagles and Native Americans

I had achieved another lifetime's goal when we rolled across the Utah state borderline into Wyoming because it was a state that I had always wanted to visit and never had until now. This is a land of cowboys, mountains and cows, cows and a few more cows. It also includes a small group of mountains, called Les Trois Tetons by early French explorers, which are part of the huge Rocky Mountain Range. They're now called the Grand Tetons but the literal translation of their earlier name, which I think is much more appropriate, is the Three Tits.

I liked this state immediately. We would never allow places to be named after people's private parts in England. Bishops Itchington and Pratts Bottom are about as good as it gets. There is also a small town called Cockermouth, and some people are up in arms about living in Butt Hole Lane, but that is another story and has no place here. Seriously, though, Wyoming is my kind of place – big sky country. I know that term is generally reserved for its neighbour to the north, the state of Montana, but the Wyoming horizon seemed to take on an almost 360º circle around me. It felt immense, and I felt very small on my motorcycle – and even smaller as I managed to slide on the gravel they use everywhere at the entrance to petrol station forecourts in Wyoming. It may save the station owner money, but on a bike it's like a proficiency test you have to undertake before you can even reach the pump and buy more fuel.

It was a direct run into Wyoming and our intention was to get to the town of Lander for an overnight halt. This meant taking Highway 28, which is long and straight and to be honest just a little bit boring.

But on each side I was entertained by the sight of herds of cattle and cowboys rounding them up, or whatever it is they do in a field with cows, either in trucks or actually riding horses. This was definitely cattle country I thought to myself, as a large pick-up truck pulling a cattle trailer roared past to overtake me. I could see the noses and faces of several surprised-looking cows peering out of the trailer's side vents as they drew alongside me and my bike. I sat behind the truck for a few minutes and suddenly started to notice specks of rain on my windscreen and on the visor of my crash helmet. Odd – the rain in Wyoming appeared to be a brownish-yellow colour – and then it hit me. The cows in the trailer ahead were pissing on me. I tried not to take it personally but decided perhaps it was time to slow down a bit. Who knows what else they might decide to throw at me?

I had no idea why I wanted to go to the town of Lander, except it would take me right into central Wyoming, closer to the Three Tits and the eastern edge of the Rocky Mountains. Plus it might allow me actually to meet some Native Americans as I had a profound curiosity about their customs and their lifestyle today in twenty-first-century North America. To date I had been cautious about asking questions of any I'd met as I felt this could be construed as being voyeuristic. As it turned out, a visit to Lander answered some of my questions but then created a whole host more.

But boy was I glad I made the choice to stop there, because Lander was simply splendid. It was like stepping back to 1957. There was a neat and tidy Main Street with prosperous-looking shops. A small river ran past the top end of Main Street and halfway down there was a small brook trickling down and under the road. There was a coffee house, some great-looking restaurants and even a microbrewery, and to cap it all there was a block party that night with everyone in Lander getting ready to have some fun. It was everything I could have hoped for in small town America – laid back, interesting and very, very friendly.

Granted much, if not all, of Lander's apparent prosperity was due to tourism and hunting plus the presence of a large military base nearby, numerous state and federal offices (the Rangers and Fish and

Wildlife Services) and a field office for the FBI. I am not certain of the reasons for the FBI's presence there but there must be far worse places to be stationed than Lander. Could there be a big cattle-rustling problem in the area and the FBI had been drafted in to go undercover? Did they have to dress up as cows? Maybe I have been riding in the sun for too long...

Lander was also home to Eagle Bronze, one of the largest statue makers and bronze foundries in the US. It was currently working on a project that had been labelled the 'largest equestrian sculpture in the world', destined for El Paso in Texas: a lifelike representation, apparently, of Don Juan de Onate, the famous coloniser of the South-West. The statue would celebrate 400 years of El Paso and was to be 36 feet high and depict Don Juan rearing backwards on his horse. The sign in the window said Eagle Bronze was willing to take on commissioned work and for a moment I was tempted to ask if they would consider doing one of me rearing backwards, out of control on a motorcycle.

Wandering down Main Street we were struck by just how friendly everyone was. The local police who were closing off the street for the evening's festivities were chatting to everyone and when I passed shop doorways people called out to us to say hello. It was nice. There was a good mix of nineteenth-century buildings and more modern shops, and while the architecture wasn't outstanding the whole town felt comfortable and lived in.

I also liked the hardware store that had a display of lawnmowers lined up on the pavement while all around townsfolk were setting up small booths for the party. None of the shops seemed to be going out of business and the gun shop across the way appeared to be doing a roaring trade as customers came and went at frequent intervals, perhaps buying supplies for a hunting expedition that weekend. Either that or they were all preparing to shoot the nosy Englishman later in the evening as part of the block party entertainment.

This all looked like it was going to be fun – so much fun that I decided to call a temporary halt to the trip so Anne and I could stay over for a couple of days to get a better feel for the place, rather than move on the next morning.

* * * * * *

That afternoon we wandered into the Lander microbrewery, on the town's Main Street, which had a huge range of beers on offer that were all brewed on the premises. I would have liked to have tried them all, but I opted for the Jack Mormon Pale Ale and decided to stick with it for the evening. It was strong, but not as strong as the 9% proof Devil's Advocate that was on offer, or a host of other similarly named brews. I liked the fact that you could buy the beer in pints or in pitchers in the bar or wander in and buy a 15.5-gallon party keg, which the brewery insisted you had to take off the premises and drink at home.

While we were sitting outside on a shady patio, or beer garden as we like to call them in England, a pleasant-looking couple asked to sit at our bench. As it turned out they were Lander residents and had lived in the town for more than 15 years. Jerry was a little evasive about what he did for a living, but he did say that for a number of years he'd run a meat business in the town, working with the hunters who would drag in bloody carcasses. He would cut them up. Not the hunters, but deer or elk, and the occasional bear.

'It's a good town to live in,' said Jerry. 'We have made a good living here with the hunter trade and in an average season we'd package up 1,200 carcasses.'

He explained that a hunter would bring in a deer or an elk and he would literally take it to pieces, like a butcher, and carve the meat up into plastic bags and freeze it for them. 'Even had to do it with a couple of bears that had been shot. People do eat bear but they aren't too nice. I wouldn't recommend it,' he said.

Right now, though, Jerry was concentrating on running 25 huskies for sledging. Winter sport was big in Lander, apparently, and running a team of dogs was clearly what fired him up and made him get up in the morning. 'Nothing quite like it, to have a team of dogs working together pulling a sled,' he said.

It was at this point that his wife Sandy suddenly interrupted the conversation. 'I am sorry to do this, but I am getting a message for you,' she said, looking directly at me. I am the biggest sceptic that ever walked the earth and categorically refuse to accept that the paranormal and the psychic world are anything more than for people who are too trusting, and simply hear and see what they want to hear and see. But my curiosity was tickled: this was an opportunity too good to miss. Sandy knew nothing about me except that I had ridden into town on a motorcycle two hours earlier and was enjoying the local beer while sitting at a table with her husband and my wife.

'I am getting a message from your grandmother who passed away two months ago. She wants to say she is very proud of you and everything will be all right,' said Sandy. 'She also knows that your mother is stubborn and the best thing you can do is forgive her.'

Sandy was correct on every point. My grandmother had died two months previously and I had fallen out with my mother. But I was also aware that people with these so-called skills have an ability to seize upon something you say to them and then capitalise upon it without you even realising. But I also got the distinct impression that Sandy didn't really want to be telling me any of this. It was as if she was being forced to, and she seemed genuinely embarrassed to talk about it. I thought I would test her abilities on one more point before letting the matter drop.

'OK, how about this,' I said cautiously. 'Can you tell me what my father is saying about me?'

Sandy looked at me for a second and then down at her hands. 'I am getting a faint feeling or a message from him,' she said. 'He says you were a good boy. That's all I can tell you as he says he didn't know you after the age of eight.'

I could have fallen off the bench at this point. Admittedly the beer was strong, but I hadn't drunk that much. How the heck did Sandy know that my father, who'd died some years ago, had only known me until I was eight years old? After that I never saw him again. I had said absolutely nothing to Sandy about myself, yet just by sitting with me she had somehow picked up on all this information about my family and me. It was a little too much for me to grasp and it made my head spin. Or maybe it really was the beer.

* * * * * *

I excused myself and wandered outside for a few minutes to regain my composure, and also to have a look at what the police were doing with a very fat man they were trying to squeeze into the back seat of their black and white squad car. Being Lander, where clearly everyone knew everyone else and everyone else's business, the police officers were being firm but cordial with their prisoner.

'Come on, Bob, you know you've had too much, so let's just take you home where you can cool off for a bit,' said one officer.

Bob looked reluctant to leave. The front of his shirt was hanging out over his shorts, he was red in the face from the exertion of being pushed, and there was a look of confusion on his bovine face. 'But I ain't done nothing wrong. They just don't like me in there, that's all. I am not too drunk and what happened last time wasn't my fault.'

Fat Bob's protestations fell on deaf police ears. They simply pushed even harder in an attempt to move his massive bulk. The rear of the police Ford Interceptor bounced down on its springs as he was finally loaded in. The last I saw of Bob was a manic-looking face grinning from the rear window, with his two thumbs sticking up at the small crowd of spectators who'd gathered to watch the fun. I think Bob had probably achieved his aim and, following an afternoon of drinking, had got a free lift home from the polite and pleasant Lander police department.

The block party was now in full swing down the road and a very bad rendition of U2's 'I Still Haven't Found What I'm Looking For', but in a modern Country & Western electronic rap style, was booming along Lander's Main Street. Maybe it was the poor acoustics of playing live in the town's high street, but the band was making a very odd noise, as was the female vocalist. She had an unusual voice that perhaps could have been put to better use calling cattle home to the ranch. She also appeared to be about a verse and a half ahead of the rest of the band and every so often would turn around, as if to plead with them to catch her up.

A group of perhaps 30 people were standing almost 50 feet away from the band, as if there was an invisible barrier that had been put up between them and the people on the stage murdering 1980s rock songs. True, the band was performing on what looked like a massive farm tractor that had been abandoned in the middle of the road, and the music was certainly not of this world, but I couldn't understand why the audience wasn't standing any closer.

That was until I saw a man in a cowboy hat and boots, with a big belt buckle that was reflecting the neon lights from the band's stage, standing above the small crowd in the bed of a large pick-up truck. He had a huge keg of beer that he was leaning against and he was dispensing ale at $1 a plastic cupful through what looked like a garden hose. He was taking money hand over fist, and I pushed my way to the front to sample this interesting way of dispensing alcoholic beverages. I had no idea what sort of beer it was, but it helped distract me from the next song emerging from the tractor trailer. It sounded similar to Bob Marley's classic track 'I Shot the Sheriff', but done in a thrash rock light opera style.

I had to turn around and start walking back to the motel when the band's lead singer managed to hold the line 'but I did not shoot the deputeeeeeeeeee' for what seemed like an entire excruciating minute. I also didn't want to get killed in the next stampede for the beer truck when the crowd were trying to escape from the band.

On my return journey to the motel I was mulling over how much I liked Lander and its friendly residents, and wondering if Sandy the psychic had somehow phoned my family in England to get the information she seemed to know about me when I ran into the Indians. To be precise and politically correct, they were two Native Americans called James and Hope and they were about to get on a 2004 Harley-Davidson Dyna.

It was the motorcycle that had attracted me first. James had done a great job on it and had replaced the stock exhaust with some nice short pipes that sounded great when he fired it up. It also had some good-looking handlebars and a mass of other sparkling chrome parts that I was having trouble focusing on. Out of the corner of my eye I could see he had the look of a Native American and, sounding like a pompous Englishman, I spoke to him.

'Great bike, by the way, but are you by any chance … er … are you…' I stammered, sounding like an English colonel in the colonies who was unsure how to address anyone who didn't look like him.

'Native American?' suggested James helpfully.

'Yes. Yes, precisely. Are you Native American and if so what tribe are you from?' I asked. Clearly the effects of the beer were kicking in because I sounded like a complete prat.

James seemed to take it in his stride, though. He was very calm and collected and made it seem perfectly normal that a tipsy Englishman was accosting him, late at night, on Lander's Main Street.

'I am from the Arapaho,' he explained. These were people I had heard about: I knew they lived in Wyoming, and in this immediate area around the Lander Valley in particular, along with the Shoshone tribe. The beer bravado was really kicking in now and I confessed to him that it had been a lifelong dream of mine to meet a medicine man. I wanted to understand more about these shamans and some of the mystic healing that they were known to be capable of performing.

James didn't bat an eyelid. 'Sure man, I understand. I can hook you up with a couple of medicine men that I know. Here, I think I've got their cell phone numbers somewhere. Why don't you give them a call? You might not get them at first as they have a sweat lodge event this weekend, but leave a message and you'll hear from them eventually.'

I declined James's kind offer, much to my later frustration. As I explained to him, it would be a little odd to leave a voice message for a medicine man that I had never met before, and downright confusing for the guy on the other end of the line to know precisely what I wanted from him. Anyway, I wasn't even sure myself what I wanted to ask or talk about.

James again seemed to understand. He said: 'I tell you what, man, why don't you head up to the res tomorrow and just ask around?'

I clearly looked confused and he had to spell it out for me.

'The res. The Indian reservation where we live. Go there tomorrow. Talk to a few people and I am sure they will point you in the direction of a medicine man willing to talk to you. There are a couple of good ones, and one of the best is a horse whisperer who does it all from his wheelchair.' And with that James started his motorcycle, his quiet but patient girlfriend Hope hopped daintily on the back, and they blasted away into the still summer night air of Lander, both no doubt thankful to get away from the idiot Englishman and his weird questions.

* * * * * *

One of the things that I continue to marvel at in the US is the way everything is designed for ease of living. There are the ubiquitous 'drive-thru' restaurants where you pull up and speak to a disembodied voice over a raspy intercom system, choose the meal you want and then drive around the corner to pay and collect it from someone standing at a window sporting an intergalactic space trooper microphone and headphone system and wearing a brightly coloured uniform with a paper hat perched on their head. This same process is also applied to banks and pharmacies across the US and even, in some cases, funeral parlours. You can pause outside a window to look lovingly at your dear departed relative or spouse lying in their coffin before heading off again in the car. Everything is done to make your life easier so you never, ever have to leave your car – or, heaven forbid, actually walk somewhere.

I was therefore somewhat intrigued as to how a launderette would work in the US. This is a concept that the English have taken from America and we have turned it into a truly depressing experience. Often the washing machines don't work and there is a peculiar smell lingering in the place with, more often than not, the local drunk sitting in there talking to a tumble-dryer. There is nearly always an unclaimed pair of enormous man's underpants screwed up into a ball in the corner and overall the place is dirtier than the clothes you have brought in to wash. The washing machine will only take coins that were minted in 1987 and it will give you back your clothes covered in strange stains or with a few things missing, like sleeves and buttons.

So it was with some trepidation that I dragged two weeks' worth of laundry downtown and into Lander's launderette. What a great surprise. Instead of a dark, dingy room filled with broken washing machines this was a big, open, clean area. There must have been more than 40 sparkling washing machines lined up, and as many driers. There was even a soap-dispensing machine that, for a few cents, allowed you the choice of a huge variety of washing powder brands presented in neatly packaged boxes. Everything was clean and everything worked and there was even an ingenious pay-as-you-go card system. You could also choose to dine in if you wanted as there was a large vending machine standing in the corner offering sugary substances and drinks.

'This launderette is good, but you have to be careful,' explained a lady standing next to me. 'I was moving apartments one day and decided to come down here and wash my entire wardrobe. Someone came in here and stole everything. I lost all of my clothes and bedding in just one morning.'

I was a little taken aback and asked her how she coped with no clothes or sheets. She explained that she put up notices around the town telling the local residents of her misfortune and to keep an eye out for her clothes.

'Do you know what?' she said. 'A couple of days later a guy turned up on my doorstep. He said his wife had taken my things from the launderette by mistake. He didn't have everything that was missing, but what he did have was stuffed into a single pillowcase. He also apologised for the bloodstains on some of the items. Turns out he had been carrying a dead deer around in the trunk of his car and somehow my clothes ended up getting covered in blood. I had to throw them all away. So you be careful and watch your clothes.'

I wondered if I would ever see my clothes again but I decided to risk it. I pressed the washing-machine button and planned to come back in an hour.

* * * * * *

A great interest of mine, as I've indicated, is the history of the Native American people. It is impossible to comprehend everything that has happened to their various nations since Europeans first set foot in North America. Experts think there were as many as 500 different nations living on the North American continent before the settlers arrived, and by the end of the nineteenth century their number had fallen to fewer than a hundred.

I had visited the fabulous Heard Museum in downtown Phoenix, Arizona, more times than my long-suffering wife cares to remember. It is a tremendous place and offers an insight into day-to-day life as an Apache or Hopi Indian several hundred years ago. Some of the exhibits are breathtaking in their beauty and simplicity. I'd go there every day if I lived close by because I like the place so much.

I am constantly astounded by the richness of Native American history, the diversity of the nations and the languages (many of which have long since disappeared) and horrified by some of the outrageous treatment these people suffered at the hands of the settlers. The Indian battles may be long over, but I feel a war of sorts is still being fought today. This was why I found a Shoshone lady called Sharky, whom I met in her shop in Lander selling some beautiful Native American craftwork, so fascinating. She was a little reluctant to talk to me at first, but once she had worked out that I was genuinely interested in what life was like for her and her tribe she was very forthcoming.

Today the Shoshone are a small tribe and they are scattered into three divisions – Northern (Idaho, Wyoming and Utah), Western (Oregon and Idaho) and Eastern (Wyoming, Colorado and Montana).

They speak a language known as Uto-Aztecan and at one point in their history had lands that stretched as far west as California's Death Valley, north into Montana, south to northern Nevada and east to Colorado. One of the most famous members of the tribe was a woman called Sacagawea, who accompanied Meriwether Lewis and William Clark, the early American explorers, on their trips into the western hinterlands.

Sharky told me Sacagawea was from the Eastern Shoshone tribe that had been pushed into the Wyoming area around 1750, after warfare with the rival Blackfoot, Lakota and Cheyenne tribes. As more settlers arrived in the nineteenth century it was inevitable that tensions arose among the indigenous people. The Shoshone took to raiding ranches and farms for food, and attacking migrants as more and more of their land was encroached upon. One of the most shameful events happened in 1863 when US military forces trapped and killed more than 400 Shoshone men, women and children near the present-day town of Preston, Idaho, in what would later be called the Bear River Massacre.

The details of this make extremely painful reading. The underlying reason for the constant friction with the settlers was that the Shoshone were rapidly losing their lands and in January 1863 were literally starving. The flashpoint was when a band of Shoshone warriors stole some cattle for food. The US military retribution was barbaric and today seems simply unbelievable.

'The old ways are going,' said Sharky. 'We are made promises by the white man even today and every time he breaks those promises.'

I was dumbfounded. Had Sharky just referred to her fellow Americans as 'the white man'? She had, but it was not meant in a derogatory way; it was just the term that her people applied to those not born within *her* tribe or race.

'Look at the reservations here. We are losing land all the time, as they need more land from us. The government allows us to build casinos but none of the money ever makes it back to the younger generation,' she explained.

I liked this lady very much. She was dapper and fast moving, and had a great sense of humour. She must have been in her early sixties and clearly had some strong opinions on the rights of the Shoshone and the wrongs of the white man. Sharky estimated that the Shoshone nation probably has around 3,000 members today, and they are outnumbered by the Arapaho nation by almost two to one in the nearby area.

'Years ago we invited the Arapaho to come and share our lands as a temporary measure while they were negotiating with the government for their own reservation. They just never left,' she said, smiling a little sadly. She was also sad about the fact that the younger generation of Shoshone didn't want to learn the old ways any more. Nobody, she said, apart from a very few, was doing beadwork. The children were more interested in video games and TV, although they would dress up and take part in the annual Sun Dance.

I said how hard it must be to be a youngster of a Native American tribe. They have one foot planted in the past and the old ways that their elders would like them to keep alive, while their other foot is firmly placed in the twenty-first century, with all that modern living has to offer. They must feel constantly pulled in two directions. Sharky agreed it was indeed a problem.

'Did you know it's now illegal to take eagle feathers here?' she asked me with a quizzical look. 'But they are part of our heritage, and they play a role in our Sun Dance Festival every year in August, as decoration for the dancers.

'A few years back, in Jackson Hole, a white man shot an eagle that was stealing fish from his lake. He was fined a large amount by the courts after the US Fisheries and Wildlife agency prosecuted him.

'But there was also a 19-year-old boy from my tribe who killed an eagle for feathers for the Sun Dance and he was sent to prison. He is still in prison now, a few years on. Where is the justice in that? He was stupid and he did wrong, but why didn't the white man go to jail too?'

I could offer Sharky no explanation. It seemed a little excessive to be sent to prison for killing an eagle and I could hear the sense of injustice in her voice.

'You're not allowed to even touch an eagle that you see dead beside the road. A few years ago I was on my way to hospital for a serious operation and I saw one that had been hit by a truck. I stopped the car, scooped it into a plastic bag and took it to the hospital with me. Put it in the fridge that was in the hospital room and nobody ever knew.' She chuckled at the memory of her defiant act.

I wished I had some answers for Sharky. She had certainly answered a lot of mine, but I felt whatever I said would sound glib and condescending so I had to content myself with just thanking her for talking to me.

As we left Anne bought a Navajo silver bracelet from her. When I asked Sharky what the symbols engraved on it meant her face took on a mischievous look and she said: 'I asked the same question of the Navajo silversmith who made it. And he told me to tell the white man it means whatever they want it to mean.' Seemed like a perfect response to me.

We had to hurry now as I was getting concerned my underwear was being stolen from the launderette and paraded around town by the resident homeless man, or used to wrap bloody deer carcasses. As it turned out, all was well and I was set for the next leg of the journey with clean clothes, free of the splattered remains of insects and road grime.

I had liked Lander a lot. It was an interesting, bright town with a lot going for it. I could have stayed another few days but we needed to get back on our bikes. We were more than 1,500 miles from home and still had three more states to ride through.

CHAPTER EIGHT

MOUNTAIN HIGH

*Thoughts on travelling – Wind River Reservation – Road construction
again – the Rocky Mountains and the Tetons – German coffee shop –
Bighorn sheep – Golf and catching alligators – Jackson's Hole*

I have never been too worried about the final destination when I'm
travelling, just interested in how I was going to get where I wanted.
I liked being on the move and seeing new towns, roads and countryside,
and being able to choose who to talk to and who to avoid. Riding a
motorcycle around the US was confirming all my ideas. I felt it was
better to have a rough idea of where we wanted to go and where to
pull up for the evening rather than a precise planned route or list of
'must-see' things. That way we might stumble across unexpected
places and interesting people along the way – and I seemed to have an
uncanny knack of being able to find the strange and the bizarre. Or
maybe they just seek me out.

On the odd occasions I had used structured agendas and guidebooks
they undoubtedly took me to tourist 'hot spots' and national
monuments swarming with people who, as far as I could see, were
only visiting so they could brag to family and friends that they'd been
there. They'd effectively ticked the tourist box, bought the T-shirt and
been photographed beside or in front of or inside 'it'. More often than
not I was disappointed with such places – not because these battle
sites, magnificent castles or places of outstanding interest were not
what they were purported to be, but because I didn't feel I was reacting
in the way I was supposed to.

Your mode of transport has a bearing on what you see, how you feel
and what happens to you, of course. Some travel writers seem to
prefer the comfort of reclining seats in the swaying carriages of luxury
trains while they cross continents looking at third-world poverty, or

they opt to cruise on vast ocean liners with everything that could possibly be wanted on board so they never need to set foot ashore. One nineteenth-century travel author relied upon a donkey as his main form of transport. It was a slowly plodding and amusing story but I felt more interested in the donkey and its welfare after the journey was finished than what the author was describing. Cars are undoubtedly convenient but perhaps a tad dull compared to the joys of motorcycling. Perhaps bikes aren't the most practical machines ever invented, but they had certainly allowed me to see (and sometimes even smell) things that I couldn't possibly have experienced in any other way.

Bicycle travel is perhaps the closest experience to riding a motorcycle. You face many of the same risks on a bicycle that you do on a motorbike, but everything happens at a much slower, muscle-ripping sort of pace. The very thought of using a bicycle to scale some of the vast US mountains we'd seen on our trips, or cross the empty, scalding hot deserts we'd experienced made my legs hurt just thinking about it.

Two of the saddest people I ever saw while travelling in the US were a husband and wife team strapped to a tandem in the middle of an Arizona desert. Their entire travel possessions, which consisted of three small bags, were tied to the frame of their bicycle. The nearest town was 60 miles behind them and the next town was at least 80 miles ahead. How did they get here and where were they going and *why* were they doing this to themselves?

It was blisteringly hot – well over 100°F – a dry heat that made you sweat in places you didn't know you had. The heavyweight and very rotund husband was purple in the face from the exertion of pedalling. He was on the front of the tandem and was making the bike weave slightly as I came up behind them on my motorcycle. His wife, a diminutive lady, was bent over her handlebars in the standard 'miserable cyclist' crouching position, and all she could see was her husband's enormous bottom that jiggled and wobbled in front of her as they rode along. What on earth would they say to each other at the end of a long day's riding?

'We've seen some great views of the desert landscape and some amazing cacti and wildlife today. Did you see that eagle gliding on the thermals, dear?' he would say. She would have no reply, as her only view would have been a pair of sweaty buttocks wrapped in fluorescent synthetic material just inches from her face. The poor woman was missing out on many things in life, including the astonishing scenery that surrounded us. She deserved a medal, or possibly a bed in an institution.

I had the same feeling of pity for a small elderly man we encountered who was manfully trying to pedal up a steep mountain incline on his racing bicycle. He too was weaving about in the road just ahead of me and when he realised that I was approaching him far too quickly he tucked himself back in again. He gave me a feeble wave as I passed by, his face a mask of utter exhaustion and total resignation. Why was he doing that to himself, I thought again?

* * * * * *

My plan of taking whichever road looked like a good option was working out well as Anne and I started to climb very quickly on Highway 287. We were already more than 6,000 feet above sea level and passing high above deep canyons and then wide expanses of pine forest interspersed with open fields where cattle were grazing. I hoped this would be a fast road to take us west out of Wyoming and into the state of Idaho. Highway 287 runs almost parallel with the wide Wind River and runs directly through the Wind River Indian Reservation, the seventh-largest reservation in the US encompassing 2.2 million acres of Indian lands. It was home to both the Shoshone and Arapaho Native American tribes, as Sharky had told us in Lander.

In the late nineteenth century the Shoshone were one of the very few Indian nations actually permitted by the US government to choose a location for their permanent reservation home. All the other tribes were dispersed around the various states to reservation lands that were as foreign to them as it would be for an Englishman sent to

China and told to start a new life. The Shoshone had opted for the Wind River Valley area as it was a traditional wintering place for them, and also an important hunting ground. But they had to fight for the right to live there. Not with the US government, this time, but with the Crow nation, who were also looking for lands after losing theirs to the encroaching migration of settlers and prospectors.

In 1866 Chief Washakie of the Shoshone sent a message with one of his warriors to the Crow to say they were welcome to hunt and live in another area close by, but Wind River belonged to the Shoshone. The Crow's response was to kill the Shoshone warrior and the Crow chieftain Big Robber (what a fabulous name) sent a message back to say the Crow would hunt and live wherever they pleased. Washakie declared war against the Crow immediately and for five days the tribes fought a running battle, but neither gained any advantage. Eventually it was decided that Washakie and Big Robber would have to fight a duel, with the victor claiming the rights to live in the Wind River area for his tribe. Washakie finally got the upper hand in this fight to the death and killed Big Robber, but he was apparently so impressed with his rival's bravery that he cut out the heart of the dead man and placed it on his lance as a sign of respect. I would hate to have seen what Washakie did to those people who really disappointed him.

Life goes on here for the Shoshone and the Arapaho, who today share the lands. It's a pleasant open area and while I felt that not a lot might happen out there, there are certainly far worse places to live. The countryside was beautiful and I could understand why the Shoshone were so keen to choose and fight for this place.

Just past the Wild River Reservation there was the ubiquitous traffic stop ahead, so we rolled to a halt as a road construction crew with enormous metal machines did improbable things with boiling hot bitumen, rollers and crushing devices. Somehow this practice always seemed to involve groups of about 20 workmen standing in a circle, with all of them watching just one man operate an enormous road-making machine. The guy on the massive machine was playing up well to his audience today, and appeared to be enjoying throwing around huge quantities of gravel in a completely haphazard fashion, much to the approval of his group of fellow workers.

It was while I was sitting there on my motorcycle, waiting for the STOP sign to turn to GO, that I looked to my left and nearly fell off my bike in surprise. There, punching the skyline, were the Rocky Mountains.

How the heck did an entire 3,000-mile-long mountain range just sneak up on me? But there they were – immense snow-capped peaks and below the sort of purplish-grey that you only ever see in travel books – the real deal. In all the years that I'd been flying to America I had only ever seen the Rocky Mountains from the window seat of a plane. Occasionally, when the plane's captain could be bothered to talk to his passengers, he'd announce that if you looked out of the window you'd see them directly below. Now, in the mid-afternoon sunshine, they looked truly magnificent, with a dark brooding appearance that changed colour by the minute as the light reflected off their slab sides and snowy peaks.

The construction worker manning the STOP sign beckoned me over. It was my turn to go and he clearly had something of importance to tell me. 'Take it easy along here, buddy,' he said. 'We have just put down 40 tons of loose gravel that will make it very hard for you on a bike. Watch out or you could fall.'

'No shit' is what I wanted to reply. He seemed to take a lot of satisfaction in imparting this news to me. Why hadn't he waited until Anne and I had passed before dropping his vast quantities of loose stones all over the road? We were the only people at this impromptu traffic stop, and no vehicles had come from the other direction. Not only that, the construction crew had also thoughtfully closed the left-hand lane so we were faced with using the right one that ran parallel to a sheer drop of hundreds of feet down to the dark valley below – with no guard rails.

This was going to be a real challenge because the loose gravel they had so thoughtfully laid down for us was some three inches deep in places and made my bike squirm and slide as the rear wheel searched for traction. There were also sharp bends at the bottom of steep hills. It wouldn't have been wise to touch the brakes on this road surface, or make any sudden movement, because the bike would simply fall over, with the ever-present risk of its rider slipping over the edge into a deep canyon. Keeping it in a higher gear helped a bit, and driving on the throttle seemed the best and only option.

Two miles became three, and then five, and still I was not out of trouble – and I was swearing a lot again because I was scared: sharp stones were bouncing off my front wheel and hitting me on the shins like small stone bullets, and rattling around the engine of my bike. Looking back on this episode it may seem as if I was being a little over-dramatic. If I had been in a car I would have paid little attention to it all, just driven through with the gravel pinging off the underside of the car and oblivious to the cliffs falling away to my right. On a motorcycle however I felt exposed – but not in the good way I was extolling earlier in this chapter!

About half a mile ahead I could just make out the end of the construction work, with two cars waiting to come through from the other side. Suddenly it was all over until the next time. I breathed a huge sigh of relief and shot up a hill on the other side to find myself at Togwotee Pass, some 9,658 feet above sea level. It was also getting much colder and the wind was whipping up and making me ride at a curious slanted angle, so Anne and I pulled over at this famous pass in the Rocky Mountains to take a break. I was tired, but I also wanted to stand on the Great Continental Divide that begins at the Seward Peninsula, in Alaska, and runs north–south through the US, Central America and on to the tip of South America.

Essentially the Great Continental Divide is a natural drainage feature. On one side and to the west all water flows in the direction of the Pacific Ocean, while on the other side the water heads eastwards towards the Atlantic Ocean. At more than 9,000 feet up the side of this mountain, I felt I was standing on the very backbone of America.

After considering all these drainage issues I glanced to my left and had a simply spectacular view of the Three Tits, or the Grand Teton Mountains. Although part of the Rocky Mountain Range, the Tetons are a smaller massif and are very distinctive in their looks because these are mountains shaped unlike any others in the area. They rise like jagged grey sharks' teeth into the sky, with the biggest one, Grand Teton, reaching 13,770 feet. The other Tetons – Teewinot, Middle Teton, South Teton, Moran, Wister, Owen, Buck and Static Peak plus a host of others – are all 10,000 feet high or more. Aside from being stacked together and looking like a massive set of dentures, and having names that sounded as if they'd been invented by Walt Disney Studios, I simply could not see how those early French explorers had decided on the name Les Trois Tetons. Either those pioneer Frenchmen were hanging out with some very odd women back then or they did not really know what women's breasts looked like. So I am with the Shoshone people on this one. They called the whole Teton range Teewino, which loosely translates as 'many pinnacles'.

What I did know, though, was that the Tetons were staggeringly beautiful. As we continued to ride west they became a permanent feature on the horizon, a constant travelling companion, and we got to see them all from a whole host of different angles over the next two days. We would ride through a dark pine forest and find them waiting on the other side, or come over a mountain pass to be met again by all the Tetons framing the horizon ahead. The best view of them ever was when I was just standing outside our Idaho motel room one evening, watching their fantastic changes of colour as the sun went down. In that twilight dusk I even tried closing one eye and squinting at them with the other, but I still could not make out the female appendages that those Frenchmen had once seen.

* * * * * *

During the thousands of miles we covered across the US I was never disappointed by the places we visited or passed through. Often a town exceeded my expectations with the quirky things I discovered there, or just because of the pleasant and interesting people I met along the way. Sometimes, though, what I had expected was not what I actually found at all, as in the case of Jackson Hole on the western fringe of the state of Wyoming.

To get there we had to ride along Highway 191, through the Bridger-Teton National Forest. Huge pines surrounded the road as it wound its way across mountain ridges and on to flat plateaus of fields. You could stop for a few minutes in these forests and see sparkling rivers cascading down the rocks into dark, cool valleys below, but you needed to keep an eye out for roaming bears and hikers. Both can be equally distracting to motorcyclists. One may attack you and eat all your food, while the other might be an aggressive 600lb carnivorous animal.

It's a tranquil sort of place, Bridger-Teton National Forest, and it lays claim to having more than 350 species of birds and 75 different types of mammals living on its 3.4 million acres. Aside from the roaming bears and hikers there are also a lot of mountain lions. And there were many times on that road that I wished for a mountain lion to appear and devour the stupid SUV or truck driver behind me, sitting inches off my bike's rear wheel while trying to find a way to get past me.

As with most national parks and forests in the US, there was a strict traffic speed limit of 50mph and sometimes even 40mph. Yet for some reason, and I assume they were eager holidaymakers looking for a campsite rather than locals, these drivers would come from nowhere in their vehicles at a furious rate of speed and then try to overtake me at some truly impossible spot with oncoming traffic appearing around the corners. I'd grown to like speed on some of the fast mountain roads we'd encountered, but this was just plain lunacy. At least eight times I found I was being tailgated by enormous vehicles whose occupants had no idea of the speed they were doing or how dangerous it was for them – and for me – to get so close to my motorcycle. If I speeded up, so did they. If I slowed down they drew even closer, trying to find a way around me. The crazy part of this charade was that as soon as they passed my bike they would then settle back to well below the speed limit and hold me up as they enjoyed the scenery or searched for a suitable site to set up camp for the night.

Frustrated by all this holiday traffic, I pulled my motorcycle over in the charming town of Dubois that still has log buildings lining its Main Street, much as it would have done when the town was first settled in the late 1800s.

According to the guidebook, my old friend and bank robber Butch Cassidy apparently lived in Dubois for six months before embarking on another crime spree. At this point in my journey I came to the conclusion that the Butch Cassidy story was similar to the legend of Queen Elizabeth I of England who, it seems, spent her entire life staying in houses and towns throughout England while ruling the country. If you actually stopped and added up all the days and nights that every house, inn and town in England claims Elizabeth spent with them she would never have been home once and would have died at the ripe old age of 357.

The same thing must be true of Mr Cassidy. If he really did stop at all these US towns I'd passed through while planning his next criminal escapade he would never actually have had the time to rob a single bank. I think Dubois was like most towns that made claims about the Cassidy legend. He may well have passed through here, but Butch probably didn't stay very long. A bit like myself.

Dubois described itself as an authentic Western town. It lies on the Wind River, surrounded by the Absaroka and Wind River Mountain Ranges. If 'authentic' means shops closing down and not a soul about, then Dubois was not selling itself short.

The woman behind the counter in the German coffee house was enthusiastic about seeing Anne and me as we were her first customers of the day, and quite possibly the only customers that day apart from an old woman who came in a few minutes afterwards. She sat mumbling to herself in the corner, staring forlornly out of the window at the passing holiday traffic that crept through the town but never seemed to stop.

I could not quite grasp why this was a 'Coffee Haus' as there was nothing remotely Teutonic about it. My limited experience of German coffee houses includes lots of pine wood panels, images of the Bavarian countryside on the walls and blond smiling people wearing leather shorts. Perhaps the name was due to the Spartan layout of the place. There was a solitary fridge and a kettle for making coffee, a few cups and a multitude of pictures and photographs of the owner's dog, but absolutely no trace of anything remotely German.

Apart from running coffee shops under false pretences, I also could not see what on earth people did in this town. Agriculture and cattle ranching were big in the area so I can only assume that Dubois provided the necessary supplies to support the local farming community. But nothing was open.

I suppose if you lived in Dubois you could always work at the National Bighorn Sheep Interpretive Center that sells itself to passing tourists as 'high, wild and on the edge'. It sounded to me more like the description of an inner city crack den than a place to learn about mild-mannered sheep. But what do I know? At one time there were apparently millions of these mountain-loving sheep roaming North America, but due to excessive hunting Bighorn sheep numbers dwindled dramatically in the early 1900s to a few thousand. A conservation programme was introduced in the 1960s and has successfully pulled them back from the brink of extinction.

At Dubois's commendable Bighorn Sheep Center you can be taken for a five-hour ride through the mountains in an off-road vehicle to look at, well, sheep with big horns. And to be fair those horns are big, sometimes weighing in at as much as 30lb. But I failed to see the attraction of looking at an ovine animal that doesn't do much but eat grass and jump around mountain ledges. I was, though, curious about the 'interpretive' title of the centre and wondered what precisely was being interpreted for visitors. I was even more intrigued by the type of people who would pay $25 each to sit in an off-road vehicle following sheep around a mountain all day. Alas, I could not find out more as time was pressing and the old woman seated in the German coffee shop was starting to make random guttural noises.

The road to Jackson runs through the Snake River Valley before descending into the town, and that morning it was busy with traffic. My notes for the day said: 'Nothing much to report, flat, dull, cold and heading into Jackson's Hole.' I was a bit confused by this town's name. History books refer to the area as Jackson's Hole: nineteenth-century hunters and trappers entered this valley area from the north and east and had to descend along steep-sided slopes, giving them a sensation of entering a hole. The town which grew up at the southern end of the valley then became called Jackson Hole, before dropping the 'Hole' entirely and today just calling itself Jackson. Good decision in my book.

It was with this attitude that I headed into a town I knew nothing about, except that some former American work colleagues used to speak in tones of wonder about the amazing games of golf that could be played there.

I'll make my apologies now. I detest golf. I am sure the game itself takes great skill and has many virtues, all of which I am afraid I am ignorant about. What I do know is that any game that has strict rules on what type of clothing you are allowed to wear as well as a hierarchical protocol that is based more upon who you are than your capabilities of playing it is definitely not for me. I am sure I am generalising, but having visited many golf courses in my past life as a car industry executive I never found one where I felt comfortable. Maybe it was because I never got to play the game but would spend the day arranging business presentations for the lunchtime break or evening gala event, while the 'real' men were outside whacking a white ball with a stick around an area that was as large as an English county.

Middle-aged men seem to adore this game. They go all gooey-eyed and talk in strange tongues of birdies, eagles and 18 holes, and they spend every moment of their spare time involved in a sport that encourages them to wear one glove and carry a massive bag of sticks around with them. Golf also allows them to avoid spending any time with their wives and families at weekends or public holidays.

The only real fun I ever had at a golf course was in Boca Raton, Florida, when a group of my colleagues returned within 40 minutes of teeing off, pasty faced and breathing very quickly from having run a long way to inform me there was an eight-foot alligator asleep on the sixth green and ask what I was going to do about it. Being the junior member of the management team and also responsible for that day's golf event for customers and our staff it was my responsibility to sort it out.

And sort it I did, with a man I telephoned called Joe who described his business in the phone book as 'Florida Nuisance Control'. This allowed him to exert his influence over an amazing list of animals from mice and rats right up to sleeping alligators on golf courses. He would catch anything, sling it into the back of his beaten-up pick-up truck and take it off to wherever he took it to, never to be seen again.

Joe was a man of very few words. He arrived 20 minutes after I'd called his office and said hello to me, but that was it. He just nodded his head when I asked if I could come and watch him in action, so we headed off in his pick-up and, sure enough, the avocado-coloured shape of an alligator was visible, lying motionless on the green at the sixth hole, enjoying a morning nap in the Florida sunshine. Joe wandered over to it to assess the situation, went to the back of his pick-up and took out a long wooden pole with a wire loop attached to it, walked back to the alligator and simply put the loop over its snout and pulled it tight around the beast's neck. The alligator bucked backwards in surprise. Joe had disturbed its mid-morning nap. It started to open and shut its mouth, displaying lines of white, jagged and decidedly unpleasant-looking sharp teeth.

But Joe was a professional and not to be thwarted. He simply stood on the alligator's neck, pulled up its head and wrapped a roll of duct tape around the confused reptile's snout. Joe then bound its rear and front legs together and, with its tail thrashing around behind it, dragged it towards his truck. In a blur of slapping alligator tail Joe heaved the heavy beast into the back of his pick-up; he had clearly done this type of job many times before.

My very English boss, David, was delighted that the game of golf could continue but he was also very keen to meet Joe and the alligator close up, and of course offer Joe a tip for his time and trouble. I think we actually paid him twice, as I had already covered his fee and tip when he first arrived on the scene. But Joe said nothing. David leaned over the back of the pick-up to get a better look and, in his best English accent, said to Joe: 'My word, he is a big one. Gosh, look at him. I say, do you mind if I ask you how you catch something like this?'

Joe just narrowed his eyes. First he looked at me, before turning his gaze back on David, and then he said: 'Very carefully, boy.'

* * * * * *

This brings me, in a very convoluted way, from Florida back to Jackson in Wyoming. Situated just south of the Grand Teton Mountains, Jackson has an enviable reputation among the well heeled and the famous as an excellent winter holiday vacation spot. There is great skiing and all manner of other snow sports in the winter, but I am not entirely sure what the town does with itself in the summer.

On our slow, traffic-clogged ride into Jackson the only bright point for me was passing the entrance to the local golf club and knowing that I would never, ever have to set foot in there. Finding somewhere to park my bike amid the holiday traffic was not easy, and I had to settle for a side street outside an expensive-looking clothing shop. The store's owner came out as I backed up to the kerb and looked at me with a pained expression on her face. Clearly motorcycles were not a welcome addition to haute couture in Jackson.

In truth Jackson was not at all what I had expected to find. I could see its attraction for the wealthy and the winter sports fanatics, but in June it was simply packed with tourists wandering aimlessly from one expensive luxury shop to another. As I sat on a balcony chewing on a rubbery hamburger, which had been presented to me by a very apathetic restaurant waitress, I looked down on the town's square and the milling throngs of people. There was a nod to Jackson's

Western past, with a stagecoach giving rides to tourists. But it just rolled around the square and no further, pulled by a couple of bored horses, while the passengers inside gazed out of the windows looking as if they had been truly short-changed.

It looked to me like Jackson had sold out. Got rid of the 'hole' from its name, and the profits to be made from the holiday trade had transformed a quaint Western town, surrounded by some of the most beautiful scenery I had ever seen, into an expensive resort and playground for the rich. Maybe I am being unfair, but a couple I passed on the street best summed up the town for me.

'Is that all there is here in Jackson, just fancy shops? I thought there would be something else,' said a small elderly woman to her husband.

He simply shrugged, pushed his cap back on his head and looked at her. 'Well it's lucky we're just passing through, honey, as it's too expensive anyways,' he said.

As were Anne and I. Just passing through. And from my balcony vantage point in Jackson's town square I could see dark storm clouds coming over the mountains, bringing with them the real threat of some serious rain.

CHAPTER NINE

FUSION & CONFUSION

Mountain rain – Englishmen in Idaho – German on a bike –
Atomic power and moon rocks – Oregon Trail – Mosquitoes –
Castration equipment – Salty lake – Perils of motorcycles –
Prisons and bowling – Turning right

The first raindrop hit me smack in the chest. And it was a big one. The sky had turned even blacker behind us as we rode out of Jackson and now, for the first time on this leg of the trip, we were facing the real possibility of getting drenched in a thunderstorm on our motorcycles. We were more than 60 miles from the next overnight halt and without any type of rain gear.

As mentioned earlier, I really try to avoid riding in the rain if I can. The motorcycle handles differently and you have to adopt a more relaxed style of riding and plan even further ahead as you look down the road. It's the poor visibility created by the spray from passing vehicles and those that you are following that causes the most problems. Your crash helmet visor mists up (unless you stop breathing) and water has an uncanny knack of getting into every item of your clothing, leaving you sodden and freezing rather than just wet and cold. No matter what the temperature, even if it's hot you'll start to get cold and before long your feet become numb and your hands ache from the combination of the wind, rain and cold. You can't feel the throttle or the pedals and your feet start to slip on the gear selector and slide off the rear brake. It's not a pleasant experience. The only options are to look for a bridge to shelter under, or pull up at a bar or restaurant for a coffee, or just carry on and grin and bear it.

I opted for the last one. Despite the heavy rain I was determined that Anne and I would make it to the town of Driggs, in Idaho, by the evening. Especially as there was nothing ahead of us for miles and there was no way that I wanted to spend any longer in Jackson. As we started to climb the edges of the Teton Mountains the rain began really coming down, bouncing off my bike's windscreen and then catching me right in the exposed part of my neck, between the top of my jacket and the bottom of my crash helmet. It stung like hell.

'Are you getting as wet as me?' asked Anne through the intercom. 'I really think we should pull over somewhere until this rain passes. What do you think?'

What did I think, indeed? I thought we should carry on. The prospect of standing by the side of the road next to our bikes in a torrential downpour had no attraction for me. I am stubborn. Once I have made up my mind I stick to it and despite Anne's possibly sensible suggestion I was absolutely determined that we should press on regardless. Anne, no doubt, was considering legal action at the very least.

My gloves had become slippery, making throttle and braking completely out of sync, and I was having a hard time seeing where I was going. I had resigned myself to a miserable two-hour journey climbing this twisty mountain road, trying to see the road ahead behind a fogged-up helmet visor while staying upright and moving forward at a sensible rate of speed. Of course you have no option on a motorcycle but to slow down when it's wet, otherwise it just gets too complicated, although there is a theory that the faster you ride a bike in the rain the drier you get. Personally I find going faster only makes the rain whip harder at you, plus you are having to contend with roads that make your bike behave totally differently from when riding it in the dry. You have to be smoother in the wet and on the constant lookout for water-filled potholes and crap that gets washed into the road. It's OK for car drivers: they simply switch on their windscreen wipers and maintain the same speed, safe and secure in the snug cabin of their vehicle and confident about the stability of having four wheels instead of two.

Right now, as the rain was pelting down, I had a large pick-up truck riding about ten feet off my rear tyre. I couldn't steer or ride normally,

I couldn't see properly and this guy seemed to have absolutely no idea of what was happening in front of him. He was just plain frustrated because instead of riding at 55mph I had dropped my speed down to 45mph and he wanted to come past. Right now.

The truck moved even closer to the back of my bike – so close that if I were to stop suddenly he would hit me squarely from behind and launch me straight off the side of the mountain road and into the valley below. I pulled to the right just a little, to let him by, and he stormed past in a wave of spray and roaring V8 truck engine noise. But as he drew level with me I managed to glance across at him and I was simply astounded. He was studying the screen of his mobile phone while he was overtaking me – and we were heading up a twisting mountain road towards a sharp right-hand bend. Then he was gone and I could breathe again. But not too easily, because my helmet visor had misted up badly and when I opened it just a fraction to gulp in air I got a face full of rain.

Suddenly, as we rounded the next corner, we were confronted by an open blue sky and sunshine. We had somehow managed to outrun the thunderstorm, and in a matter of minutes it was warm and I was starting to dry out. We had also crossed the state border via the Snake River Mountain Range, leaving Wyoming behind us and moving into the flat arable fields of Idaho. This is the land of the potato.

Now that is probably grossly unfair of me as Idaho is the sixth fastest-growing state in the US in terms of population and has a huge range of industries. But about the only thing I had ever known about Idaho was that some of the finest potatoes in the world came from there. Somewhere in the region of 60% of all the potatoes grown in the US come from Idaho.

So it was with a great sense of satisfaction that as we pulled into the small town of Driggs I saw an enormous fibreglass potato (and I mean enormous) mounted on the flatbed of a red 1950s Ford pick-up truck. I wasn't entirely sure why it was there or what it was advertising, but this was clearly a statement of some sort, as was the large bra hung from the horns of a concrete buffalo's head over the doorway of a former bank in Driggs's Main Street. Yet again, though, everything looked closed and there was nobody about. Nobody, that is, apart from an elderly Englishman who struck up a conversation with me outside the motel where Anne and I had decided to stop for the night.

'Nice-looking bike,' he said, as he watched me unload my saddlebags. 'I used to ride a bike when I was younger.'

I wanted to ask him what on earth he was doing in a very quiet town in the middle of Idaho, talking to a stranger outside a motel, but before I got the opportunity he immediately volunteered a few things about himself.

'I'm from England, you know, and I'm on a summer holiday with my wife and some friends. Where are you from, and where have you come from?' he asked me.

Before I had a chance to reply he went on to say: 'I live near London and it's really busy around there. Have you ever been to the UK? So this trip to the US is a bit of a relief for the wife and me. We have just had the elections and got a new government, and the weather hasn't been too good, so we thought we'd take a look at America for a holiday. We've never been here before. Do you know how far it is to Colorado? We thought we'd like to go there tomorrow.'

I explained that Colorado was really quite some way away, probably six hours of driving, and maybe it was a little ambitious to attempt getting there and back by the following morning. He nodded, and immediately cut me off.

'This country is huge. Not like the UK. We have a lot of traffic there and it can take forever to get anywhere but it's really just an island and everything is within easy reach. Not like America. You can't even get a good cup of tea here in the US, can you?'

He hadn't really listened to a single word I had said about the route to Colorado. Clearly he was just having a great conversation with himself and was using me as an interested bystander. Again I tried to say something to him, but then the sliding door of a mini-van, parked close by, opened up and a small grey-haired woman stuck her head out and beckoned to him to come and get in.

'Come on, Stan,' she said. 'Mavis and John are ready to go. We thought we might go to Salt Lake City for the evening. Do hurry up, dear.'

Stan raised a quizzical eyebrow at me. I was expecting him to ask for directions but instead he said: 'You should go to England one day. You'd love it. You Americans love our history and we have a lot of it.'

I just nodded. I had met probably the only other Englishman in eastern Idaho and he had thought I was American. To be fair, though, he had not given me much of a chance to speak. I also knew it was more than 280 miles to Salt Lake City so I wouldn't be seeing him again in the morning. Probably just as well, as he'd be keen to tell me more about our shared country of birth.

* * * * * *

It was the same ritual every morning for me before setting off to ride wherever the road took us. I'd unlock the motorcycles and then spend 10 minutes peering at engine bits and prodding things. I didn't really know what I was looking at or what I was looking for. But my basic routine consisted of checking the tyres were still inflated and there was oil in the engine and, on one occasion, taking a screwdriver to a brake caliper to see if the pad was still in place. Fortunately my Harley-Davidson had obviously been built with mechanical incompetents like me in mind. In 8,000 plus miles I never had a single problem. Nothing fell off. Nothing broke. And no matter how badly I rode it, it always started first time and never once let me down. Out there, in the middle of North America, I felt I let *it* down on many occasions.

I am a bit of a sceptic at heart and have never felt inclined to give names to mechanical objects or refer to them as 'her' or 'him'. Nor did I believe all the stories about bonding with your motorcycle. Lots of people had told me about how attached they had become to their bikes for various reasons and how they could never, ever bear to sell them. I liked my bike very much the day I bought it, but I felt then that I could quite happily sell it for another. After all, it was just a motorcycle – a means of transport, albeit a fun, exciting and sometimes downright dangerous way of getting about.

But something strange was happening. I definitely looked at my bike in a different way in Idaho. I felt more comfortable and at ease with it now, with several thousand miles behind us. I knew its limitations and it clearly knew mine. It had taken me up mountains, across vast plains and through deserts and it had been 100% reliable. This is not some sort of testimony to encourage you to go out and buy a Harley-Davidson, but because of all the things I had experienced with it I had developed a real respect for my bike. Which was why, when I met a German biker in a car parking lot in Idaho Falls, I totally understood the look of pride in his eyes when I asked him about his MZ motorcycle.

Frank was a 65-year-old former engineer from Frankfurt on the trip of a lifetime. He had recently retired from the automotive industry and was on a six-month journey across the US on his rare and special MZ sports bike. He seemed delighted when I said I had heard of MZ (Motorradwerk Zschopau) and knew of their roots in the former East Germany. I knew they had gone bust in 2008 but that there was a plan to relaunch the brand with former Grand Prix motorcyclists Ralf Waldmann and Martin Wimmer taking control of the company. Frank said many people in the US had been fascinated by his bike, which looked something like an Italian sports motorcycle, and that he had gone to enormous lengths to get it properly equipped as a touring motorcycle, with custom panniers and luggage racks specially made for it.

'I love motorcycles,' he explained. 'I once rode from Frankfurt to Modena in Italy and back in just over a day. Not stopping for sleep or anything but fuel and food.'

In my book that was some achievement, as it's a good 636 miles each way and on a sports motorcycle it must have been tough.

'Yeah, my back hurt a bit after that trip,' he laughed. 'But it was good fun. You have to go fast and just keep going. If you stop for long, you're finished.'

This time, though, Frank had opted for a more leisurely six-month cruise across the US and he said he was enjoying himself immensely. 'Everybody's been great. Everybody likes my bike. This is a dream come true, so I am having a really good time.'

I was having a good time too, until just outside Idaho Falls when we hit the longest road construction site we'd come across on our travels. There were ten miles of road works, the carriageway had been torn up and, of course, it had been sprinkled liberally with a good loose topping of gravel. My previous encounters with US road construction had sometimes been several miles long, but this was the biggest by far and every inch was just like riding on a shingle beach. There was, though, a sign which the construction crew had thoughtfully put out for passing bikers like me: 'Motorcyclists Take Care for the Next 10 Miles.'

I had no choice but to push on as there were more than 330 miles to cover and we needed to get to the other side of Idaho and into Oregon before nightfall. This was not good. My bike squirmed through the loose stone chippings which covered the uneven road surface, and I had to try and stay focused, delicately balancing staying upright, maintaining a smooth speed and on no account changing gear or braking as that would end in immediate disaster as I would undoubtedly fall off and then get run over by the long line of impatient cars sitting right behind me. The oncoming traffic was also driving through gravel but it was not keeping to the reduced speed limit. Consequently I was being showered in chippings flicked out by their tyres, which hit me like small bullets and made rattling noises as they bounced off my motorcycle, causing me to squeal like a baby every time one hit me in the leg or arm.

Every so often there would be a small pothole that my front wheel would fall into, making the whole bike shudder and jump while the rear wheel slewed round as it scrabbled through the loose stones. It was like some sort of hideous obstacle course that seemed to go on for ever and ever. In reality it was probably no more than 15 minutes, but by the end my hands were numb from the vibration coming up through the front forks and I was drenched in sweat from the sheer exertion of keeping the bike in a straight line. As I reached the end of the construction there was another sign: 'Thank you for driving carefully and for your patience.' I wanted to punch whoever had put that sign up. Very hard.

* * * * * *

We were now on Highway 20, a fast road heading due west through flat, open Idaho countryside that took us straight past the oddly named Experimental Breeder Reactor (EBR). My initial thought was that this was some sort of weird US government animal procreation centre. As it turned out, it was even weirder than that. Essentially it was a decommissioned nuclear research reactor located in the middle of the Idaho high desert.

Originally it had been designed to validate nuclear theories, but in 1951 it became the world's first electricity-generating nuclear power station when the research scientists there managed to work out a few things and got it to produce sufficient power to light up four light bulbs. As they started to get the hang of nuclear physics they moved on to joining the right wires up to things and then they got the reactor to produce sufficient electricity to power the entire EBR-I building.

These scientists clearly felt they were on to something, but it seemed to me that they then started to get a little overconfident and were soon throwing nuclear fusion parts around and joining up all their available wires until, on 29 November 1955, the EBR-I reactor – and I quote here from the guidebooks – 'suffered a partial meltdown'. To their credit, the boffins managed to patch the reactor up (I am not at all sure how they did this) and then carried on proving and disproving nuclear theories and generally messing around with plutonium until 1964, when the US government pulled the plug and stopped everything for reasons that, to this day, are still not particularly clear.

In 1966 President Lyndon Johnson agreed to EBR-I's closure and it was then designated a national landmark. Ten years later it was announced that the place could throw open its doors to the general public. However, there are strict regulations as to when you can visit and only at specific times of the year. I am assuming this is when radiation contamination levels drop off a bit and visitors don't all leave with a curious green glow and some of their body parts morphed into strange shapes. Now I don't know about you, but there is nothing on this planet that could drag me to stand in or around a concrete building, in the middle of a desert, where people had been playing around with nuclear fusion. Not only had the eggheads been experimenting with things they didn't entirely understand, they'd even admitted they had managed to cause a partial nuclear meltdown there.

Just to add to the atomic theme, at the EBR-I site there are apparently a couple of experimental nuclear-powered aircraft engines on display. These never made it into the air on an aircraft as the programme was cancelled in 1961 when it became evident to the scientists that they really did not fully understand what they were dealing with, and strapping nuclear engines on to something airborne was probably not a very good idea. Anyway, to my mind they can call the engines whatever they like, but a flying thing with radioactive propulsion is nothing more than a nuclear bomb. I am very glad they stopped when they did.

The nuclear propulsion and atomic energy theme is big in Idaho, and Highway 20 snaked us past the Lost River Mountain Range and straight into the pleasant town of Arco. In the history book of nuclear power Arco has earned itself a place as the first town in the world ever to be powered by atomic energy. It even had a sign over the city's civic office and recreation hall in Main Street proudly stating 'First City in the World to be Lit by Atomic Power'. The truth of the matter is a little less dramatic. For less than one hour on 17 July 1955 the nearby National Reactor Testing Station (NRTS) provided 20,000 kW of energy to the town. I am not sure if this was enough to light four light bulbs or the entire town, but it was just a brief flicker of atomic power and a glimpse into the future for everyone. It never happened again as five years later the NRTS also had a significant reactor meltdown, resulting in the deaths of three people – it's labelled the worst nuclear accident ever in the US – and since then Arco has had to content itself with its brief one hour of fame.

In 1977, the NRTS changed its name to the Idaho National Engineering Laboratory – possibly to distance itself from some of the mishaps it had encountered in the previous decade – and then became more politically correct when it was re-christened the Idaho National Engineering and Environmental Laboratory before finally settling for the Idaho National Laboratory (INL) in 2005. It is still there today, occupying some 890 square miles of Idaho desert, and it is a top-secret establishment and inaccessible to the public as there are 'ongoing' experiments they are still working on. It's estimated that around 50 nuclear reactors have been built at INL, with only three still working, which makes me slightly nervous and suspicious as to what happened to the other 47. Maybe Arco will get its name in atomic lights a little longer the next time, if they can get the sums right and join all the wires up correctly.

Behind the town I was surprised to see a whole series of giant white numbers painted on the side of the rock face. At first glance I thought they might be the current radiation levels of the various atomic experiments conducted nearby that had subsequently gone wrong. I stopped and asked a woman in Arco's Main Street what they were for and she told me that every year the graduates from Arco High School climb up and paint the year of their class on the side of the hill. By my calculations they must have been doing it for almost 40 years as the whole rock face was daubed with numbers. It looked like some immense mathematical problem that a mad scientist was trying to work out but couldn't find the solution to.

I like tradition, however, and this seemed to be a good one. It would have taken them a lot of effort and time to scale the rock face and then paint their class year in 20ft-high numbers. I was impressed. It was far better than anything I'd come across in the UK, where graduating students tend to resort to cross-dressing, drinking their weight in cheap booze, having a fight, wearing a traffic cone on their heads, passing out and then being arrested. The approach of the Arco students appeared to be a far more genteel and sensible way of leaving your mark on society.

* * * * * *

Just 20 miles up Highway 20 from Arco was a landscape of extraordinary dimensions. It was called the Craters of the Moon National Monument Preserve and that magnificent title just doesn't do it justice. Covering 1,117 square miles, it looked as if someone had taken an enormous barbecue full of cold coals and emptied it all over the landscape. There were miles and miles of black volcanic rocks moulded into weird and wonderfully distorted shapes, made even stranger by erosion from the desert wind. It was a geologist's wildest dream. This area even has its own unique species of vegetation.

Experts estimate that the last volcanic eruption there was some 2,000 years ago, but that volcanoes had been blowing their tops for as long as 15,000 years, covering the entire region in dense black and brown stone. I pulled my motorcycle over at a tourist vantage point to have a closer look and it felt so utterly peculiar and strange that I seriously wondered if I was actually still standing on planet Earth. The landscape was totally unlike anything I'd ever encountered in my life. There wasn't a sound, apart from an occasional passing car. It had to be one of the loneliest and oddest places that I'd ever been.

Time was pressing, however, and we still had more than 200 miles to go before getting to the next motel in Oregon that evening. There was no option for us but to take Interstate 84, which drags you west through Idaho and on into the flat lands of the Harney Basin in eastern Oregon.

* * * * * *

As I swung down the slip road and joined the light freeway traffic I suddenly realised that, for the first time in weeks, I was totally fine with riding on an interstate. This was nothing like my Californian experiences. There were just a few 18-wheeler trucks plodding along and none of the crass madness that seems to possess everyone driving cars and SUVs in my adopted home state. I actually relaxed and even had time to take in the scenery, which was flat open grassland with absolutely nothing happening.

I began to pay attention to the passing trucks and what they were carrying, especially noticing one that blasted past me loaded with pigs. I could see porcine snouts poking out of the trailer's side apertures, and several curly tails, and then I got a strong waft of pig crap. This was a truly dull road. If I was having to resort to looking at pigs' backsides for entertainment I needed to do something about it. At the earliest opportunity we dived off the freeway with the intention of heading west into the Snake River Valley, and we soon found ourselves in countryside rich in fields and enormous tractors. It was very like Europe to look at, with neat and tidy lanes and busy farms, except that everywhere there were massive pieces of agricultural machinery and huge pick-up trucks, and the roads were literally like a maze. I felt I was going round and round in circles. Every road looked the same.

I knew I really was lost when I came to a sign for the town of Murphy that gave me two options – either right or left. Eventually I took a chance and followed a small road that I hoped would take us over the Idaho–Oregon border and into the town of Vale. More by luck than judgement I made the right choice, and soon we were heading along a small back lane that eventually led us to Vale. This small town played an important role in the development of the US West Coast in the nineteenth century and I was interested to see what it looked like today.

Vale was the first town on the settlers' migratory route which was to become known as the Oregon Trail. These early pioneers had to set off from the east of the United States in April in order to ensure that there was sufficient grazing along the way for their animals. It took around six months to complete the arduous 2,000-mile trek and they travelled either on foot, on horseback or in wagons. Experts estimate that more than 400,000 immigrants came through this area on the Oregon Trail between 1841 and 1869, and they were either intending to make land claims or find business opportunities on the West Coast. Some were part of the 1848 Californian gold rush to Coloma.

Vale was then the gateway to the west and in its heyday was a thriving town where people could restock with provisions before continuing their journeys north into Washington and south to California. But when the Union Pacific and Central Pacific railroad companies completed the nation's first transcontinental railway in 1869, the Oregon Trail lost its importance. Rail travel was infinitely quicker, faster and safer than slogging through the mountains of the western US on a horse or dragging an unwilling mule behind you.

With the days of the Oregon Trail over, Vale's fortunes appeared to have ended too. Today its main claim to fame was having no fewer than 30 wall murals scattered around the town to celebrate the fact that the Oregon Trail started here in 1843. The Vale business community began fundraising in 1993, as part of the 150th Oregon Trail anniversary year celebrations, and people started furiously painting murals all over the town, only pausing for breath in 2006 when the last one was completed. They are pretty impressive, but to my eye Vale itself had definitely seen better days, for many of the shops were closing or had closed down.

There was a proper 'biker bar' in town called the Sage Brush, though, with darkened windows facing Vale's Main Street and motorcycle paraphernalia up on its walls. A number of motorcycles were parked outside. The bar was staffed by a friendly woman who appeared from a multitude of different doors every few seconds as she moved furniture around the bar, served drinks, cooked food and talked to everyone who came in. She insisted on giving me a ton of literature about local motorcycle enthusiast groups and bike rides; I didn't have the heart to tell her I had no intention of passing this way again for some considerable time.

There was nobody else in the bar except for a trio of motorcyclists from California, among them a loud, annoying woman who seemed very pleased with herself. She had spotted that our bikes were from California too and she started to interrogate me about what I was doing there, but she quickly lost interest in me when her meal arrived. She and her two male travelling buddies were to reappear after lunch as we rode alongside the beautiful Malheur River on Highway 20, overtaking Anne and me three times at crazy speeds as if to show they were extremely proficient motorcycle riders and we really should pay attention to them.

* * * * * *

The countryside in eastern Oregon was breathtaking. Beautiful hills, desert scrub and winding rivers – I was surprised at what I found there, including the 18-wheeler truck that was embedded into a rock face after a particularly nasty accident with a bored-looking sheriff's deputy standing beside it, trying to figure out what had caused it. The driver was nowhere to be seen.

We pulled into the town of Burns for an overnight halt. I was a little cautious about checking into our motel at first as it appeared to be either catering for the tastes of local paedophiles or the owner had a child fixation. There were bronze statues of children playing, in various poses, littered all around the front of the building. It felt just a little bit creepy.

Burns was a small but clearly prosperous farming community and as this was early summer it had a lot of interesting social activities going on, including Old Timer Fiddlers performing at the Country Music Jamboree that weekend, which looked fun. Hopefully the fiddlers were musicians and not residents of our motel. According to the town's local newspaper, the *Burns Times & Herald* ('Covering Hanney County Like The Sagebrush' proclaimed its banner strapline), I had just missed the 2010 Oregon High School Rodeo finals in nearby Prineville. Darn it.

My eye was caught by the lead story in the newspaper that said a local father and son had finally been indicted by a federal grand jury for causing multiple fires in the surrounding countryside. That was bad in itself, but it soon became apparent that the duo had not just been setting fires in the area on a spur of the moment whim but had been at it for the past 24 years. It astonished me. They'd been responsible for causing damage to more than 45,000 acres of public land for nearly a quarter of a century but they were also charged, according to the newspaper report, with 'threatening to assault firefighters by setting fires beneath and around firefighters during fire suppression'. The list of charges against them involved using an aircraft without proper medical certification in a restricted government area as well. These two were definitely in big trouble, but what a great story.

Apart from these seriously professional arsonists I could find nothing else exciting to report about Burns except for some particularly aggressive mosquitoes the size of small sparrows that were waiting for me after dinner, outside the restaurant next to our motel. They were like a group of small street muggers. I am sure they took five pints of blood off me as I ran around the car park, trying to escape them by flailing my arms, and then stumbling around in the darkness amid a multitude of statues of bronze children while I tried to find the entrance door and safety back inside the motel.

The six or so mosquito bites I suffered paled into insignificance when I noticed the 'annoying' Californian woman motorcyclist and her two friends suddenly pull up on their bikes at the reception of the Paedo Motel a few minutes later. They were unaware of the massive carnivorous insects that were waiting for them so it was with a great sense of satisfaction I heard her shouting and dashing around outside as the mosquitoes really got stuck in. I felt there was a god of some sorts after all.

* * * * * *

Burns did have one outstanding feature for me in the form of one of the most magnificent agricultural hardware stores I have ever encountered. I am a sucker for places like this. I like nothing better than to examine all the products and try to work out what you could do with them, and indeed why you would need to do that with them. Being a big farming community there were shelves and shelves of things that I had absolutely no idea what you could use them for. But I was totally entranced.

I knew I was on to a really good thing when I passed the 'For Sale' board at the store's entrance, where customers were encouraged to post adverts. Apart from being able to purchase a couple of very fine-looking pigs – I was tempted, but unsure how I would get them on to my motorcycle – or the interesting proposition of buying a somewhat mangy-looking pony whose description said that it did not like to be ridden, there was a picture of a man sitting inside an enormous motorised fibreglass cow that ran on wheels. For only $500, the advert said, I could buy this mechanical cow from the smiling man in the photograph. It came with a three-speed gearbox and engine and you drove it with your head poking out of the middle of the cow's back. The advert also claimed that, once ensconced in the cow, I could expect to get up to heady speeds of 25mph.

I was enthralled. I think its purpose was to familiarise horses with being around cattle on ranches. Or maybe I misunderstood the advert altogether and it was an alternative mode of transport for people to go to work on in Oregon. Clearly a lot of time and effort had gone into making it, and for such a bargain price. I was certain I could find a use for a motorised cow. I just needed to think through this purchase decision properly and then try and persuade Anne how much we needed it in our garage at home.

For 15 minutes I wandered happily up and down the store, looking at aisle after aisle of fishing rods, gun accessories and hunting equipment. I even examined the various farm animal foodstuffs that were on display and spent more than a few minutes studying the cattle castration section, until a pleasant and smiling assistant wandered up and asked if I needed any help. I was holding in my hands a Newberry Castrating Knife at the time – the de luxe version, according to the label – so I was a little unsure how to answer his question. The implement looked more like a medieval torture tool than an agricultural knife. How on earth was I going to get out of this one? I had no real interest in purchasing a castrating tool but I didn't want to appear as if I were some kind of weirdo just hanging around his hardware store ogling animal mutilation instruments.

'I'm sorry, I'm just looking,' I said. I knew as soon as I'd said it that it sounded very bad, as if I was sizing up the knives before choosing the precise castration tool that I really wanted for my collection back at home. I thought I'd change the subject and said quickly: 'Do you have a clothing section, as I am interested to see what you have got there?'

The sales assistant didn't bat an eyelid. Perhaps it was completely normal for a potential customer to go from the cattle castration section to the ranch hand and cowboy fashion aisles. I beat a hasty retreat and found myself in an enormous area of cowboy hats, tartan shirts, jeans, boots and leather chaps. There was literally everything I would ever need to kit myself out to look like a real cowboy or possibly, as an Englishman with no ranch or horse, a complete and total prat.

Now there are many in the motorcycle community who swear that you need to wear leather chaps over your trousers when riding a bike. There are also some very odd members that say you don't need to bother wearing trousers under chaps at all. But we will skip over this. The hardcore bikers say that chaps can keep you warm on your motorcycle, protect your legs from objects that are thrown up off the road and will help considerably in preventing gravel rash on your skin when you fall off and slide up the road.

I, on the other hand, still needed to be convinced. It was probably the leather-clad biker character in the Village People band of the 1970s that had put me off the idea. Leather chaps also seemed to be incredibly complicated items of clothing, with a multitude of belts and buckles. I am sure it would take me a good half hour just to put some on and then at least a week to take them off. Men and leather trousers just don't work, in my opinion, although I do know that they are hugely popular in certain trendy sections of German society, along with pastel-coloured eyeglasses, bright yellow jackets with the sleeves pulled up and pop songs from former *Baywatch* actor David Hasselhoff, or Der Hoff as they call him in Munich.

So it was with some surprise I found myself holding up to my waist a pair of suede-fringed leather chaps while admiring myself in the clothing section's full-length mirror. Could I get away with looking like this, I wondered? I picked up another pair that appeared to have half a sheep glued to the front of each leg and stood contemplating myself again. Perhaps these would only look good on a film cowboy such as Roy Rogers or John Wayne. I was brought swiftly back to earth by a gentle cough from someone standing directly behind me.

It was the sales assistant again. 'Find everything you are looking for sir, or do you need some help?' he asked.

'No, no. I'm fine,' I stammered. 'Just browsing. You have a lot of good stuff here. I don't know where to start. Maybe I need to look at the boots?'

'Just take your time and let me know if you need any help.' And he instantly disappeared, this time behind what looked like a cross between a bear trap and a Roman siege catapult. I had spent far too much time in the store and I was certain that, before long, they would be calling the local police to have me ushered out of there. But it had been great and I had enjoyed myself immensely. I just wish I had bought that motorised cow.

* * * * * *

It was going to be a long day, with more than 360 miles to cover through southern Oregon and into the top eastern corner of California. That sounds like a relatively short and easy journey and in a car it probably is. You just set off and can most likely drive the entire distance within the space of six or seven hours. You probably don't even need to stop for fuel and will arrive at your destination maybe a little tired but none the worse for the experience.

Travelling on a motorcycle for hours at a time, however, can beat you up pretty bad. Never mind the obstacles you have to encounter on two wheels rather than four, or the constant changes in weather or the fact that at best you only have a range of around 210 miles in a tank of petrol so you are constantly scanning the horizon for the next fuel stop. Or not, in my case. No, the really hard thing is having to contend with other vehicles whose drivers simply don't see you, then being hit by mystery objects that are flung up off the road by passing traffic, together with the enormous variety of insects that somehow manage to hit you and your bike all the time. At the end of a journey of 360 miles a motorcyclist will arrive very tired, arms aching from keeping the motorcycle upright, filthy dirty and covered in the carcasses of dead flies, beetles and butterflies. You may even find a collection of dead bees on your saddle, like the ones I discovered at the end of my ride in Idaho. To this day I am still trying to work out how they got under my backside and then all died without stinging me.

* * * * * *

I decided we were going to ride a direct southerly route along Highway 395 that would take us through the Lake Chewaucan basin and on to the Oregon–California border with the aim of getting to Susanville, in northern California, by nightfall. On the way we would pass the astonishing sight of Lake Abert which, according to the guidebooks, is an endorheic body of water. I didn't know what that meant either and to save you time I have looked it up. It turns out that this is a drainage basin that retains water but has no outflow to rivers or oceans. That to my mind is a stagnant pond.

Lake Abert is topped up only occasionally by snowmelt waters from the surrounding mountains and the odd summer thunderstorm. It was created by a much larger glacial lake that has long since disappeared and today it is flanked on its eastern edge by the stunning Abert Rim – a steep escarpment that rises over 2,500 feet above the lake's edge and runs for almost 30 miles. Dramatic would be an understatement for the Abert Rim. In the early morning light, North America's longest fault scarp (where two masses of rocks have been pushed together so blocks of stone are literally extruded up out of the ground) looked like an ancient crusader castle towering up above Lake Abert.

This lake is so salty that large white crusts have accumulated along the water's edge and on first sight, as we passed alongside, it looked as though it was frozen solid, with snowdrifts on its shores. It was almost silver in the morning light and yet this massive body of water that is approximately 15 miles long and a mile wide was only seven feet deep. Nothing can live in it apart from a type of shrimp, which apparently grows in abundance in the saline water and attracts a host of migrating marine birds and wildfowl from all over North America. It's also considered to be 'very unsuitable for people to swim in'. If you can't swim in it, use a boat on it or drink the water the only other option for humans is birdwatching – and boy, there were a lot of birds.

Huge flocks of Canada geese were waddling up and down the lake's saline shores while terns and what looked like oystercatchers rummaged around in the rocks on the salt beaches. I think I also spotted some grebes and a small group of avocets. This would be a birdwatcher's heaven, as well as being a truly spectacular lake. As the sun rose higher in the sky the surrounding mountains were mirrored in the waters. There wasn't a soul about and I felt like I was the first person ever to gaze on this peculiar and enormous stretch of water. The US had astounded me yet again with the sheer natural beauty of its wild open spaces.

* * * * * *

'Hey, that's a real nice bike,' said a disembodied voice that appeared to be coming from the other side of a petrol pump that I was using to fill my motorcycle's gas tank.

I spun around in surprise to look at the owner of the voice, but before I could spot him he went on to say: 'Yeah, I used to have a Harley myself, but I gave it all up when a good friend of mine got himself killed on his bike one night. Truck hit him and spread him up the road and I never wanted to ride again.'

I found the voice of doom lurking the other side of the pump in the form of a friendly-looking middle-aged man who was filling up his car with fuel while continuing to study my bike. 'Had another friend who lost a leg when a car he hit pushed him into a crash barrier on the freeway. He won't ride again and nor will I. He is lucky to be alive.' Mr Cheerful nodded his head in satisfaction, obviously keen to pass on to me this wealth of information about mayhem and destruction involving motorcycles.

I have found that in my time riding in the US there are two clear groups of people. The first lot know nothing at all about motorcycles and, perhaps understandably, they don't need to know about them or even care about them. Then there is a second group of people who also seem to know nothing about bikes or riding apart from the fact that they do know of someone who was fatally injured, dismembered, suffered brain damage or had some truly frightful injury inflicted upon them because they chose to ride on two wheels. Not once has a single member of this latter group ever told me a great story about someone they knew who had a tremendous motorcycle ride across an empty desert, or rode up a lonely mountain road, or just went out for a ride and still came back with their limbs intact.

Of course I know and appreciate that riding a motorcycle is a dangerous avocation. Of course I could be killed each time I get on my bike. But I have weighed up the consequences and decided I will take my chances, so I don't understand why these people feel it is important to remind me what might happen when I ride a motorcycle. I am sometimes tempted to regale these death mongers with stories about hideous car crashes I have witnessed because fundamentally, what lies at the bottom of their smug satisfaction, is that they think they are safe in their cars and by riding a motorcycle I most definitely am not.

This in turn underlines another problem I have with what US motorcyclists call 'cagers' or, to you and me, car drivers. If they have never ridden a bike they have absolutely no appreciation of how difficult they, as car drivers, make it for us motorcyclists. They are blissfully unaware of the presence of bikes on the road most of the time, and they are incapable of judging closing speeds, checking their mirrors correctly before pulling over into another lane or changing direction when a motorcyclist is behind them. Frankly they seem to have no idea of how downright dangerous it is for a bike rider to have a car get within 20 feet of their rear tyre.

I mentioned some US accident statistics at the beginning of this book, and they certainly all included a number of contributing factors, but I can guarantee that the biggest killers of motorcyclists are other vehicles. It seems to be overlooked by the purveyors of gory motorcycle stories that they too are involved in this destruction derby, whoever's fault it was, or whether the rider was wearing a crash helmet or not, or was drunk.

'Yep, I'll never ride again and I don't know as if I miss it really. Be careful out there and ride safe,' said the man at the gas station. I nodded to show I had at least heard him and his tales of caution, and then watched as he finished fuelling his car and drove off down the road with the petrol tank cover on the side of his car flapping in the breeze.

* * * * * *

I had a guilty secret. I had some feeling of trepidation about reaching the northern Californian town of Susanville. This was our overnight halt after a long day of hard, fast riding through Oregon to ensure we got back into California before heading due west to the ocean, getting on to Pacific Coastal Highway 1 and heading south for home. It was not that Susanville, a former logging and mining town, had a bad reputation. In fact I really knew nothing about the place, except that on its outskirts was the maximum security High Desert State Prison of California. Built in 1995 to house 2,000 inmates it was now close to bursting point, with nearly 4,000 young men incarcerated inside. And that was the problem.

I was not concerned about escaping inmates, many of whom were serving life sentences for particularly gruesome crimes, it was just that I felt sure the motel where we would be stopping would be full of their relatives visiting them. I had totally irrational visions of being assaulted by an angry parent who had been denied access rights to their son or somehow being sucked into a life of crime just by stopping and staying in the same town as them. Stupid, narrow-minded and even perhaps a bit pathetic of me, but that's what I felt. To be fair, though, my judgement was perhaps clouded by being absolutely exhausted after that ride of 360 miles through the desert. Just to make me feel a real jackass, I didn't meet a single person who wasn't polite and helpful, and none were connected in any way to the inmates of the penal establishment just up the road.

Susanville is tucked into the north-eastern corner of California and looks an uneventful sort of place. It bore little resemblance to any of the small towns I had encountered in the southern part of the state and its history was unassuming, apart from the fact that it was once known as Rooptown. Presumably the town now relies directly or indirectly on that massive prison for much of its income.

However, I was touched by the support the local townspeople were giving to their sons, daughters, fathers, mothers, brothers and sisters serving in the US military, either in Afghanistan or Iraq. Along the Main Street were large individual banners and photographs of every one of Susanville's men and women serving overseas. I simply could not get over how young most of them looked, which made it particularly poignant. This collection of posters looked more like photographs of schoolchildren than active members of the US military forces. That made me stop and think.

* * * * * *

'I am very sorry, sir, you cannot have any more beer. My manager knows that you have had two bottles and that is your limit here,' said the apologetic waitress in the Susanville restaurant where we had stopped for dinner.

I could have fallen off my chair – and not because I was inebriated. Never in all my years of moderate (some would say immoderate, but they lie) drinking have I ever been told in either a restaurant or a bar that two half pints of beer was my absolute limit. It had been a *very* long day and I was thirsty, and having a few beers seemed to me like a good way to unwind. I had been thinking of ice-cold beer for the last two hours of my journey. I tried pleading with the waitress but then realised I was sounding like a whining child or someone who really did have a drink problem.

The waitress was adamant. There would be no more beer served for me in this restaurant. I looked around me and it was busy with families and groups of friends, eating and talking and not drinking beer. Why on earth, I wondered, had the restaurant manager been keeping an eye specifically on me and precisely what I had been drinking? It transpired, according to the waitress, that the manager, and she alone, had the one key to the wine and beer cabinet and she kept a careful eye out for customers like me who were clearly drinking well beyond their capabilities.

So it was with a heavy heart and a raging thirst that we got up to leave the restaurant in order to amble across the road to the one place in town that Anne reckoned might serve me another beer – Susanville's bowling alley. Never before in my life had I had any inclination to set foot in a bowling establishment. I hated the very thought of being made to wear their ridiculous shoes, so I wouldn't damage the wooden floors. I also knew the shoes would still be warm as other people had been wearing them only minutes before me. Then I would be faced with the prospect of having to hurl an enormously heavy black cannon ball, with three holes drilled into it that didn't fit my fingers, down an immense wooden alleyway towards a target that seemed to be several miles away on the horizon.

Within minutes, though, I had grasped the essence of this game. It wasn't hard. The object was to hit as many as possible of the white bottle things at the other end of the runway with the heavy black sphere. Also, the shoes I had been handed by the friendly bowling alley staff were not too warm. They were not exactly new, but I don't think they'd been worn that evening.

I also began to like the way that there was some sort of machine that replaced the fallen skittles with a brand-new set every time you knocked the previous ones over. This process involved a series of mechanical jerks and loud crashing noises and you didn't even have to lift a finger. This bowling game was actually turning out to be quite fun. My scepticism about bowling had all but disappeared, until it became apparent that the Susanville skittle-replacing machine was not working properly. Every so often an employee would resignedly wander off around the back of the alley amid all the pulleys, wires and metal cradles and poke at things with a broomstick until it all started moving again.

A man after my own heart, I thought. If in doubt about the workings of mechanical machines I also find that poking them with a stick often helps. You never actually achieve much, but there is something immensely satisfying about watching mismatched cogs and whirring chains chew up a wooden stick before the entire contraption comes to a complete halt and seizes up altogether. Then, and only then, do you call in the professionals to get the machine going again.

My enthusiasm for all things bowling had now really started to warm up. The cannon ball that I had just hurled down my chosen run magically reappeared next to me within a few seconds of my throwing it several miles away – all without me having to move an inch. This was great. This was an entirely static sport that needed very little input from me, apart from lobbing the occasional ball. And my happiness reached a new level when a tray was poked through a hole in the wall behind me with several bottles of beer precariously placed upon it. I had to pay, of course, poking dollar bills back through the hole. I never once saw who was actually supplying me with the beer or for that matter ever got to speak to them, but at least he didn't tell me I'd had too many.

When my score reached an apparent 18,471 on the screen above my lane, which then flashed lots of red crosses while making a high-pitched buzzing noise, it seemed to be time for me to call it a night. I never quite got to work out how to keep score myself, but it had been immensely good fun just hurling the cannon balls in haphazard fashion around the bowling alley. Sometimes they made it to the end of my lane and sometimes they didn't. Occasionally I think I joined in other people's games as well, when my ball missed my lane entirely. The staff at the Susanville bowling alley were perhaps also relieved to see me leave, especially the guy with the broomstick who'd seemed to spend more time poking around in the jammed skittle crates in my area than anyone else's. But what a great night it had been in Susanville.

* * * * * *

It was time to hit the road again. We needed to get across the top of California, just above San Francisco, on to the infamous Pacific Coastal Highway 1 (PCH1) to head south and home. To reach the ocean meant that I was going to have to navigate us over the Sierra Nevada Mountains and down into the Sacramento Valley before striking west towards the Pacific. It sounded easy on paper but it was much harder in actual practice.

I knew that this was going to be a truly memorable ride. The Sierra Nevada Mountains (meaning 'Snowy Mountains' in Spanish) stretch some 400 miles from the Susan River in the north of California down to the Tehachapi Pass just north of Los Angeles. Approximately 70 miles at its widest, this mountain range is like a backbone sticking out of mid- and northern California. It is generally agreed among the experts that the Sierra Nevada Mountains were formed more than 100 million years ago from granite deep under the earth. A mere 4 million years ago uplift started, and then erosion by glaciers exposed the rock and formed the light colour they are today. Due to the various stages of this geological uplift the Sierra Nevada Mountains have a widely differing range of elevations and consequently there are apparently five different climate zones.

The mountains actually get higher the further south they go into California. Starting at around 5,000 feet in the north, where I planned to cross them, they rise to nearly 14,000 feet with Mount Humphreys, near Bishop, California, before culminating in Mount Whitney, near the town of Independence, at 14,505 feet. This makes Mount Whitney the tallest peak found in 49 of the states that make up the mainland US. Only 16 other mountains are taller – the biggest being Mount McKinley at 20,320 feet – and all 16 of those are in the state of Alaska. So there you go, some geographical information that you never knew or thought you would need.

It was a brilliant, bright sunny morning as I loaded up the saddlebags on the motorcycles and started to work out a route with Anne that would take us away from Susanville and towards Chico in the Sacramento Valley. We would then go across the notorious Interstate 5 and on to the foothill roads of the Coast Range Mountains that overlook the Pacific Ocean. In total it would be a ride of probably 250 miles.

They have some great slang words in the US motorcycle world and one of my favourites is 'chicken strips'. This refers to the sidewalls of your bike's tyres. If you are a good, fast, hard rider who can crank your bike over in the corners like a professional, then your tyres, and particularly your rear tyre, will be the same uniform matt black colour all over. Have a look some time at the rear tyres of any parked motorcycles you see in the street and they will tell you an awful lot about the capabilities or otherwise of their riders. If you are a scaredy-cat wuzz like me, however, then you will have nice shiny sidewalls on your tyres that you can probably see your face in. Actually I am being unfair to myself. I probably don't have the reviled chicken strips on my bike's tyres but something more akin to chicken nuggets.

For some reason I have absolutely no problem with fast, slow or even indifferent left-hand corners, so the left side edge on my bike's rear tyre is properly worn down. I do, though, have an innate fear of right-hand corners and nothing on god's earth would make me crank my bike hard over in a right-hander. This made for some interesting riding on sinuous, twisty mountain roads such as the spectacular route I had planned that would take us up into the Sierra Nevadas before dropping us down to the Sacramento Valley in the heartlands of central California.

Leaving Susanville I had really hoped for a quick run out of town, but within less than a mile the traffic was at crawling pace following what appeared to be a US navy battle cruiser on a trailer being hauled up the mountainside by no fewer than two trucks. It was being followed by six police cars and a procession of traffic. Quite why there was a need for a marine vessel in the Sierra Nevada Mountains was beyond me. So instead I opted for Highway 36, just outside Susanville, a road that would take us straight up into the Sierra Nevadas. It also had a lot of left-hand corners so I could make great progress along the straights, through the narrow passes and around left-hand bends, but then I had to drop to a snail-like speed whenever I needed to go right.

As we reached the very western edge of the Sierra Nevada Mountains we were confronted by the most amazing view of the Sacramento Valley. Through the hazy sunshine I could literally see for miles and miles as the flat valley floor panned out straight ahead and also to my left and right. It was superb. I'd never experienced such a panoramic vista in my life. I could see small towns, farms, hills and roads. It was like looking at a real-life map that someone had thoughtfully left open for me.

CHAPTER TEN

HEADING FOR HOME

*Clearlake – Napa Valley and wine – Motorcycle clubs –
Golden Gate Bridge – Rain and mist – Carmel – Pacific Coastal Highway –
Sea lions – LA traffic – Homeward bound*

From the very first moment I met her I liked Mary, the barmaid at the Clearlake motel we stopped at that evening. She was a no-nonsense sort of woman who knew her own mind, and she didn't care what you thought of her. If Mary didn't like you I was certain she wouldn't waste any time in telling you. She was a lady in late middle age and had clearly seen it all and done it all in her life.

'I ran away from home in Missouri at the age of 17,' she told me. 'I have had a few husbands, lost a few husbands, and I have lived here in Clearlake for 40 years. But it's not the same any more. People just don't come here.'

The town sits right next to the largest freshwater lake in California, called Clear Lake. It's the tenth largest lake in the US and experts estimate that it has 100 miles of shoreline, it's at least 480,000 years old and it's there due to a geological fluke. The lake's bed sits on a massive block of stone which tilts north at the same degree that the lake fills with sediment, thus keeping the water at roughly the same depth across its entirety.

It used to be a hugely popular holiday resort about 60 years ago, with people coming from all over the US to enjoy what the town and the lake had to offer. And the gnat population of California came too. Things got so bad back then that in the evenings there were piles of dead gnats beneath Clearlake's streetlights, looking like dirty snow. The gnat swarms of the 1940s became so dense that people driving cars along the lake's edge reported having to stop every quarter of a mile to clean off the dead insects from their windscreens and headlights.

A decision was made in 1949 that the only way to control the gnat population and encourage people to keep coming to Clearlake for their holidays was the abundant use of the chemical insect killer DDT, and it was sprayed in enormous quantities all around the lake. This man-made pesticide attacked the insects' central nervous systems but also had a number of unpleasant drawbacks. DDT killed the gnats and the holidaymakers did return for a while, but in 1953 the effects of the DDT wore off and the gnats returned with a vengeance. The solution back then was to throw even more DDT about. Unfortunately such huge quantities were sprayed around Clearlake that not only the gnats died but a lot of the local wildlife, and fish and birds too. And people mysteriously stopped coming to the town.

To compound Clearlake's problems further, high quantities of mercury were then found in the water due to the nearby Sulphur Banks Mine that had extracted seven million pounds of mercury from the ground before closing in 1957 and leaving Clearlake with an even bigger environmental problem than the DDT. Even today there are high levels of mercury from the mine in Clearlake's water and also in the fish that are caught there. Expectant mothers and young children are encouraged by health organisations to limit the number of local fish they eat because of their high mercury content. I think that's why the town is so quiet. The combination of DDT and mercury poisoning may be why people moved elsewhere for their recreational activities and holidays. Just saying.

Of course Mary had her own opinion about Clearlake's problems. 'It's all to do with the town council,' she said. 'They make all sorts of promises and have done so for years and years, and they've done absolutely nothing. We have been told we were to get new roads, schools and housing, but nothing. I still live down a dirt track to my house. Can you believe that?'

I would believe anything that Mary told me. She was that sort of lady, and definitely not a person to be argued with. I raised the delicate subject of the US having a new president and suggested that maybe this would lead to things improving for people in Clearlake.

Mary looked at me incredulously. 'You really think that is going to happen? The government is just as bad as the town council here. Nothing has happened and nothing will ever happen. Obama has not done anything yet. And I don't think he ever will.'

Mary wasn't complaining, just stating the facts as she saw them. She was surrounded by an interesting group of bar regulars in the motel that included a French chef from a nearby hotel, a woman who claimed to have ridden to the Sturgis bike rally in South Dakota and to every other motorcycle event in the US, and a random long-term guest. They all nodded in agreement. The town council had done nothing and no new president of the United States of America was going to make a blind bit of difference to Clearlake's fortunes.

I wandered downtown to have a look at the lake. On a shaky, partly rotten wooden pier I walked out over the water expecting to see three-headed fish and giant mutated waterfowl thanks to the man-made chemical cocktails that had been thrown around here. Instead I was very pleasantly surprised. There was nobody about and it was a still quiet evening. Clear Lake's water looked clean and pure and I could see a number of normal-looking fish swimming in the weeds below me. A man was tying up his boat after a day's fishing and he had some enormous specimens tied together on a line that he was lifting on to the edge of the jetty. It all looked idyllic. The sun was setting and a warm summer's breeze was blowing across the water. What a great place for a holiday, I thought. Then I felt something bite my arm. It was a gnat. They were back and this time it was personal. I just hoped for Clearlake's sake that right there and then nobody was reaching for the can of DDT again.

* * * * * *

I was genuinely excited as we set off – I always looked forward to the prospect of getting on my motorcycle each morning and wondering what I was going to find, but that day I was more enthusiastic than normal. The route I had planned would, I hoped, take Anne and me due south, away from Clearlake and through the famous Californian wine-growing region of the Napa Valley, past the outskirts and hills of San Francisco, and across the Golden Gate Bridge. We would then drop straight on to one of the most dramatic and famous roads in the US – Pacific Coast Highway.

I had checked the weather ahead on the motel's TV that morning and had been promised clear sunny skies as far as San Francisco and then wind, rain, fog and sea mist, and below-season temperatures from then on to Carmel on the Monterey Peninsula. Oh hell.

The road to Napa Valley was exactly like a small English country lane, except without the smart-looking women wearing headscarves and walking their Labrador gun dogs in the middle of the road, or angry red-faced farmers driving their tractors in the middle of the road, or errant badgers weaving around in the middle of the road. Writing this has reminded me how many things seem to be drawn to the centre of country roads in England. I had nearly hit all three of these on a number of occasions, and many other rural obstacles as well.

This Californian road was very narrow and on occasions downright dangerous as I faced oncoming traffic trying to get around the multitude of tight hairpin bends. Quite how I had ended up here, at the northern end of the Napa Valley, I was not really sure, but Highway 29 had appeared from the map to be the most direct route into one of the world's and the US's biggest wine-production regions. The road got tighter and tighter, with some seriously sharp corners that snaked back around on themselves before eventually spitting me out at the sleepy market town of Cobb and so into the Napa Valley.

This region has an enviable reputation as a great wine-growing area. It is also one of the oldest counties in California, having been created in 1850, but what amused me most about it were the arguments surrounding the origin of the valley's name of Napa. Some people say it is derived from a Native American word meaning Grizzly bear, or motherland, or even fish. Others say Napa is a Patwin tribal word for house. There seemed to be more than a few translations of the word Napa going on here, which made me think that life for the local Native

Americans must once have been fraught with real danger if they were using the same word for house as they did for bear.

There are countless books, travel guides, magazines and a ton of information about the Napa Valley written by people far better qualified than me, but what I can tell you is that wine growing here has been going on since the early nineteenth century and that more than 140 vineyards had been established a hundred years later. Napa was to suffer badly under the US prohibition laws of the 1920s, when the sale of alcohol was forbidden throughout the country. Then a particularly virulent root louse came and attacked all the vines up and down the valley. Wine production almost came to a complete standstill in Napa because of this and it wasn't until the 1960s that the vineyard owners began to turn things around. Today it's regarded as one of the greatest wine-producing regions of the world – up there and on a par with France and Italy.

I found it really strange riding along Napa's straight roads, surrounded by vines, because it felt exactly as though I *was* in France or Italy. It was in part due to the topography, but also because so many of the countless vineyards we passed had Italian or French influences in their architecture. It was lovely and sunny, and there were signs everywhere inviting passing tourists in for a wine tasting, but while that was very tempting it was only 10.00am. I had enough trouble riding a motorcycle sober, let alone with a few glasses of wine inside me.

We were soon through Napa and on the outskirts of San Francisco, heading around the top of the Bay area. The sun had gone and there were heavy grey clouds on the horizon, and what appeared to be dense fog rolling in off the Pacific Ocean. Good gracious, I thought, this is California, not England. And it was the middle of June. It began to feel exactly like a summer day in the UK – cold, damp and miserable – which was also a good description of me at this point. My jeans were soaked from the mist rolling in off the sea, and I was sliding around on the saddle of my motorcycle because it was drenched. My hands were cold and I couldn't see a darn thing as the visor on my helmet was constantly misting up with my breath.

I also realised that I was moving right into outlaw motorcycle club territory.

* * * * * *

I mentioned earlier in this book about some of my diverse interests, but another of them was definitely US outlaw motorcycle clubs. Apart from seeing a solitary Hells Angel riding like a man possessed on the freeway, with his colours flying on the back of his leathers as he tore through early morning traffic, I had not met or seen a single member of one of these clandestine groups of hard-core motorcyclists.

The Hells Angels have a long association with Oakland in San Francisco's Bay area. In part this is due to their long-term and current worldwide president, Ralph 'Sonny' Barger, who epitomises the outlaw biker lifestyle. He has written several interesting books about his life with the Hells Angels, and he comes across as a shrewd and clever man whose marketing abilities would not have been wasted if he had chosen another path and worked in America's corporate business world. Barger says he has now retired – he has moved to Arizona – but his management of the Hells Angels has left a deep impression on this worldwide club that can still be seen today.

I am no expert when it comes to outlaw motorcycle clubs, but I do know there are strict rules and regulations about who can join, and even stricter ones on when you can leave their ranks. Today much Hells Angel activity is under constant scrutiny from the US law enforcement organisations, particularly the offices of the Alcohol, Firearms and Tobacco departments.

I'd been told by a far more experienced motorcyclist that you should never approach a club member, and on no account should you ever ask them any questions about their activities. It seemed like a reasonable position to take, but I was still fascinated by the whole outlaw motorcycle club lifestyle and why they do it. I had never had any real contact with a Hells Angel at that time, or any experience of encountering them.

That was all to change one Saturday morning in Southern California as I headed over to the local dealership to buy some parts for my bike. As I stopped at an intersection I could hear the sound of a lot of motorcycles coming up behind me. My bike was the only vehicle waiting at the stoplight. Suddenly I was surrounded by a group of some 20 fearsome-looking men with equally fierce-looking motorcycles. All of these guys were members of the Vagos motorcycle club. This was an outlaw club. I had never even heard of them, but after some research when I got home I discovered they were up there in the notoriety stakes with the Hells Angels and their deadly rivals, the Mongols.

These Vagos guys didn't even look at me, or acknowledge me. I was cursing my luck – I felt that only I could get mixed up in a pack of hard-core bikers – but the real problem was that I didn't know what I should do next. Should I ride with them? Or ought I to wait and let them all pass me by? As the lights turned green I had no option but to move off because I had at least six of them sitting right behind me. I accelerated forward and then checked myself. I did not want to appear as though I was trying to race them away from the lights. So I started to slow down.

This made the six behind me slow down too, while their fellow members roared away into the distance and on to the next stoplight. In a flash the six stragglers were all around me. One very large bearded guy had huge ape-hanger handlebars on his motorcycle that raised his hands almost 12 inches above his shoulders; he looked across at me, shook his head, and simply shouted: 'Asshole...'

He was right. I had just ridden like an asshole, but they hadn't exactly given me a lot of options. So that was my closest experience to date of an outlaw motorcycle club in the US – being called an asshole by them. At least they hadn't beaten me up or set fire to my motorcycle, but I suppose there was always next time.

* * * * *

San Francisco's inclement weather had kept most of the sensible motorcyclists inside that day, apart from one stupid Englishman who really should have known better. The roads leading me around the city were exactly like those I had seen for years on TV cop shows and in every film shot of this city, seemingly an endless wave of steep hills. Tall pastel-coloured houses lined the streets. It was just like a backdrop from the movies, except for one thing. The sun was not shining and there was a heavy marine fog sitting about 100 feet up over my head. It was damp and cold again, and the San Francisco early morning traffic crawled slowly around the city.

That morning, as I rode around the city, I'd caught occasional glimpses in the distance of the Golden Gate Bridge, which takes Highway 101 right across San Francisco Bay. The bridge's red frame stood out starkly in the morning light, surrounded by the mass of sea fog that swirled around it. Built in 1937, the Golden Gate Bridge is held up by approximately 80,000 miles of steel wire and is 1.7 miles long. It was once the largest suspension bridge in the US and even today is an instantly recognisable landmark. I had always wanted to drive or ride across it.

As I got closer the fog intensified so that entire sections of the bridge appeared to completely disappear. Occasionally just one of the famous red towers would stick out, and then disappear again in a white shroud of fog. I was deeply disappointed. I had envisioned a Golden Gate crossing in bright California sunshine, with the opportunity of looking at the city of San Francisco on my left and the bright blue of the Pacific Ocean on my right. Maybe I'd even get a glimpse of the former Alcatraz Penitentiary that sat on top of a rock on an island out in the bay. But it was not to be. I found myself sitting in bumper-to-bumper traffic riding a motorcycle over one of the world's most famous bridges without being able to see a damn thing.

I became even more disappointed when I discovered that I had to pay $6 for the privilege of crossing the Golden Gate Bridge on this foggy day in June if I wanted to head south. As I got on to the bridge I made a quick decision and dived ahead of the traffic behind me, aiming for the far right-hand lane in the vain hope of seeing something. Anything. But the blanket of white fog came up to the side of the bridge and stopped before continuing again on my left side, entirely blanking out the city of San Francisco. I was reduced to looking at the Pacific Ocean, running under the bridge, between the gaps in the road. This was a stupid thing to do as I needed to pay attention to what was happening ahead of me. Staring at the road moving underneath me made me feel dizzy and disorientated. If I wasn't careful I was going to end up having a big accident on the Golden Gate Bridge.

The nice woman at the toll booth on the other side of the bridge relieved me of my $6 crossing charge with a flashing white smile. When I complained about the weather and the fact that I hadn't seen anything she said: 'Well, honey, why don't you turn right around and go back the other way? At least you don't have to pay a toll going north.'

I sort of understood her flawed logic, but I still wasn't going to be able to see anything. I felt the mystique of the Golden Gate Bridge could wait until another time, when it wasn't foggy and I could actually see further than 20 feet around me.

* * * * * *

There was still a clammy cold dampness in the air as we rode along Highway 101. This route would take us about 12 miles due south from San Francisco and on to Pacific Coast Highway (PCH), and then straight down to Los Angeles and home to Orange County, Southern California.

Sea mist was rolling in off the Pacific Ocean in patchy clumps, making the road ahead very difficult to see, and at times I lost all perspective of where I was on it. Somewhere to my right was the ocean and over to my left a dramatic rocky landscape. Heck, this was PCH, one of the most famous driving roads in the world. It runs for some 600 miles north to south, literally following the extreme western edge of California right next to the Pacific Ocean. And again I couldn't see a damn thing.

A stiff breeze had now got up and I settled back on my motorcycle for a miserable three-hour journey. There was no traffic, which surprised me as this was vacation time and a lot of people drive up and down this spectacular road just for the hell of it. PCH has featured in countless films and books and is considered one of the most beautiful roads in the world. But it appeared that I was not going to be able to see much of it on this journey. I resigned myself to riding through dense wet fog until we got to the town of Carmel-by-Sea that afternoon, cursing my luck about being out on this fabulous road on such a day. Then suddenly the fog cleared and Anne and I shot into a broad valley of sunshine, with blue skies, the glittering expanse of the Pacific Ocean and fabulous beaches and coves laid out to our right.

Not only that, there was some form of highly entertaining aerobatic display going on in the ocean, with a group of people tied to enormous brightly coloured kites being dragged through the surf at a very fast rate. The wind was so strong these kite surfers were being pulled right out of the water. They were spinning and leaping into the air before being dropped back down again into the crashing waves. It looked amazing. It also looked cold and bloody hard work. These guys had taken the art of surfing to a new level. They still had surfboards, but these were harnessed to a small paraglide parachute, and they were being blown around the shoreline really, really quickly. I stopped to watch them and wondered how they managed not to hit each other or get their lines entangled. It was a very odd spectacle to suddenly stumble across as we emerged from the mist.

PCH was literally dug into the side of the California cliffs in the 1930s, and as well as hugging the coast it has some fantastic bridges spanning deep canyons that run into the ocean. It was extreme nature at its very best. I had never seen a road like it and it was certainly one of the best I had ever ridden – dramatic scenery, craggy shorelines, crashing ocean waves that are so close you feel you could reach out and touch them, and an empty, fast, twisting road that compelled you to ride faster and faster. It ticked all the bike-riding boxes for me and was a superb few hours of riding. I had to stop every 20 minutes or so to pull into lay-bys just to peer down at the Pacific Ocean and try and take in all this astonishing scenery. It really was nature gone wild.

* * * * * *

When we hit snarled-back traffic at Carmel-by-Sea, due to a huge golf tournament, and the fog and rain came back again, however, I felt like a junkie who had had just experienced an enormous high only to come crashing back down again. Carmel is not exactly my most favourite US town. There's nothing actually wrong with it, it's just that I think it is very twee, very expensive and appears to be catering only for people with six-figure incomes. This was a town that elected cinema great Clint Eastwood as mayor from 1986 to 1988. It also describes itself as a dog-friendly town and allows people to bring their pampered pooches into restaurants, and really anywhere else their dogs choose to go. It is also full of fine art shops with some astonishingly bad paintings being sold at astonishingly high prices.

Carmel did redeem itself a little in my book with a few very odd by-laws that included a prohibition on wearing high heels without a permit. This one was introduced to prevent lawsuits arising from pedestrians tripping or having an accident caused by the town's sidewalk paving slabs. Alas, that law is not currently being enforced. I had liked the idea of applying for a high-heeled shoe licence, and wondered what would happen if you did not have a permit yet had chosen to stride around the town in six-inch stilettos.

I also liked the Shell gas station in front of our motel. The ultra-conservatism of this immensely affluent community meant that even major oil corporations had no choice but to follow the rules. No gaudy yellow and red Shell logos had been permitted here, and the result was a muted brown and cream fuel station more reminiscent of the 1930s, to blend in with the surrounding town's buildings. It looked very cool.

I began to wonder if Carmel made visitors to the town wear a regulation uniform on certain days of the week so as not to spoil the look of the place. And as I wandered the manicured streets of tidy shops and restaurants that evening I spotted a sign in an estate agent's window that amused me. 'Buying a house here by the sea is a little nearer to heaven', it stated. More like hell, I thought.

* * * * * *

There was something definitely going on down by the ocean's edge as we began the 330-mile ride down PCH into Los Angeles. There were lots of cars parked beside the road and a small crowd of people staring at something down on the beach. This I had to see. As I got off my bike I got the first strong whiff of shit. I hoped this had nothing to do with me scaring myself again on my motorcycle. I wandered over to where a group of people were busily taking photographs, and talking and pointing. Peering over the fence I saw a group of big, brown, hairy, cylindrical animals lying on the beach – Californian sea lions, and lots of them.

Some of them were immense and must have been at least 12 feet long and weighed several hundred pounds. They were lying haphazardly up and down the beach on their backs, on their fronts, scratching and making loud roaring noises, and attempting to bite each other. They looked a bit like a group of British holidaymakers I had once seen in Spain, but without the sunburn, tattoos and beer cans.

The sea lions looked up lazily at the people taking photographs of them, and they occasionally barked as if to acknowledge the human presence before rolling over again to doze in the morning sun. I did wonder, though, who was actually watching whom. We, the humans, were being kept well back from the sea lions because we were herded into a viewing area and had to peer through a small glass fence at them. The sea lions, on the other hand, were lying and relaxing on a big empty expanse of Pacific Ocean beach watching us. I think they had the better deal.

* * * * * *

This was a fast ride back to Los Angeles. PCH still clung tight up against the rock face, with the Pacific Ocean across to my right, and as I came around a corner I was confronted by one of the most famous landmarks on the western US coastline – Big Sur, or in Spanish, the

Big South. This is essentially where the Santa Lucia Mountains rise out of the Pacific Ocean and move eastwards inland.

Over the years Big Sur has attracted many visitors, particularly artists, impressed with the dramatic scenery and the wild coastline. It is a truly spectacular 90 miles of ocean, cliffs and peaks, and nothing I can write here would do it justice in any way. The best thing I can say is that it feels like standing on the very edge of the world, so that at any moment you could step off and disappear into the blue oblivion of the Pacific Ocean. Yep, it's that good.

The scenery and fast swooping road had been truly fantastic, with PCH living up to all the expectations that descriptions by friends and family had engendered, but I was now in a rush to get home. It wasn't because I'd had enough of this fabulous route and all that it offered, but I was getting very tired of the stupidity of car drivers as Anne and I made our way down the coast. Entering the bottleneck of Santa Monica, just north-west of downtown Los Angeles, the Pacific Ocean was still there on the right but the previously fast-moving empty road had changed to stop and go, with traffic lights and intersections every few hundred feet, and small businesses and apartments were starting to emerge alongside the road.

We were at the very edge of the massive sprawling conurbation that makes up the eastern edge of Los Angeles, and PCH had to snake through all its craziness before heading out and into Orange County and beyond towards San Diego. The LA traffic was just horrendous. Maybe it was because it was the weekend, but nobody seemed to care what they were doing out on the road. Cars and SUVs were stopping abruptly or swerving across lanes without signalling and, despite the recent changes in California law, drivers were still talking on their mobile phones.

I was constantly fighting to keep my motorcycle away from the cars and trucks that were careering close to me on the congested road, or avoiding drivers who would suddenly pull to a halt just to get a parking slot near the beach without checking the rear-view mirror as to what was behind them. It was completely and utterly nuts.

I opted for the right-hand lane on a really busy section as this seemed to be moving quicker than the left lane that had a long stream of cars waiting to turn up a side street. Anne was about two car lengths behind me when a driver in a black Mercedes suddenly decided he'd had enough of waiting in the left lane and pulled right, straight out into Anne's path.

Anne slammed on her motorcycle's brakes and I could hear her shouting in surprise as she slid towards the pavement, but she managed to bring her bike to a halt without hitting the Mercedes or some nearby pedestrians waiting at a crossing. It was a very close thing and I was incensed – so angry, in fact, that I went charging after the Mercedes driver. He whipped past me, back into the left-hand lane, and tried to get away. I began shouting profanities at him while chasing him up the road, and then the traffic lights turned to red and he had no option but to stop. He looked very sheepish, and was clearly trying to avoid eye contact with me, but he had left his passenger side window down.

'You fucker,' I shouted. 'What the hell were you thinking? Didn't you see that motorcycle? Why the fuck did you pull out like that without looking?'

I was furious on two counts. First, because he had nearly knocked my wife off her motorcycle, but second, because we had spent the past few months riding through eight US states on some wickedly dangerous roads, covering many thousands of trouble-free miles (although I'd caused a few problems) only to get almost within sight of our house for something as stupid as this to happen. Although I didn't want to admit it at the time, I guess it also reminded me that I could be knocked off my motorcycle anywhere, any time, any place.

The Mercedes driver was a young guy, about 30 years old. He looked across at me and said: 'I'm really sorry, dude. I didn't mean to do that. I'm in a hurry and I am really late. I am though really, really sorry. Please don't make this out to be a big deal.'

I got a glimpse of myself in one of my bike's mirrors. I had six weeks' worth of beard, I was filthy dirty on a great big black Harley-

Davidson and I looked very angry, even to me. Heck, I'd be sorry if I saw myself in my rear-view mirror coming up the road and shouting and cursing.

'Well it is a big deal,' I said. 'Use your frigging mirrors, man, if you are going to pull out like that. Just don't drive around without looking. You could have killed her.'

There was nothing more to be discussed. The lights changed to green, I had said my piece, and the Mercedes driver sloped off into LA's early evening traffic. A year ago I wouldn't have said boo to a goose. Being English, I would probably have apologised to the guy. But a road trip around the US on a motorcycle definitely changes you – physically and mentally.

* * * * * *

I had seen some astonishing things while out on the back roads of America. I'd met some very interesting people and witnessed things I could never have dreamed of in a million years. I'd ridden more than 8,000 miles through every kind of landscape from mountains to wide-open empty deserts. One thing was certain: there are many amazing things out there in the US if you take the chance and explore beyond the bright lights of the famous cities and all the popular tourist places.

My impression was that small town America was alive but not exactly kicking. The US, like the rest of the world, stands at a crossroads thanks in part to the economic meltdown that had started in 2007. As yet there was no end in sight. There was still, though, a true spirit of hope in this nation. I'd constantly been reminded of how proud Americans are of their country, noting the huge number of Stars and Stripes flags that I'd seen flying everywhere from a shack in the desert to the mansions in the Los Angeles hills. The American Dream is still there, but perhaps at the moment just a little harder for people to realise.

I had experienced just how big North America really is – and how diverse, with so much out there to see and do, interesting people to meet and small towns to visit. A whole range of bizarre and funny things had happened that appealed to my English sense of humour. There are, of course, any number of scary things we might have encountered on the road in the US, and they could happen to anyone, but I never once felt intimidated or frightened by what I saw or found out there. Maybe, from my English perspective, I was ignorant about certain situations and didn't fully appreciate what was going on around me at the time, but I can honestly say that London seems far more aggressive and dangerous to me than anything I'd encountered while travelling in the US.

I felt I now had a better understanding of the country and its people. I might only have lightly scratched the surface, but travelling through America's backwaters had certainly taught me a few things. I'd known almost nothing about some of the states we rode through before I went to them. I left each one a little wiser either due to some experience on the road or by actually stopping and talking to people. In this age of electronic mail, videos and computers city people don't seem to have time actually to talk face to face to each other any more. But they do out there in small town America. I'd experienced it first hand, with complete strangers stopping to say hello to us or tell us something unexpected. My appreciation and respect for this huge nation called the United States of America was unwavering. I had hoped to discover something profound about the US's new president, but time and again people in the small towns I travelled through showed little interest in Barack Obama, or had few opinions about him. There were a few signs on buildings saying things like 'If you voted for Obama you lost the right to complain', but overall I got the feeling that small town America was holding its collective – and perhaps cynical – breath. Obama clearly still had to prove himself.

If I'd been in a car I would never have seen some of these things or met some of the people we encountered along the way. From the saddle of my motorcycle I got to see, up close and personal, the real, raw beauty of the American landscape and it's far, far better and more diverse than anything you will ever see on film or in a photograph. I'll remember those broad horizons, staggeringly beautiful mountains and the silence of the deserts for the rest of my days.

I also learned to ride a motorcycle just a little better. If I could just get those right-hand corners sorted I might find I'd stop going round and round in left-hand circles all the time. As I pushed my bike back into my garage in Santa Ana, California, at the end of the final leg of our journey, I stopped for a second to take a look at it.

It was really dirty. It was absolutely covered in layers of road grime and dead insects. And so was I. In the twilight of that Californian evening I started to think to myself that I could do that road trip, every single mile of it, all over again, beginning tomorrow morning. But this time I'd go even further. Maybe I will. After all, *it seemed like a good idea at the time*.

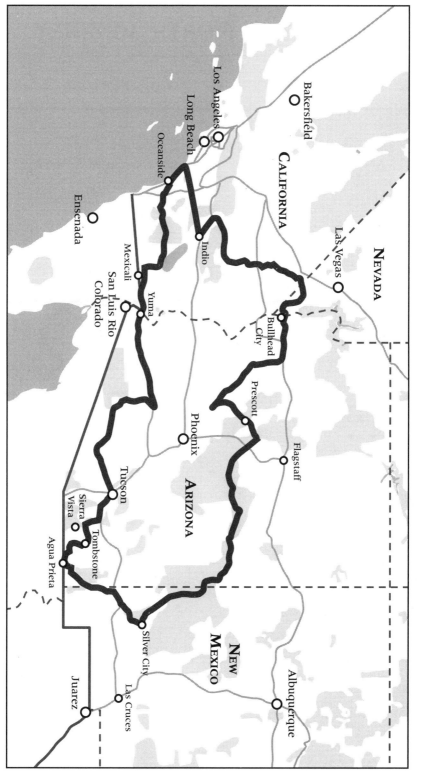

MAP OF THE SOUTH JOURNEY

MAP OF THE NORTH JOURNEY

INDEX